THE PLAYS
OF
JACK LONDON

THE PLAYS

OF

JACK LONDON

With an Introduction by Clay Reynolds

IRONWEED PRESS
NEW YORK

Ironweed Press, Inc.
P.O. Box 754208
Parkside Station
Forest Hills, NY 11375

Manufactured in the United States of America.
Ironweed American Classics books are printed on acid-free paper.

Cover painting: Frederic Remington,
"The Scout: Friends or Foes?" c. 1900–05, oil on canvas.
© Sterling and Francine Clark Art Institute,
Williamstown, Massachusetts.
Courtesy of Sterling and Francine Clark Art Institute.

Library of Congress Cataloging-in-Publication Data

London, Jack, 1876–1916.
  [Plays]
  The plays of Jack London / with an introduction by Clay Reynolds.
    p. cm. — (Ironweed American classics)
  Includes bibliographical references.
  ISBN 0-9655309-7-3 (pbk. : alk. paper)
    I. Title. II. Series.
  PS3523.O46 A19   2000
  812'.52—dc21   00-044896

CONTENTS

INTRODUCTION

The discovery that Jack London (1876–1916) wrote plays may come as a surprise to even the most ardent students of his career, but it should not. London regarded himself as someone who could and would write almost anything for money, and he was at times a shameless self-promoter. That he would try his hand at one of the most popular literary forms of his day seems only natural.

London's literary reputation has risen and fallen over the years in accordance with the political and ideological climate, and it is easy to forget that he was arguably the most popular prose writer of his time and perhaps the most successful in capturing the intellectual zeitgeist of early-twentieth-century America. London set forth his vision of post-frontier America in such works as *War of the Classes* (1905), *The Iron Heel* (1908), *Martin Eden* (1909), and *Revolution and Other Essays* (1910). In formulating his literary philosophy he drew upon the ideas of Karl Marx and Friedrich Nietzsche, his two principal influences, but as illustrated in his naturalistic masterpieces *The Son of the Wolf* (1900), *The Call of the Wild* (1903), *The Sea Wolf* (1904), and *White Fang* (1906), also found inspiration in the writings of Charles Darwin, Herbert

Spencer, Edward Bellamy, and George Frazer. London's works —like those of Stephen Crane, Frank Norris, and Theodore Dreiser—embodied the new critical force that would become the hallmark of American literature throughout the Modernist period.

For all his literary sensitivity and social consciousness, London was a product of the commercial publishing establishment. Throughout his career he was a self-defined hack, a writer who regarded his work both as a means to a paycheck and as a vehicle for political and artistic expression. Although he craved—and, to some extent, enjoyed—critical acclaim, he unhesitatingly exploited the popular forms of his time; this is perhaps best seen in *Tales of the Fish Patrol* (1905), based on his own rough-and-tumble experiences as a youth on the San Francisco wharves, or in *John Barleycorn* (1913), an autobiographical and highly melodramatic account of the evils of alcohol. London knew when to play to the orchestra—and when to play to the balcony. Given his recurring financial problems and almost obsessive desire to maintain his popularity, London frequently put aside his aesthetic principles in search of a broader audience.

But London never completely dropped his didactic pose, always seeking to season his work with a bit of social criticism. Even his less elevated works reveal the influence of literary luminaries such as John Milton, George Bernard Shaw, and, to a lesser extent, Oscar Wilde and Rudyard Kipling. One of America's most prolific writers (he reportedly wrote over a thousand words a day at the height of his career), London seemed always to be searching for new forms of literary expression. Highly egotistical, he believed that, if properly instructed, he could write successfully in any genre.

It seems inevitable, then, that at some point he would turn to drama as yet another outlet for his ideas and talents. But London discovered that playwriting posed far greater challenges than prose. His plays at times betray his shortcomings as a writer as well as his inability to meet the restrictive demands of the dramatic form. Nevertheless, they offer a fascinating glimpse of a writer in his prime attempting to master an elusive and volatile genre while grappling with changing literary times.

London was by no means the first American fiction writer to direct his ambitions toward the stage. A number of nineteenth-century American writers sought to extend their work to the theater. William Dean Howells published more than two dozen dramatic works. Henry James composed a number of short sketches and one-act "parlor plays," several of which were privately performed in the United States and England, but after his play *Guy Domville* was hooted off the stage by an outraged audience in 1895, he abandoned any hopes of persuading another theatrical producer to undertake a full-length script. Other writers of the period—Mark Twain, Bret Harte, Hamlin Garland, Upton Sinclair, Sherwood Anderson, Edith Wharton, Sinclair Lewis—also dabbled in the dramatic form, sometimes attempting adaptations of their own works or collaborating with professional playwrights in the same endeavor. But such triumphs as *Ben-Hur,* based on Lew Wallace's historical novel, were a rarity in American theater. On the whole, American novelists had little success as dramatists.

This failure was in part due to a seldom recognized distinction that Americans of this period made between private and public entertainment. To the American Victorian mind, it was one thing to read, in the privacy of one's own home, fiction that was deemed unsavory or outré; it was quite another to view a performance of such material in a public forum. This distinction, which may seem silly today, was an important one at that time, and the failure to recognize it may well have contributed to the novelists' failures as playwrights.

Throughout the nineteenth century the American stage had

flourished on imported works, principally from Great Britain. It was no happenchance that Abraham Lincoln was attending a British parlor comedy the night he was shot at Ford's Theater, or that such thespian families as the Booths, Barrymores, and Hernes who dominated the boards from coast to coast won the hearts of America's theater patrons with comedies and dramas from abroad. The critical consensus was that American plays lacked artistic merit. Plays with popular appeal generally took the form of adventures and pageants based on historical events or frontier characters, or of spectaculars that offered little in the way of dramaturgical innovation.

American playwrights seemed to find their stride in melodramas, as evidenced in such plays as Augustin Daly's *A Flash of Lightning* (1868), Bronson Howard's *The Banker's Daughter* (1878), and Bartley Campbell's *The White Slave* (1882). Although melodramas were often sensational (*The White Slave*, for example, turns on the mistaking of a white girl for a black one), by and large they were morally conservative and directed toward the more genteel sensibilities of Victorian-era audiences.

The conventions of the melodrama were well established by the turn of the century. Typically, the plot centered on a struggle between a hero of sterling character and a wealthy, lecherous villain over the virtue and fortune of a beautiful ingenue. This formula had become so deeply ingrained in the minds of American audiences that plays which failed to exploit it had little chance of success. A love triangle or class-division complication usually provided a titillating twist to the standard story. More often than not, dramatic irony, wherein the audience knew full well what was "best" for the hero and heroine who were being duped by villainous forces, was the principal source of suspense as well as the setup for the mandatory happy ending. These stock plot devices were aided by physical elements such as secret or purloined documents, chases through the wilderness, and mysterious locked strongboxes. The plays relied on pat speeches and canned dialogue, as well as tableaus, off-stage violence, and predictable outcomes. Coincidences, misdirected communications, last-minute rescues, and cases of mistaken identity were also common. Genuine catharsis, alas, was not.

By the last two decades of the nineteenth century such clichéd fare had reached the point of self-parody. The moral lessons contained in the plays were simplistic and obvious; social criticism was innocuous, if it existed at all; and genuine social engagement was all but absent. Audiences came to the theater prepared to boo and hiss at the villains, just as they cheered and applauded the heroes; sometimes the patrons became so demonstrative that performances had to be halted and extra intermissions called. Patrons typically enjoyed a buffet and an open saloon and sang along with a medley of popular songs before and after the performance. Vendors outside the theater often sold flowers and overripe vegetables to be used by the audience to express their approval or disapproval for a given play or performance. On the whole, the theatergoers behaved as they might have at a period baseball game.

American drama, from Manhattan's "Great White Way" to San Francisco's grimy theater district, had reached a nadir by the last decade of the century. While drama was rapidly evolving in Europe, in the United States it was still mired in the traditions of the antebellum period. The introduction of electrical lighting, sound amplification, and recorded music transformed the American popular stage on a technical level, but the substance of the plays remained largely unchanged.

One of the more significant changes took place in the mid-1880s, when Dion Boucicault introduced "scenic realism," a new method of directing and acting that stunned audiences with its verisimilar presentations. Till then, directors had shown little concern for verisimilitude. Players usually worked on a "raked stage," sometimes tilted as much as thirty degrees upward from the flat floor of the house or the "orchestra," which was merely a cordoned-off area where musicians sat during musical productions. Rather than speaking in a natural, conversational way, the players would declaim their lines, even stepping onto the apron of the stage and into the limelight when reciting longer speeches. Physical interaction, particularly violent confrontations or loving embraces, was kept to a minimum, and obvious devices like asides, eavesdropping, and secretion of characters in plain view were frequently employed. Sets were little more than painted backdrops (which could then be easily rolled up and transported); makeup was exaggerated and costuming dictated less by accuracy than by budget.

A more significant change was being effected by the actor and playwright William Gillette. A veteran of Mark Twain's play *The Gilded Age,* by the mid-1880s Gillette was a seasoned actor and producer. In 1896, his second "Civil War Play," *Secret Service,* debuted in New York. Performed on a flat stage, with authentic costumes, the play offered a realistic story of espionage and politics, marked by natural dialogue and character interaction as well as genuine plot development and intrigue. Although it is indebted to melodramatic conventions, the script works as well today as it did a century ago, and its frequent revivals testify to the modernity of Gillette.

Even though those innovations were a far cry from Stanislavsky's method-acting technique or Piscator's experimental theater, they represented an abrupt shift in the way plays were written, and many playwrights were quick to adapt their work to the new methods. Moving away from the traditional melodrama, Clyde Fitch offered such plays as *Captain Jinks of the Horse Marines* (1901), *The Climbers* (1901), *The Girl with the Green Eyes* (1902), and *The City* (1909), while others converted stock melodramas into more realistic and modern forms. The efforts of the American playwrights to modernize American drama would finally succeed in producing a literary product competitive with the European imports.

In the first decade of the twentieth century, using the American professional stage as a vehicle for the promotion of a writer's celebrity seemed to be a tempting and logical step in any author's career. The failure of Henry James, Mark Twain, William Dean Howells, and others to make the transition did not discourage London. Perhaps more than any other writer of his generation, he was confident of his ability to mine any literary vein with success. As a habitué of the professional theater in San Francisco, London doubtless found it natural to try writing for the stage.

In 1904, London found himself in desperate need of money. Faced with huge debts, largely as a result of his pending divorce from his wife, Bess Maddern, he wrote to the drama critic of the *San Francisco Call,* Blanche Partington, proposing to write several "curtain raisers." Shortly thereafter, Ethel Barrymore, at the time a budding starlet, contacted London and asked him to compose a play especially for her; and the script, *Scorn of Women,* adapted from his Yukon story "The Scorn of Women" (1901), was completed in 1905.

Barrymore rejected the play out of hand and went on to take a role in Ibsen's *A Doll's House.* As if anticipating the rejection, London had also approached Minnie Maddern Fiske, a cousin of his ex-wife's, and suggested that the play was being written for her. Fiske's acting career was in decline, and London hinted that associating her name with his might revive it. But when she read the play, she too rejected it. Undeterred, London took the script to Blanche Bates, who had been a sensation in David Belasco and Luther Long's *The Darling of the Gods.* Bates, however, turned down the script, taking instead a part in Belasco's *The Girl of the Golden West.*

Ultimately published as a book in 1906, *Scorn of Women*

closely follows the plot of the short story. Set in the mining town of Dawson in the Northwest Territory, the play centers on the efforts of two women, Freda Moloof and Mrs. Eppingwell, to save the "Eldorado King" Floyd Vanderlip from the wiles of the avaricious Loraine Lisznayi. Despite his frontier masculinity, Vanderlip is unable to resist the charms of any woman who approaches him—"a man whom women of the right sort can tie into knots." Loraine, a penniless but attractive vagabond unaccountably stuck in the frozen North, finds the wealthy, gullible Vanderlip an easy mark. Her plan is to induce him to run away with her "down the river," where presumably she will gain control of his fortune.

Freda, a professional dancer with a sordid reputation, and Mrs. Eppingwell, the wife of a government agent, get wind of Vanderlip's plan to leave Dawson secretly in the company of a woman, although initially they do not know whom. Each plots separately to hasten the arrival of Flossie, Vanderlip's fiancée from California who is coming across the ice to join him, and both Freda and Mrs. Eppingwell send fresh dogs to meet Flossie's sled party and hurry her to Dawson before Vanderlip can leave. Each believing that the other has designs on Vanderlip, they are unaware of the other's efforts to effect the same end, a situation that gives rise to considerable misunderstanding and miscommunication throughout the play.

The plot seems straightforward enough, but London imposes an unnecessary degree of complexity and, consequently, no clear dramatic structure emerges. The play relies heavily on the melodramatic formula, as exemplified by the nick-of-time rescue in the final act. Among the principal characters, the wily servant Sitka Charley is the least broadly drawn, his pidgin English and obsequious demeanor betraying London's racial bias. In the scene where he is beaten with an inflated bladder, Sitka Charley is used in much the same way that ethnic characters are frequently used in melodramas, that is, as an ignorant object of buffoonery. To his credit, though, London dispenses with the standard love triangle, and in sharp contrast to the one-dimensional women common in melodramas, his female characters are complex and fully realized individuals. Freda's and Mrs. Eppingwell's strength of purpose moves the plot forward and prevents it from collapsing during the farcical, chaotic second act. When they stand unmasked before each other at the costume ball, their conflict reaches a dramatic crescendo and becomes genuinely poignant.

The most powerful scene in the play occurs in the third act, when Vanderlip and Freda are waited on by her maid, Minnie. As the banter between Vanderlip and Freda moves from flirtation to pointed seduction, tension mounts in a way that few melodramas could sustain. When Vanderlip realizes that Freda has played him for a fool, his violent reaction recalls the best of London's "brutes." Frustrated in his attempt to thwart the cunning ways of women, Vanderlip angrily uses force to take what he thinks has been teasingly dangled in front of him. The scene unquestionably depicts an attempted rape, or as close to one as was possible in 1906. In the manner of Norris or Dreiser, London portrays Vanderlip as a man who is driven by his raw, naturalistic ego but is ultimately stymied by social and innate limitations. This scene foreshadows the works of Eugene O'Neill, who would stun the theater world a decade later with his portrayal of brutish male behavior in *The Hairy Ape* and *The Emperor Jones*. The theme would be explored again thirty years later by Clifford Odets and Sidney Kingsley and would be perfected fifty years later by Tennessee Williams in *A Streetcar Named Desire*.

London's next known attempt to write a full-length play did not occur for another five years. In January 1910, London saw Olga Nethersole playing the lead in *The Writing on the Wall,* a progressive melodrama by William Hurlbut staged at the Oakland Theater. He apparently sent his compliments to the actress, who invited him to her dressing room; there they agreed that he would write a play for her, although it is not known who originated the idea. London was more cautious than he had been with Ethel Barrymore. He asked Nethersole to outline what she would want in a play, and in a series of letters exchanged over the next several weeks, tried to establish a motif and situation that would be agreeable to her. But London ultimately disregarded her suggestions, turning instead to another source, Isaac Friedman's 1907 reform novel, *The Radical,* as the basis for his plot and theme. Cast loosely in the mold of the "reform melodrama," the play, *Theft,* was completed within three months, an amazingly short period of time even for a writer of London's prolificacy.

Set in Washington, D.C., the play opens in the home of Senator Thomas Chalmers, a bought-and-paid-for politician controlled by his father-in-law, Anthony Starkweather, a robber baron par excellence. The conflict is established early in the first act, when Chalmers and Ellery Hubbard, a journalist and henchman of Starkweather's, are discovered discussing a speech to be given by the Oregon congressman Howard Knox. A social and labor reformer, Knox is preparing to expose Starkweather's corrupt political machinery in a speech the following day, but lacks the evidence to substantiate his charges. Starkweather, in turn, is planning to use his influence with the press to challenge Knox's credibility and destroy him politically. The dynamics of the conflict are complicated by the romantic entanglement between Knox and Margaret Chalmers, who is both Starkweather's daughter and the senator's wife.

Theft falls back on many of the conventions of the melodrama—the love triangle, purloined documents, the threat to the purity of a young woman. In addition, the story is burdened at the outset with too many characters who are only auxiliary to the main events: Margaret's mother, sister, and son; Starkweather's secretary, Felix Dobleman; the minister, Rutland; the labor agitator John Gifford; the secretary of the Japanese embassy; and the wife of the Peruvian minister. These secondary characters clutter the play and serve to add an unnecessary act to an already overlong script. More important, the conflict between Knox and Starkweather becomes altogether muddied with the emergence of Margaret and Knox's adultery as a competing element in the story line.

The play also favors the declamatory style of melodramas. London's repeated use of propagandistic monologues detracts from the authenticity of the play's dialogue. In the first act, for example, Knox attempts—at a tea party, no less—to recapitulate the socialist critique of capitalism. Similarly, a good deal of Margaret's dialogue consists of speeches about social injustice and the subjugation of women. But such criticism may be somewhat beside the point. *Theft* is essentially a polemical work, unique to that brief period in American history, just before World War I, when socialism had the semblance of a mass movement. In 1910, the Socialist Party had close to 60,000 members, and within two years would double that number and claim over one thousand members in public office. In the 1912 presidential election its candidate, Eugene Debs, would receive nearly a million votes, some six percent of the total.

Scholars have often disparaged London's radicalism, and his understanding of Marxism was indeed at times imprecise. Still, London did more to popularize socialist thought than any other writer of his era, producing some of the finest proletarian literature in American letters. Temperamentally, if not ideologically, London was closer to the Bolsheviks than to the reform-minded members of the Socialist Party, and he became increasingly troubled by what he regarded as the rightward drift of the party. Founded in 1901, the Socialist Party subscribed to the revolutionary rhetoric of Marxism, but in practice it resembled the social democratic parties of Western

Europe, emphasizing electoral and reform politics over armed struggle. In the winter of 1909, shortly before beginning work on *Theft,* London wrote, "I shall stand always for keeping the Socialist Party rigidly revolutionary. If the socialist movement in the United States goes for opportunism, then it's Hurray for the Oligarchy and the Iron Heel." *Theft* reflects his concerns over signs of opportunism within the movement. Although he was by no means a model party member, his criticism was often trenchant, even prophetic, and in the figure of Knox, he serves a warning to the cadres who would allow personal interests to cloud their judgment or compromise their principles.

Such sectarian considerations aside, *Theft* is above all a wholesale attack on capitalism. London's critique is based largely on Marx's, and the play, in its seemingly unstudied presentation of Marxist tenets, gives some indication of London's skill as a political propagandist. His definition of "theft," as explained by Knox in the first act, is derived from Marx's labor theory of value, a linchpin of Marxist political economy. Through Knox and Margaret, London asserts that the capitalist wage system is tantamount to "theft" and profits to "fruits of thievery," "stolen from those who did the work." For London and like-minded socialists, exploitation is an irreducible fact of capitalism.

For all his inflammatory language, London does not overindulge in ad hominem arguments. Like Marx, he regards "the monstrous vileness, the consummate wickedness of present-day conditions" as the natural consequence of capitalism and not necessarily as the result of moral turpitude on the part of those responsible. His characterization of Starkweather is particularly telling. As if anticipating the sociology of Max Weber, London traces the spirit of capitalism to its Protestant cultural origins and depicts Starkweather not as some avaricious Moloch but as a Jesuitical ascetic, imbued with "rigid New

England morality." "Absolutely certain that civilization and progress rest on his shoulders and upon the shoulders of the small group of men like him," Starkweather is as convinced of the sanctity of his mission as Knox is of his. But London is careful to stress that their conflict is just part of the larger historical struggle between capital and labor—of the "great social and cosmic process" that "does not depend on one man."

It was perhaps the polemical tone of the play that caused Nethersole to decline the script. On the other hand, her decision may have had more to do with a question of taste than with any perceived demerits of the script. Like the attempted rape scene in *Scorn of Women,* the strip search of Margaret in the third act, compounded by the falling screen and the revealed humiliation, constituted a serious affront to Victorian moral sensibilities. The casual view of adultery taken by the hero and heroine is perhaps the most scandalous aspect of the script. Margaret is a wife and mother; her demonstrable desire to be Knox's lover—even though she resists it in the name of political priorities—would have been poorly received by audiences in 1910.

Regardless of Nethersole's reasons for rejecting the script, London once more found himself with a play that would never be performed in his lifetime. It was ultimately staged in 1955 by the Lithuanian National Drama Theater, in the only recorded production it has ever had. Notwithstanding its unfortunate history, *Theft* is unquestionably the most intriguing of London's plays and stands as one of the first political plays written from an explicitly socialist perspective, particularly by someone of London's literary stature. Again, he demonstrated a unique kind of artistic prescience. Within thirty years' time the reform play would find a home on Broadway and would inspire the American theater's battle cry, "Drama as Weapon." From Claire and Paul Sifton's agit-prop drama, *1931—,* to Clifford Odets's *Waiting for Lefty* and *Awake and Sing!* to the Federal Theater Project's *One-Third of a Nation* and *The Cradle Will Rock,* drama would serve as a platform for the advocacy of political and social change during the Great Depression.

Although a few scholars have attributed as many as seventeen plays, wholly or in part, to London, the consensus is that he truly authored only three full-length plays—*Scorn of Women, Theft,* and *The Acorn Planter* (1916)—and three one-act plays—"Her Brother's Clothes" (1910), published posthumously as "The Birthmark" in *The Human Drift* (1917); "The First Poet" (1911); and "A Wicked Woman" (1917), an adaptation of his own short story. Ironically, London would enjoy commercial success with his light, comic one-act plays. All three were produced, the most successful being "Her Brother's Clothes"/"The Birthmark," which played in San Francisco, Minneapolis, Boston, and New York.

Gold (1910, 1913), an adaptation of London's story "A Day's Lodging" (1907), and *Daughters of the Rich* (1915), a one-act play, have been attributed, at least in part, to London.[1] But subsequent research convincingly suggests that he merely lent his name to the true authors—Herbert Heron and Hilda Gilbert, respectively—in the guise of a collaborator, presumably in return for some sort of remunerative arrangement. None of the other plays attributed to him have survived either in published or manuscript form.[2] While it is possible that he

1. *Gold,* with Herbert Heron (Oakland: The Holmes Book Co., 1972); the 1910 script was revised in 1913, but neither version was ever produced. *Daughters of the Rich* (Oakland: The Holmes Book Co., 1971); the play was originally copyrighted by Hilda Gilbert in 1915.

2. Other plays attributed to London are "The Return of Ulysses—A Modern Version" (1898–1900); "The Great Interrogation" (1905); "As It Was in the Beginning" (1905); "Billy the Kid" (1910); "Mayor of Goldland" (1911); "War" (1912); "Babylonia" (1913); and "The Damascus Road" (1913). At least five of the plays are said to have been written collaboratively: "The Great Interrogation" and "As It Was in the Beginning," with Lee Bascom (Mrs. George Hamilton Marsden); "War," with Joseph Noel; "Babylonia," with C.P. Clement and Edward Gage; and "The Damascus Road," with Walter H. Nichols. "The Great Interrogation," "As It Was in the Beginning," and "The Damascus Road" were based on London's short stories, "The Great Interrogation" (1900), "The Story of Jees Uck" (1902), and "South of the Slot" (1909), respectively.

did work on some of these lost scripts, there is no evidence to support the contention.

Some bibliographies of London's primary work indicate by omission of the other titles that he wrote only one full-length play, although all three were published and reviewed as books. The play most often cited as London's own is his last, *The Acorn Planter*. The play was commissioned in 1914 by San Francisco's Bohemian Club, of which London was a long-standing member, for the club's "Jinks" of 1916. The "Jinks" was an annual production staged by club members to celebrate the organization's efforts to conserve the redwood grove in which it held its annual retreat. Each "Jinks" was performed in an amphitheater in the grove, on a stage flanked by giant redwoods. Previous "Jinks" had been written by George Sterling, Rufus Steele, and Porter Garnett, among others, and most of them followed pseudo-classical analogues, adapted from such sources as folktales, Greek and Roman mythology, and Arthurian legends.

London had apparently lobbied to write the "Jinks" for some time. Once invited to do so, he chose as his theme the conflict between the Native Americans of California and the encroaching white settlers. He very likely relied on such sources as Stephen Powers's 1877 volume, *Tribes of California*, for Native American legends and songs. Divided into four segments—a prologue, two acts, and an epilogue—the play calls for "efficient singers accompanied by a capable orchestra." London opens the text with an "Argument" outlining the play's thesis and plot. The principal characters are Red Cloud, the War Chief, the Shaman, and the Dew Woman, all Nishinam Indians, in whom "are repeated the eternal figures of the philosopher, the soldier, the priest, and the woman—types ever realizing themselves afresh in the social adventures of man"; and the Sun Man, the representative and leader of the white settlers. Other characters, both Native American and white, function as extras and chorus. The segments are separated by vast numbers of years; but all the scenes take place in the redwood grove, and the characters are altered only by the progressive modernization of their costumes, weapons, and tools.

There is little dramatic action in the play, which is punctuated by lengthy songs. In the prologue, set in "the morning of the world," an argument arises between Red Cloud and the War Chief as to which course—war or kindness—is the better one for the Nishinam to follow. Red Cloud, the Acorn Planter of the play's title, points to the richness and bounty of the earth and argues for the kindness of the human spirit and the patience of the planter. The War Chief declares that war is the only path to security and peace for the Nishinam, and suggests that Red Cloud is too passive to be a leader, as it has been through war that other tribes have been subdued or defeated. To quell the argument, the Shaman tells of a legend predicting the coming of the Sun Man and the destruction of the Nishinam.

The first act moves the action forward ten thousand years. The forest has become barren and the streams have dried up. As Red Cloud and the War Chief argue over what to do, a party of shipwrecked sailors appears, singing of their courage and their misfortunes. They are led by a captain whom the Nishinam immediately call the "Sun Man," as he fits the physical description of the legend—yellow hair, blue eyes, and, of course, white skin. The captain also carries a musket, which represents "thunder in his hand." Although Red Cloud insists that the sailors be treated with kindness, the War Chief calls for their slaughter to thwart the prophecy, and the warriors, responding to his battle cry, kill them.

When the second act opens, another hundred years have passed. The land is fertile once again, but Red Cloud fears that the Nishinam will be punished for the treacherous killing of the Sun Man. Reports come in that the Sun Man and his followers are advancing on the grove from all directions. Upon their arrival, the Sun Men summarily slaughter all the Nishinam. Dying, Red Cloud recognizes that the Sun Man has triumphed not because he is a superior warrior but because he is a superior planter and cultivator. By killing the first Sun Man, the Indians have betrayed their heritage as planters and thereby sealed their fate.

As a theatrical piece, *The Acorn Planter* is not without its shortcomings. Even in the context of an allegorical production, the lyrics sound contrived at times, and the songs seem disproportionately long, giving the impression of an operetta rather than a play with musical accompaniment, as mandated by the "Jinks" guidelines. Although London obviously borrowed from Native American songs, legends, and other folklore to create his story, his portrayal is unlikely to elicit admiration or sympathy for Native Americans. It is almost as if London took only the surface elements of Native American culture and discarded the substance. London's Native Americans are stereotyped to such a degree that only the most bigoted audiences of 1916 would have appreciated them.

The most troubling aspect of the play is its thesis, which is informed by London's Social Darwinist views. Apparently attempting to reconcile the theme of the play with the philosophy of the Bohemian Club, London argues, in effect, that whites enjoy a natural right to the land because they are better cultivators than Native Americans. "You planted well, but not well enough," the Sun Man tells Red Cloud as the chief lies dying. "Your fat valley grows food but for a handful of men. We shall plant your fat valley and grow food for ten thousand men." In other words, before the arrival of white settlers, Native Americans deserved to live on the land in peace because they were the best cultivators on hand. But once white settlers reached the New World, Native Americans became impediments to progress and had to be dispossessed of their land, if necessary with violence, for they were not making optimal use of it. This thesis echoes the ideology of manifest destiny and rationalizes the white conquest of California (and, by extension, the rest of America), reflecting London's belief in the "white man's burden" and in the supposed natural responsibility of the white civilization for cultivating the earth—a belief that most members of the Bohemian Club undoubtedly shared.

Also evident in the play is London's long-held notion that so long as there is hunger in the world, there will be war. Like most Americans in 1915, London was concerned about the war in Europe and the possibility that the United States would be drawn into it. By London's own admission, the play is an indictment of what was widely seen as German aggression. In the character of the War Chief, he is condemning those who would choose war over cultivation and peace. But London, breaking rank with the Socialist Party, supported intervention and, in the second appearance of the Sun Man, offers a cautionary message to those who would emulate the bellicose War Chief.

The Acorn Planter may be significant more as a personal manifesto than as a play, for it represents, albeit in allegorical form, a summation of London's social and political philosophy. Vividly illustrated is the contradictory tension found in much of his work between his egalitarian, socialist impulses and his exclusionary, elitist predisposition. For all its limitations, *The Acorn Planter* provides a unique insight into London's literary and political legacy.

Like his two previous full-length plays, *The Acorn Planter* was rejected. The "Jinks" committee found the songs too long and the effort required to "fix" the play too great, and chose instead Frederick Myrtle's *Gold: A California Forest Play.* London died shortly after the publication of *The Acorn Planter,* and we can only speculate whether he would have continued experimenting with the dramatic form.

Given London's enormous success in other genres, some may be inclined to view his plays as curiosities, but that would be a misjudgment. Long neglected, London's plays serve as valuable historical benchmarks, shedding light on the reactionary and progressive trends in American theater. They anticipate some of the most important changes that American drama would undergo after World War I, and should be read with care for their raw expression of his literary estate.

Clay Reynolds
University of Texas at Dallas

SCORN OF WOMEN

ACT I
Alaska Commercial Company's Store at Dawson

ACT II
Anteroom of Pioneer Hall

ACT III
Freda Moloof's Cabin

Time of play, 1897, in Dawson, Northwest Territory.
It occurs in thirteen hours.

CHARACTERS

FREDA MOLOOF: A dancer.

FLOYD VANDERLIP: An Eldorado king.

LORAINE LISZNAYI: A Hungarian.

CAPTAIN EPPINGWELL: United States government agent.

MRS. EPPINGWELL: His wife.

FLOSSIE: Engaged to marry Floyd Vanderlip.

SITKA CHARLEY: An Indian dog driver.

DAVE HARNEY: An Eldorado king.

PRINCE: A mining engineer.

MRS. MCFEE: Whose business is morals.

MINNIE: Maid to Freda Moloof.

Dog punchers, couriers, miners, Indians, mounted police, clerks, etc.

ACTORS' DESCRIPTION OF CHARACTERS

FREDA MOLOOF: A Greek girl and a dancer. Speaks perfect English, but withal has that slight, indefinable foreign touch of accent. Good figure, willowy, yet not too slender. Of indeterminate age, possibly no more than twenty-five. Her furs the most magnificent in all the Yukon country from Chilcoot to St. Michael's, her name common on the lips of men.

FLOYD VANDERLIP: An Eldorado king, worth a couple of million. Simple, elemental, almost childish in his emotions. But a brave man, and masculine; a man who has done a man's work in the world. Has caressed more shovel handles than women's hands. Big-muscled, big-bodied, ingenuous-faced; the sort of a man whom women of the right sort can tie into knots.

LORAINE LISZNAYI: A Hungarian, reputed to be wealthy, and to be traveling in the Klondike for pleasure and love of adventure. Past the flush of youth, and with fair success feigning youth. In the first stages of putting flesh upon her erstwhile plumpness. Dark-eyed, a flashing, dazzling brunette, with a cosmopolitan reputation earned in a day when she posed in the studios of artist queens and received at her door the cards of cardinals and princes.

CAPTAIN EPPINGWELL: Special agent for the United States government.

MRS. EPPINGWELL: His wife. Twenty-five to twenty-eight years of age. Of the cold order of women, possessing sanity, and restraint, and control. Brown hair, demi-blond type, oval-faced, with cameo-like features. The kind of a woman who is not painfully good, but who acts upon principle and who knows always just what she is doing.

FLOSSIE: Eighteen or nineteen years of age. Of the soft and clinging kind, with pretty, pouting lips, blow-away hair, and eyes full of the merry shallows of life. Engaged to marry Floyd Vanderlip.

PRINCE: A young mining engineer. A good fellow, a man's man.

MRS. MCFEE: Near to forty, Scotch accent, sharp-featured, and unbeautiful, with an eager nose that leads her into the affairs of others. So painfully good that it hurts.

SITKA CHARLEY: An Indian dog puncher, who has come into the warm and sat by the fires of the white man until he is somewhat as one of them. Should not be much shorter than Vanderlip and Captain Eppingwell.

DAVE HARNEY: An Eldorado king, also a Yankee, with a fondness for sugar and a faculty for sharp dealing. Is tall, lean, loose-jointed. Walks with a shambling gait. Speaks slowly, with a drawl.

MINNIE: Maid to Freda. A cool, impassive young woman.

POLICEMAN: A young fellow, with small blond mustache. An Englishman, brave, cool, but easily embarrassed. Though he says "sorry" frequently, he is never for an instant afraid.

ACT I

Alaska Commercial Company's store at Dawson. It is eleven o'clock of a cold winter morning. In front, on the left, a very large wood-burning stove. Beside the stove is a wood box filled with firewood. Farther back, on left, a door with sign on it, "Private." On right, door, a street entrance; alongside are wisp brooms for brushing snow from moccasins. In the background a long counter running full length of room with just space at either end for ingress or egress. Large gold scales rest upon counter. Behind counter equally long rows of shelves, broken in two places by ordinary, small-paned house windows. Windows are source of a dim, gray light. Doors, window frames, and sashes are of rough, unstained pine boards. Shelves practically empty, with here and there upon them an article of hardware (such as pots, pans, and teakettles), or of dry goods (such as pasteboard boxes and bolts of cloth). The walls of the store are of logs, stuffed between with brown moss. On counter, furs, moccasins, mittens, and blankets, piled up or spread out for inspection. In front of counter many snowshoes, picks, shovels, axes, gold pans, ax handles, and oblong sheet-iron Yukon stoves. The feature most notable is the absence of foodstuffs in any

*considerable quantity. On shelves a few tins of mushrooms, a
few bottles of olives.*

*About the stove, backs to the stove and hands behind their
backs, clad in mackinaw suits, mittens dangling from around
their necks at ends of leather thongs, earflaps of fur caps
raised, are several miners. Prince stands by stove. An Indian
is replenishing the fire with great chunks of wood. Mounted
police pass in and out. Sitka Charley is examining snowshoes,
bending and testing them. Behind the counter are several
clerks, one of whom is waiting upon a bearded miner near
end of counter to right.*

MINER: (*pathetically*). No flour?

Clerk shakes head.

MINER: (*increased pathos*). No beans?

Clerk shakes head as before.

MINER: (*supreme pathos*). No sugar?

CLERK: (*coming from behind counter and approaching stove,
visibly irritated, shaking his head violently; midway he
encounters Miner, who retreats backward before him*). No!
No! No! I tell you no! No flour, no beans, no sugar,
nothing!

*Warms his hands over stove and glares ferociously at Miner.
Dave Harney enters from right, brushes snow from moccasins,
and walks across to stove. He is tall and lean, has a loose-
jointed, shambling gait, and listens interestedly to Clerk
and Miner. He evinces a desire to speak, but his mustached
mouth is so iced up that he cannot open it. He bends over
stove to thaw the ice.*

MINER: (*to Clerk, with growing anger*). It's all very well for
your playing the high an' lofty, you sneakin' little counter
jumper. But we all know what your damned company is
up to. You're holdin' grub for a rise, that's what you're
doin'. Famine prices is your game.

CLERK: Look at the shelves, man! Look at them!

MINER: How about the warehouses, eh? Stacked to the roof with grub!

CLERK: They're not.

MINER: I suppose you'll say they're empty.

CLERK: They're not. But what little grub's in them belongs to the sourdoughs who filed their orders last spring and summer, before ever you thought of coming into the country. And even the sourdoughs are scaled down, cut clean in half. Now shut up. I don't want to hear any more from you. You newcomers needn't think you're going to run this country, because you ain't. (*Turning his back on Miner.*) Damned cheechawker!

MINER: (*breaking down and showing fear, not of Clerk, but of famine*). But good heavens, man, what am I to do? I haven't fifty pounds of flour for the whole winter. I can pay for my grub if you'll sell it to me. You can't leave me starve!

DAVE HARNEY: (*tearing the last chunk of ice from mustache and sending it rattling to the floor. He speaks with a drawl.*) Aw, you tenderfeet make me tired. I never seen the beat of you critters. Better men than you have starved in this country, an' they didn't make no bones about it neither— they was all bones, I calkilate. What do you think this is? A Sunday picnic? Jes' come in, eh? An' you're clean scairt. Look at me—old-timer, sir, a sourdough, an' proud of it! I come into this country before there was any blamed company, fished for my breakfast, an' hunted my supper. An' when the fish didn't bite an' they wa'n't any game, jes' cinched my belt tighter an' hiked along, livin' on salmon bellies and rabbit tracks an' eatin' my moccasins. (*Jubilantly.*) Oh, I tell you this is the country that'll take the saleratus out of you! (*Miner, awed by being face-to-face with an old-timer, withers up during harangue and at finish shrinks behind other miners and from there makes exit to right. Drawing paper from pocket and presenting it.*) Now, lookee here, Mister Clerk, what'd you call that?

CLERK: (*glancing perfunctorily at paper*). Grub contract.

DAVE HARNEY: What's it stand for?

CLERK: (*wearily*). One thousand pounds of grub.

DAVE HARNEY: Say it again.

CLERK: One thousand pounds of grub.

DAVE HARNEY: An' how much sugar?

CLERK: (*looking for item on paper and reading*). Seventy-five pounds.

DAVE HARNEY: (*triumphantly*). That's the way I made it out. I thought my eyes was all right.

CLERK: (*after a pause*). Well?

DAVE HARNEY: Well, that mangy little cuss around at the warehouse said I could only get five hundred on that piece of paper, an' nary sugar. What's that mean?

CLERK: It means five hundred pounds and no sugar. Scale-down went into effect today. Orders.

DAVE HARNEY: (*wistfully*). An' nary sugar?

CLERK: Nary sugar.

DAVE HARNEY: That grub's mine, an' that sugar. I paid for it last spring. Weighed my dust in on them scales there.

CLERK: Can't help it. Orders.

DAVE HARNEY: (*wistfully*). An' nary sugar?

CLERK: Nary sugar.

DAVE HARNEY: (*meditatively, in low voice*). Curious, ain't it? Mighty curious—me ownin' two five-hundred-foot Eldorado claims, with five million if I'm wuth a cent, an' no sweetenin' for my coffee or mush. (*Whirling upon Clerk in sudden wrath, Clerk retreating wearily to behind counter.*) Why, gosh dang it! This country kin go to blazes! I'll sell out! I'll quit it cold! I'll—I'll—go back to the States! I'll—I'll—see the management!

Strides rapidly toward door to left.

CLERK: Hold on! (*Dave Harney stops.*) The boss is busy. Vanderlip's with'm.

DAVE HARNEY: He's buckin' the sugar proposition, too, eh?

CLERK: No, he ain't.

DAVE HARNEY: Then here goes. Dave Harney don't wait on Vanderlip or any other man.

Jerks open door marked "Private."

Vanderlip appears in doorway, just entering.

VANDERLIP: Hello, Dave. What's the rush?

DAVE HARNEY: Hello, Vanderlip. Got any sugar to sell?

VANDERLIP: No, but I want to buy—

DAVE HARNEY: (*interrupting*). No sugar, you can't do business with me.

Rushes through door, slamming it after him.

General laugh from miners about stove. Clerk throws up his arms despairingly.

Vanderlip looks backward through door, which he pulls open for a moment, and laughs at Dave Harney.

Loraine Lisznayi enters from right and pauses at door to brush snow from moccasins.

VANDERLIP: (*sees Loraine Lisznayi, starts across to meet her, but stops midway to speak hurriedly to Sitka Charley*). How about those dogs, Charley?

SITKA CHARLEY: I get um all right by and by.

VANDERLIP: I want them right away, today.

SITKA CHARLEY: Yesterday you tell me tomorrow.

VANDERLIP: Today, I tell you, today. Never mind the price. I must have them—good dogs. Tonight, twelve o'clock, have them down at the water hole all ready, harnesses, grub, everything in shape. And you're to drive them downriver for me. Sure?

SITKA CHARLEY: Sure.

VANDERLIP: (*over his shoulder as he continues to cross to right*). Never mind the price. I must have them.

Crosses on over to right to Loraine Lisznayi, an expression of joy on his face. Sweeps off his fur cap and shakes her hand.

LORAINE: You must do better than that. Had there been a woman here, your face would have given everything away.

VANDERLIP: I can't help the gladness getting into my face, Loraine.

LORAINE: Don't call me Loraine. Somebody might hear. And we can't be too careful. And you mustn't talk but for a moment, Floyd.

VANDERLIP: (*grinning broadly*). There you go, calling me Floyd. Somebody might hear. But who's afraid? I'm not. Let 'em hear. I'm glad of it! Proud of it that you're mine. The dearest little woman in the world, and mine, all mine!

LORAINE: (*glancing furtively about and finding that nobody is paying any attention*). Hush, dear. Wait until we are safely away, and then I shall be proud before all the world to have you proud of me. You are such a man! Such a man!

VANDERLIP: Just wait until I get you into that Mediterranean palace. We'll make 'em sit up with this Klondike gold of ours. People don't know how rich I am, Loraine. Nor do you. I've got pay claims over on Dominion Creek nobody dreams of, and—

LORAINE: I don't care how much you've got, or how little. It's you, you big, big man, you, my hero, that I care for. You'll grace a palace like a prince, and I've known a few princes, too.

VANDERLIP: And queens, too, didn't you say?

LORAINE: Yes, and queens, too. And they will be proud and glad to know you. They don't have men like you over there—real men. You'll create a sensation.

VANDERLIP: (*anxiously*). But this living in palaces—sort
of softening and fattening, ain't it? I don't like fat.
(*Looks her over critically.*) You don't incline that way,
do you?

LORAINE: (*laughing*). You foolish, dear man, of course not.
Do I look it?

VANDERLIP: (*slowly*). Well, you look round—and plump.

LORAINE: I've always been plump like this. I'm like my
mother. She was that way. She never got stout, and
neither shall I.

VANDERLIP: (*anxiety going out of face, being replaced by
satisfaction*). Oh, you're all right, Loraine, you bet.

LORAINE: But you must leave me now, Floyd. Somebody may
come in at any moment. Besides, I've a few little things to
buy for our journey.

VANDERLIP: And they're fixing my money for me in there.
(*Nodding toward door at left. Loraine betrays keen and
involuntary interest.*) Letters of credit, you know, and all
that. Can't carry much dust. Too heavy. And by the way,
keep the weight down. Don't buy too many little things.
Dogs are dogs, and they can only haul so much.

LORAINE: Only enough for me to be comfortable.

VANDERLIP: A woman needs so almighty much to be comfortable. But it'll be all right. Two sleds'll carry us, no
matter how comfortable you make yourself. Bring plenty
of footgear, moccasins, and stockings, and such things.
And be at the water hole at midnight with your whole
outfit. Be sure that Indian of yours has enough dog food.
I'll get my dogs today sometime.

LORAINE: Which water hole?

VANDERLIP: The one by the hospital. Don't make a mistake
and go to the other one. It's way out of the way.

LORAINE: And now you simply must leave me. And you mustn't
see me again today—not till midnight, at the water hole,

by the hospital. You know I can scarcely bear to have you out of my sight. But these women—oh, they are such suspicious creatures!

VANDERLIP: Good-bye, then, until tonight.

Turns to go toward left.

LORAINE: (*softly*). Floyd! (*Vanderlip turns back.*) You must go to the ball tonight. I've begged off, but you must go. It will avert any possible suspicion.

VANDERLIP: I was going anyway, just to drop in for a while. I—that is, you see—I promised Mrs. Eppingwell I'd go.

LORAINE: (*jealously*). Mrs. Eppingwell!

VANDERLIP: Of course, but it's all right, Loraine. She don't count.

LORAINE: Of course not. But then, Floyd, I care so much for you that I can't help a little jealousy—but there, there, you *must* go. Good-bye, dear.

VANDERLIP: Good-bye, dear, dear Loraine.

Turns to go toward left.

LORAINE: (*softly*). Floyd!

VANDERLIP: (*turns back, waits, and after a pause*). Well?

LORAINE: (*with sweet reproof*). I've been hearing things about you, sir.

VANDERLIP: What's up now?

LORAINE: Oh, you seem to have—how shall I say?—a penchant for foreigners.

VANDERLIP: (*mystified*). Darned if I know what you're talking about. Penchant—is that something to eat?

LORAINE: (*laughing*). Well, then, there is a certain woman, supposed to be Greek, at any rate a foreigner like myself, but with the most adorable accent—or so the men say—

VANDERLIP: (*interrupting*). Freda, you mean.

LORAINE: (*fastidious expression on face*). Yes, I believe that is the woman's name.

VANDERLIP: (*laughing jovially*). There ain't anything in it. I don't care a rap for her—not a rap.

LORAINE: Then there's that Mrs. Eppingwell. I can't help thinking you are a little devoted to her.

VANDERLIP: (*showing slight embarrassment*). Oh, well, I've only seen her in a social way—that's all, in a social way.

LORAINE: And you do love only me? (*He nods.*) Then tell me that you do.

VANDERLIP: (*with impulsive eagerness, half-lifting his arms as if to embrace her and controlling himself with an effort*). Oh, I do, Loraine. I do, I do.

LORAINE: It is sweet to hear you say it. And now you really must go. Good-bye, dear, good-bye.

He crosses stage to left and goes out.

She starts to cross stage to rear, but is approached and stopped by Sitka Charley.

SITKA CHARLEY: (*gruffly*). Good morning.

LORAINE: (*sweetly*). Good morning, Charley.

SITKA CHARLEY: (*bluntly*). You got my money?

LORAINE: Oh, let me see. How much is it?

SITKA CHARLEY: Two hundred dollar.

LORAINE: I'll tell you. You come to my cabin tomorrow morning, and I'll give it to you.

SITKA CHARLEY: (*not letting on that he knows she is lying*). Tomorrow morning you give me money?

LORAINE: At my cabin, don't forget.

SITKA CHARLEY: All right, tomorrow morning.

He turns abruptly and starts to go toward stove.

LORAINE: (*calling*). Oh, Charley! (*He turns back to her.*) Is Dominion Creek very rich?

SITKA CHARLEY: Dam rich.

LORAINE: And do you know whether Mr. Vanderlip has any claims there?

SITKA CHARLEY: Me no know.

Starts to go.

LORAINE: (*detaining him*). But Mr. Vanderlip is very rich, isn't he? You know that?

SITKA CHARLEY: Vanderlip dam rich.

Sitka Charley turns abruptly and goes back to stove. Loraine crosses stage to left rear to counter, where a clerk waits upon her.

Enter Mrs. Eppingwell and Mrs. McFee from right. Both engage in brushing snow from moccasins.

MRS. EPPINGWELL: (*finishing first, and looking about the store as if in quest of someone*). . . . as I don't see anything of Captain Eppingwell, and he is the soul of promptness.

MRS. MCFEE: (*still brushing snow*). Mayhap we are a bit early, Mrs. Eppingwell. But as I was saying, it's verra dootful morals the giving of this masked ball. Masked, mind you, with every low dance-hall creature a-dying to come and put decent folk to the shame of their company. I speak my mind, and it's ay shameful that honest bodies must be so sore put. There'll be ruffians and gamblers with masks over their sinful faces, and who's to know? And there's that Freda woman. 'Tis said she plays with the souls of men as a child with a wee bit of a pipe plays with soap bubbles. And there's all the rest—bold hussies!—who's to stop them from flaunting their fine feathers in our faces? Who's to stop them, I make free to ask?

MRS. EPPINGWELL: (*smiling*). The doorkeeper, of course. It is quite simple. Masks must be lifted at the door.

MRS. MCFEE: Ou, ay, verra simple, I should say. Belike you'll undertake the doorkeeping, and belike you'll know the face of every rapscallion of them.

MRS. EPPINGWELL: We'll get one of the men who do know— Mr. Prince, for example. There he is, by the stove. We'll ask him to be doorkeeper.

Prince goes to rear and joins Loraine.

MRS. MCFEE: (*with more than usual asperity*). And how comes it Mr. Prince should know the children of sin and still be company for decent bodies?

MRS. EPPINGWELL: Because he is a man, I imagine. (*Mrs. McFee snorts.*) There is Sitka Charley. I suppose you would bar him if he wanted to come?

MRS. MCFEE: (*judicially*). Why, no, he's a verra good soul.

MRS. EPPINGWELL: Yet I'm sure he knows all the children of sin, you call them.

MRS. MCFEE: But he's an Indian, and he doesna dance.

MRS. EPPINGWELL: (*laughing*). Then I suppose I shall not shock you by speaking to him. (*Approaches Sitka Charley while Mrs. McFee goes to counter and is waited on by a clerk.*) Good morning, Charley. Have you seen Captain Eppingwell?

SITKA CHARLEY: (*nodding good morning*). Yes.

MRS. EPPINGWELL: How long ago? Was he here?

SITKA CHARLEY: I see um last night.

MRS. EPPINGWELL: Oh! (*Laughing.*) I've seen him later than that. But he was to meet me here.

SITKA CHARLEY: Um.

MRS. EPPINGWELL: (*trying to make conversation*). It is rather cold this morning.

SITKA CHARLEY: Um.

MRS. EPPINGWELL: How cold?

SITKA CHARLEY: Sixty-five below. Any dogs to sell?

MRS. EPPINGWELL: Still trying to buy dogs! For whom this time?

SITKA CHARLEY: Vanderlip. He want eight dogs.

MRS. EPPINGWELL: (*startled and interested*). Mr. Vanderlip?

SITKA CHARLEY: Um.

MRS. EPPINGWELL: What does he want with dogs?

SITKA CHARLEY: Um. Got dogs?

MRS. EPPINGWELL: (*a sudden thought striking her*). Yes, I've dogs to sell. Or rather, Captain Eppingwell has.

SITKA CHARLEY: Fresh dogs? Strong dogs?

MRS. EPPINGWELL: (*considering*). Well, no. You see, he just arrived yesterday. It was a long trip.

SITKA CHARLEY: Yes, me know—sixteen hundred miles. Dogs all bones, all played out, no good.

MRS. EPPINGWELL: How soon does he want the dogs?

SITKA CHARLEY: Right away, now, today.

MRS. EPPINGWELL: What does he want the dogs for?

SITKA CHARLEY: (*stolidly*). Um?

MRS. EPPINGWELL: What does Mr. Vanderlip want the dogs for?

SITKA CHARLEY: That no Sitka Charley's business. That Vanderlip's business.

MRS. EPPINGWELL: But I want to know.

SITKA CHARLEY: Then you ask Vanderlip.

MRS. EPPINGWELL: Tell me.

SITKA CHARLEY: Much better you ask Vanderlip, I think so.
A pause, during which Sitka Charley merely waits, while Mrs. Eppingwell seems to be thinking. When she speaks, it is in a changed, serious tone.

MRS. EPPINGWELL: Charley, we have traveled the Long Trail together, you and I.

SITKA CHARLEY: Um.

MRS. EPPINGWELL: We journeyed through the Hills of Silence. We saw our last dogs drop in the traces. We staggered and fell, and crawled on our hands and knees through the snow because we had not enough to eat, and it was very cold. We had our last food stolen—

SITKA CHARLEY: (*eyes flashing, face stiffening, grimly and with satisfaction*). Captain Eppingwell kill one man who steal food. I kill other man. I know.

MRS. EPPINGWELL: (*shuddering*). Yes, it was terrible. But we kept the faith of food and blanket, you and I, Charley.

SITKA CHARLEY: And Captain Eppingwell.

MRS. EPPINGWELL: And Captain Eppingwell. And by that faith of food and blanket I want you to tell me the truth now.

SITKA CHARLEY: Um.

MRS. EPPINGWELL: (*eagerly*). Will you?

SITKA CHARLEY: (*nodding his head*). Um.

MRS. EPPINGWELL: (*hurriedly*). Mr. Vanderlip wants dogs, fresh dogs—why?

SITKA CHARLEY: He make a long travel, many sleeps.

MRS. EPPINGWELL: Where? When? Tell me all.

SITKA CHARLEY: Um travel downriver. Um start tonight.

MRS. EPPINGWELL: He goes alone?

SITKA CHARLEY: (*shaking his head*). No.

MRS. EPPINGWELL: Who goes with him?

SITKA CHARLEY: Me go.

MRS. EPPINGWELL: (*irritably*). Yes, yes, of course. But you don't count. Anybody else?

SITKA CHARLEY: (*nodding his head*). Um.

MRS. EPPINGWELL: (*triumphantly*). Just as I thought. Tell me, Charley, it is—it is this—er—this horrid woman? You know.

SITKA CHARLEY: Um, this bad woman—this dam bad woman. Um, she go with him tonight, twelve o'clock, the water hole. She meet um there.

MRS. EPPINGWELL: (*eagerly*). Yes, yes. And then—

SITKA CHARLEY: And then she go with um, many sleeps, down the river.

MRS. EPPINGWELL: And you will get the dogs?

SITKA CHARLEY: Sure, I get um. (*Enter Dave Harney from left, striding angrily.*) I get um now—Dave Harney. Good-bye. *Starts in the direction of Dave Harney.*

MRS. EPPINGWELL: Wait a minute, Charley.

SITKA CHARLEY: (*over his shoulder*). I come back. You wait. (*Approaches Dave Harney.*) Hello, Dave. Cold today.

DAVE HARNEY: (*whirling upon him savagely*). You betcher life

it's cold—regular freeze-out, with me frozen. But I'm goin'
to quit it, quit it cold. I'll harness up my dogs and hit the
high places for a land of justice where a man can get what
he's ordered a year before and paid for.

SITKA CHARLEY: Got any dogs to sell?

DAVE HARNEY: Got any sugar to sell?

SITKA CHARLEY: I buy um dogs.

DAVE HARNEY: I'm buyin' sugar.

SITKA CHARLEY: I got no sugar. You got dogs. I buy dogs—
eight dogs—how much?

DAVE HARNEY: Five hundred dollars a dog.

SITKA CHARLEY: Um—eight dogs—four thousand dollar.

DAVE HARNEY: Dogs is wuth what you're willin' to pay for 'em.

SITKA CHARLEY: Um.

DAVE HARNEY: Look here, Charley, I used to be a miner, but
I'm a businessman now. Got any sugar?

SITKA CHARLEY: No sugar.

DAVE HARNEY: I'll throw a lot off them dogs for some sugar.
No sugar, they cost you four thousand.
Turns to go.

SITKA CHARLEY: (*making no movement to detain him*). Um.

DAVE HARNEY: (*over his shoulder*). Four thousand, Charley.

SITKA CHARLEY: Um.

DAVE HARNEY: They're wuth it if you want 'em real bad.

SITKA CHARLEY: All right, Dave. I buy.

DAVE HARNEY: Bring the dust around to my cabin at one
o'clock.

SITKA CHARLEY: I buy now.

DAVE HARNEY: No, you don't. I'm goin' back to tell 'em what I
think of 'em, the skunks! They've got sweetenin' in plenty
for their own mush and coffee. You betcher life they have,
and I'm goin' to get some of it or know the reason why.
Storms out through door to left.
Sitka Charley returns to Mrs. Eppingwell.

SITKA CHARLEY: That Dave Harney all the same one big robber. But I get um dogs all right.

MRS. EPPINGWELL: Tell me about this—er—this woman, Charley, this Freda—Freda Moloof her name is, isn't it?

SITKA CHARLEY: (*showing plainly that his attention has been called off from the consideration of Loraine Lisznayi*). Oh, Freda!

MRS. EPPINGWELL: (*smiling*). You call her Freda.

SITKA CHARLEY: Everybody call her Freda. Um good name. Me like it.

MRS. EPPINGWELL: Well, what kind of a woman is she?

SITKA CHARLEY: Um good woman.

MRS. EPPINGWELL: (*with an angry movement of arm and clenching of hand*). Oh!

SITKA CHARLEY: (*looking surprised and getting stubborn*). Me know Freda long time—two years. Um good woman. Um tongue speak true. Um just like you, no afraid. Um just like you, travel Long Trail with me. No afraid, very soft heart; sorry for dogs; no ride on sled when dogs tired. Um tired, but um walk. And um tongue straight; all the time speak true. I am Sitka Charley—I know.

MRS. EPPINGWELL: Yes, yes. Go on.

SITKA CHARLEY: (*considering*). Freda no like men.

MRS. EPPINGWELL: Now, that is too much, Charley. How about Mr. Vanderlip?

SITKA CHARLEY: (*shrugs his shoulders*). I know Freda long time. Freda know Vanderlip short time. Maybe Freda like Vanderlip. I don't know. But before she never like men, that I know. Maybe you like Mr. Vanderlip, I think. (*Mrs. Eppingwell smiles, and Sitka Charley grows more positive.*) Vanderlip come your cabin all the time. You ride on Vanderlip's sled. I know. I see. Maybe you like Vanderlip.

MRS. EPPINGWELL: You don't understand, Charley. I have reasons for being nice to Mr. Vanderlip.

SITKA CHARLEY: (*skeptically*). Um.

MRS. EPPINGWELL: And, Charley, you mustn't tell anybody what you have told me about Mr. Vanderlip going away tonight with that—that woman.

SITKA CHARLEY: (*weighing her words*). Maybe I tell Freda.

MRS. EPPINGWELL: (*stamping foot angrily*). Don't be foolish, Charley. She is the last person in the world who ought to know. Of course you'll not tell her. Tell no one. (*Sitka Charley hesitates.*) Promise me you'll not tell. Promise me by the faith of food and blanket.

SITKA CHARLEY: (*reluctantly*). All right, I no tell.

MRS. EPPINGWELL: They say Freda is a dancer. Have you seen her dance?

SITKA CHARLEY: (*nodding his head, a pleased expression on his face*). I see um. Very good dance. Um dance at Juneau, two years ago, first time I see. Treadwell Mine no work that day. No men to work. All men come Juneau and look see Freda dance. Freda makum much money. Um speak to me. Um say, "Charley, I go Yukon Country. You drive my dogs, how much?" Then Freda travel Long Trail with me.

MRS. EPPINGWELL: They say many men like her.

SITKA CHARLEY: (*nodding head vigorously*). Um, sure. Me like her too, very much.

MRS. EPPINGWELL: (*smiling tolerantly*). And they say she makes fools of men.

SITKA CHARLEY: Sure. Dam fools. Men just like bubble. Freda just make play with um—smash!—just like that. Everybody say so.

MRS. EPPINGWELL: What kind of a looking woman is she?

SITKA CHARLEY: You no see um?

MRS. EPPINGWELL: No. What does she look like?

Freda enters from right.

SITKA CHARLEY: (*looking at Freda*). Um there now.

MRS. EPPINGWELL: (*not understanding*). What?

SITKA CHARLEY: (*nodding head toward Freda*). Um Freda there.
*Mrs. Eppingwell turns involuntarily to look. Freda pauses on
entering, starts as though to retreat at sight of the crowd,
then stiffens herself, face and body, to meet it, and proceeds
to brush snow from moccasins. There is silence in store.
Then a perturbation amongst miners about stove, men
craning their heads over one another's shoulders to look at
Freda. The clerks look at her. Everybody looks at her.
Mrs. McFee turns up her nose several degrees and, plainly
advertising a highly moral rage, walks over to Mrs. Eppingwell.*

MRS. MCFEE: (*to Mrs. Eppingwell, but glaring at Freda*). It's my
way of thinking that it is high time for decent bodies to
be going.
Sitka Charley glares angrily at Mrs. McFee.

MRS. EPPINGWELL: (*in low voice*). Hush. It is a public place,
and she has as much right here as you or I. Don't insult
the poor woman.

MRS. MCFEE: (*snorting*). In my way of thinking the insult's the
other way around. Come you, Mrs. Eppingwell, we must
go. The verra air is contameenated.

MRS. EPPINGWELL: (*pleadingly*). Do please restrain yourself,
Mrs. McFee. Don't make a scene.

MRS. MCFEE: (*raising her voice*). I'll no restrain myself, and I'll
no wait for you if you see proper no to come now. The
hussy!
*Mrs. McFee, nose high in the air, turns to make exit at right.
Freda has just finished brushing snow and has risen erect.
Mrs. McFee, passing her to go out the door, sniffs audibly
and draws aside her skirt. Freda makes no movement, though
her lips tighten. Exit Mrs. McFee. Freda tries to hang up
wisp broom, but her hand trembles, misses peg, and wisp
broom falls to floor. She picks it up and this time hangs it
properly. Turns and goes to right rear to counter, where
clerk waits upon her.*

SITKA CHARLEY: (*glaring after Mrs. McFee, angrily*). That womans no like Freda. What for?

MRS. EPPINGWELL: (*speaking gently*). No women like Freda.

SITKA CHARLEY: (*stunned, slowly*) You no like Freda?

MRS. EPPINGWELL: (*more gently even than before*). No, Charley, I do not like Freda.

SITKA CHARLEY: (*showing anger*). What for you no like Freda?

MRS. EPPINGWELL: I cannot explain. You would not understand.

SITKA CHARLEY: (*more anger*). Me Sitka Charley. Me understand. What for you no like Freda?

Capt. Eppingwell enters from right.

MRS. EPPINGWELL: I— (*Catching sight of Capt. Eppingwell.*) There is Captain Eppingwell now.

Capt. Eppingwell brushes moccasins quickly and goes immediately to Mrs. Eppingwell. Sitka Charley, still angry, joins group about stove.

CAPT. EPPINGWELL: Early, as usual, Maud.

MRS. EPPINGWELL: No, merely on time. It is you who are late.

CAPT. EPPINGWELL: Impossible! (*Looks at his watch and smiles triumphantly.*) I knew it. On time to the tick of the second.

MRS. EPPINGWELL: (*smiling*). Not by Dawson time.

CAPT. EPPINGWELL: Oh, of course. I haven't changed my watch. I'm still going by sun time. Sorry.

MRS. EPPINGWELL: (*smiling*). I forgive you. It is the first time, but I really can't count it against you.

CAPT. EPPINGWELL: (*looking closely into her face*). What's wrong?

MRS. EPPINGWELL: Archie, you're the dearest man I know. Of course there is something wrong, and of course you knew it as soon as you set eyes on me. Well, I am beaten.

CAPT. EPPINGWELL: The Ever-Victorious-One beaten! Impossible! I'll not believe it.

MRS. EPPINGWELL: I am, just the same. Here I have been

trying to save Floyd Vanderlip, counteracting that evil woman's influence, having him to tea and dinner and giving him no end of my time, and Flossie isn't here yet, and he runs away with Freda Moloof tonight. It's all arranged and everything.

CAPT. EPPINGWELL: But—but—wait a minute. Enlighten me. I am only a poor traveler. Who is this Flossie? And why shouldn't this Vanderlip man—whoever he is—run away if he wants to?

MRS. EPPINGWELL: How ridiculous of me! I forget you've been away. You know who Freda Moloof is?

CAPT. EPPINGWELL: Surely, surely. She has the most magnificent furs and the most magnificent dogs in all Alaska. A fascinating creature, I—er—understand. She plays with men as a child plays with bubbles.

MRS. EPPINGWELL: It seems to me I've heard that before.

CAPT. EPPINGWELL: It has become a saying in the country.

MRS. EPPINGWELL: I have heard of men who whistle women up as they would whistle dogs. She must be the type of woman that whistles men.

CAPT. EPPINGWELL: (*warmly*). All she has to do is look at a man.

MRS. EPPINGWELL: (*smiling*). You speak as though she had looked at you.

CAPT. EPPINGWELL: (*smiling*). A very interesting woman.

MRS. EPPINGWELL: Well, anyway, she has cast eyes and wiles upon Floyd Vanderlip.

CAPT. EPPINGWELL: But why shouldn't she? This is a free country.

MRS. EPPINGWELL: Wait a minute. I'm trying to explain. Floyd Vanderlip is engaged to marry someone else.

CAPT. EPPINGWELL: O-o-h!

MRS. EPPINGWELL: Floyd Vanderlip is a big, strong man. For five years he chased Eldorados over the ice fields, living

on moose and salmon and working like a beast. He never
had an idle moment in which to be wicked. Then he
struck it on Klondike and is worth millions and millions.
Also, he sat down for the first time in five years and
rested. He remembered a girl who was waiting for
him down in the States—a young thing—and sent for
her to come in. They were to be married as soon as
she arrived. He has a cabin all ready. Well, that's Flossie.
She is coming in over the ice now—he's told me all
about it—and ought to be here any day. I've been
looking for her and looking for her till I am almost sick.
Then this Freda Moloof cast her spell upon him. I heard
the gossip—

CAPT. EPPINGWELL: And proceeded to take a hand. I begin to
understand.

MRS. EPPINGWELL: I did my best to break her influence. The
time and thought I've wasted upon that man! It's almost
scandalous the way I've devoted myself to him! Sitka
Charley believes I am in love with him—told me so to my
face. And it's all wasted, card parties and everything.
What was I against the only woman in Klondike who
possesses a piano and a maid? And tonight he runs away
down the river with her.

CAPT. EPPINGWELL: With Freda Moloof?

MRS. EPPINGWELL: With Freda Moloof. There she is now,
buying things for the journey most probably.

CAPT. EPPINGWELL: (*turning to look at Freda and turning back
again*). I must say she couldn't have done better if he is
worth all you say he is. I remember him now, a strapping
fellow, brave as a lion and all that.

MRS. EPPINGWELL: Yes, but he's caressed more shovel handles
than women's hands, and that's the trouble with him. And
I don't know what I shall do.

CAPT. EPPINGWELL: You could scarcely serve an injunction
on him.

MRS. EPPINGWELL: I don't know what I'll do. Floyd Vanderlip is not the sort of man to appeal to. To try to impress him to do the right thing would be like setting fire to a powder mill. I wish I knew how near Flossie is. There hasn't been a courier or a mail carrier in for weeks and weeks. The mail from Dyea is twenty days overdue. *Enter Mail Carrier, carrying leather mail pouch. He is clad in a long squirrel-skin parka reaching to his knees, the hood drawn over his head and ears and leaving only face exposed. Face and mouth are iced up, making speech impossible. He does not stop to brush snow from moccasins, but proceeds rapidly to cross to stove.*

CAPT. EPPINGWELL: There is the man who can tell you about Flossie. Shall I ask him?

MRS. EPPINGWELL: Oh, the mail carrier? At last! And in the nick of time. Yes, do.

CAPT. EPPINGWELL: (*stepping into the path of the Mail Carrier*). What's the news? (*Mail Carrier makes dumb show that he cannot speak, waving his arms and pointing to his iced mouth and then to the stove. Capt. Eppingwell laughs and lets him pass. To Mrs. Eppingwell.*) He's so iced up he cannot speak. Wait till he thaws out, and then I'll get hold of him. In the meantime—

MRS. EPPINGWELL: (*interrupting*). In the meantime you must meet the Lisznayi.

CAPT. EPPINGWELL: The Lisznayi!

MRS. EPPINGWELL: Yes, she is a fascinating woman, our latest acquisition. An Old World Hungarian with all the do and dare of the New World blood. She was a friend of the Queen of Romania. Posed as a model for the Queen. Had cardinals and princes at her beck and call. Plenty of money, of course, position, and all that. Came into the Klondike out of sheer love of adventure, and possibly because she was bored. You'll enjoy her, I know. There she is over there. Do you care to?

*Mrs. Eppingwell and Capt. Eppingwell walk over to left rear
to Loraine Lisznayi and Prince.*

*Mail Carrier tries to get to stove, but is blocked by miners,
who are demanding: "What's the news?" "How's the trail?"
"Any letters for me?" "And me?" "And me?" "Where did you
meet O'Brien? He left ten days ago." "How's the ice on Thirty
Mile River?" etc., etc. To all of which Mail Carrier replies by
waving his arms and thrusting through the crowd till he gets
to stove, over which he holds his face.*

*Dave Harney enters from left, still in towering rage, but his
face lights up, as though struck by a sudden thought, when
he catches sight of Mail Carrier. He strides over, clutches
Mail Carrier by the arm, and draws him to one side.*

DAVE HARNEY: (*in a whisper*). Got a noospaper?

Mail Carrier nods head.

DAVE HARNEY: How many?

Mail Carrier holds up one finger.

DAVE HARNEY: I'll give you twenty dollars for it.

Mail Carrier shakes head.

DAVE HARNEY: (*bidding rapidly, each bid being met by a shake
of Mail Carrier's head*). Twenty-five. Thirty. Thirty-five.
Forty. Fifty.

Mail Carrier nods head and goes back to stove.

*Freda walks forward toward stove and beckons to Sitka
Charley, who leaves group about stove and comes to her.*

FREDA: Tell the mail carrier I want to speak to him, Charley.

SITKA CHARLEY: (*obediently*). Um. (*Sitka Charley crosses to
stove, where Mail Carrier is pulling the ice from his mouth.*)
Freda want talk some with you.

MAIL CARRIER: (*turning to look at Freda, nods head and
mumbles incoherently, at same time starting to go to Freda
and still pulling ice from mouth. He shakes hands with
Freda and speaks thickly at first.*) How do do, Freda.

FREDA: How do you do, Joe. What kind of a trip did you
have?

MAIL CARRIER: Pretty rough, but I made good time just the same. Passed everything in sight.

FREDA: That is what I wanted to ask you about. Did you pass the outfit of a girl, or, rather, of a young woman?

MAIL CARRIER: Coming in by herself, with a dog puncher and an Indian?

FREDA: Yes. Where did you pass her?

MAIL CARRIER: Yesterday afternoon, about three o'clock. They were making camp early. She was pretty tired, from the looks of her.

FREDA: When should she get in?

MAIL CARRIER: I talked with the dog puncher. He said they'd camp tonight at Mooseback and come in tomorrow. That's twenty-five miles, and if they don't start too late, they'll make Dawson by the middle of the day.

FREDA: What kind of a girl is she?

MAIL CARRIER: Good. How do you mean?

FREDA: I mean, what kind of a looking girl is she? How did she strike you?

MAIL CARRIER: Oh, one of the soft and clingy kind, I guess I'd call her. You know, the kind that needs lots of cuddling and petting. Pretty, yes, danged pretty. Blue eyes, wavy hair, and all the rest—trembly lips and teary eyes—smiley and weepy, you know, all in the same moment. But gee, Freda, I can't stand here gassin' all day. I got about a thousand dollars' worth of letters to deliver—a dollar apiece and cheap at the price. I'll see you later. So long.

FREDA: All right, Joe. Tell Sitka Charley I want to see him, will you?

Mail Carrier returns to stove, picks up mail pouch, and sends Sitka Charley to Freda.

Capt. Eppingwell comes to Mail Carrier, and is leading him off to Mrs. Eppingwell when Dave Harney interposes.

DAVE HARNEY: Hold your hosses, Joe. How about that dicker for the noospaper? You said yes to fifty.

MAIL CARRIER: (*pulling out his gold sack and drawing news-paper from pocket and giving both to Dave Harney*). All right. Just weigh the fifty into that.
Dave Harney takes gold sack over to scales, produces his own gold sack, and a clerk weighs from one sack into the other.
Mail Carrier accompanies Capt. Eppingwell to Mrs. Eppingwell. Capt. Eppingwell, Loraine Lisznayi, and Prince move along counter toward right and inspect mittens and moccasins.

FREDA: What time tomorrow has he decided upon starting?

SITKA CHARLEY: No tomorrow. Today, tonight, twelve o'clock tonight.

FREDA: (*startled.*) Tonight! Are you sure?

SITKA CHARLEY: Um.

FREDA: You said tomorrow.

SITKA CHARLEY: Vanderlip um change mind. Look like much hurry.

FREDA: And the Lisznayi woman?

SITKA CHARLEY: She wait water hole. Um meet her there. One Indian drive her dogs. Me drive Vanderlip's dogs.

FREDA: But Vanderlip mustn't go tonight. I tell you, Charley, he simply mustn't.

SITKA CHARLEY: (*incredulously*). Um.

FREDA: Not only that, but you must help me to keep him from going.

SITKA CHARLEY: (*angrily*). What for, Freda? I am Sitka Charley. I buy dogs, I sell dogs, I drive dogs. I help you dogs, yes. What for I help you other things? Vanderlip all the same one big chief. Um womans like um. (*Holding up fingers.*) One, two, three womans like um. That um womans' trouble. No Sitka Charley's trouble. What for, Freda?

FREDA: Why, what are you thinking about?

SITKA CHARLEY: I think you one big fool, Freda.

FREDA: (*smiling sadly*). And I think you are right, Charley,
  when I look back.

SITKA CHARLEY: No look back. Right now. What for you make
  fool with Vanderlip? Him no good. Him big fool too.

FREDA: Oh, I see. You think I am in love with him.

SITKA CHARLEY: (*with satisfaction*). Um.

FREDA: You really think so?

SITKA CHARLEY: Um. What for you say he must no go tonight?
  Um?

FREDA: Listen, Charley. You must help me, and I'll tell you all
  about it. There is a little girl coming in over the ice to
  marry Vanderlip—

SITKA CHARLEY: (*interrupting excitedly*). One more woman!
  Um Vanderlip one dam big chief. (*Holding up fingers.*) One
  woman, two woman, three woman, four womans.

FREDA: (*surprised*). Four women?

SITKA CHARLEY: Um. Four womans.

FREDA: Who are they?

SITKA CHARLEY: (*holding up fingers*). Little girl come in over
  ice—one. Lisznayi woman go 'way with um—two. Freda
  no want Lisznayi woman go 'way with um—three. Mrs.
  Eppingwell—four. One—two—three—four—womans.

FREDA: (*surprised*). Mrs. Eppingwell! Oh, you told me about
  her once. She was the woman who was with you on that
  trip through the Hills of Silence. She is a very brave
  woman. I have heard much of her, and I like her. If I were
  a man, I could love her. She must be very good, and sweet,
  and kind.

SITKA CHARLEY: Sure. And um hard like iron sometimes. But
  um no like you. Um say so. What for um no like you?

FREDA: (*gently*). No woman likes me, Charley.

SITKA CHARLEY: All men like you.

FREDA: (*with touch of anger*). All men are fools.

SITKA CHARLEY: What for womans no like you?

FREDA: (*meditatively*). And she likes Vanderlip. How do you know? What do you know?

SITKA CHARLEY: No can tell. I promise.

FREDA: Promised whom?

SITKA CHARLEY: Mrs. Eppingwell. Um Mrs. Eppingwell very good woman.

FREDA: But she has a husband. It is not good for her to like another man. What do you think?

SITKA CHARLEY: (*perplexedly*). I think I don't know. I think all um womans crazy. What for all um womans like this Vanderlip man?

FREDA: (*decisively*). Well, I don't.

SITKA CHARLEY: (*skeptically*). Um.

FREDA: Let me show you, Charley, and then you will know why I want you to help me. And remember, you mustn't tell a word of any of this to anyone.

SITKA CHARLEY: (*debating the proposition*). Um—maybe I tell Mrs. Eppingwell.

FREDA: (*angrily*). Don't be silly, Charley. You mustn't tell anybody. Promise me now.

SITKA CHARLEY: (*with despairing perplexity*). All right, I no tell.

FREDA: Now this little girl is coming in over the ice—her name is Flossie. She has lived a soft life down in California, where the sun is warm and there is no snow. She does not know hardship, nor the trail, and she is having a hard time now on the trail. Think of it! Sixty-five degrees below zero this morning, and she is out in it, walking, walking, walking, her breath freezing, her mouth icing up, her eyebrows rimed with frost. And she is very stiff, and sore, and tired. Every step of the trail she takes in pain. It is like a bad dream to her, Charley. But she sees, always before her, at the end of the dream, an awakening at Dawson, in the arms of the man who is to marry her. But, Charley, what if when she gets to Dawson there is no Floyd Vanderlip? No man to marry her? It will break her heart. It will be no happy awakening from a bad dream, but the beginning of a worse dream. And she is a little girl, Charley—not a strong woman like me who does not care. She will care, and she will know nobody, and she will cry, and cry, and cry. Did you ever hear a woman cry, Charley? Think of it, she is only a little girl.

SITKA CHARLEY: Um. More like baby.

FREDA: Yes, put it that way, more like a baby. She cannot stand pain.

SITKA CHARLEY: Oh, on trail, too much walk make um hurt.

FREDA: No, no. (*Holds hand to heart.*) Pain here.

SITKA CHARLEY: Um. I know. Um sick. What um call—heart disease. I see one man sick that way. Um fall down dead, just like that.

FREDA: (*irritably*). Oh, you don't understand.

SITKA CHARLEY: (*puzzled*). I don't know. Womans all crazy.

FREDA: (*smiling*). I think I can explain. Last summer you were in a canoe race on the river. You paddled very hard, but you lost. (*Putting hand to heart.*) And it hurt you—

SITKA CHARLEY: (*interrupting*). Um. Um. Paddle like hell. No win race. (*Stroking first one arm and then the other.*) Much tired right here. (*Putting hand over heart.*) And um much hurt right here, no tired, just hurt like rheumatism, because I am sorry I lose race. (*Nods head repeatedly.*) Um. Um.

FREDA: The very thing. She doesn't know it, but she is racing against this Lisznayi woman. Flossie must get here before the other woman steals her man. And you must help her win the race. Will you?

SITKA CHARLEY: You know this Flossie girl?

FREDA: No.

SITKA CHARLEY: No?

FREDA: Never saw her in my life. But she is coming into a strange country without a friend or a dollar when she gets here. She will have great trouble. And you know, Charley, it is not good for a woman to be without friends or money in this country.

SITKA CHARLEY: (*puzzled as much as ever*). Don't know Flossie girl. No like Vanderlip man. What for you care? . . . Much foolishness. All womans crazy. . . . All right, I help.

Mail Carrier has finished interview with Mrs. Eppingwell, received gold sack back from Dave Harney, and gone out with mail pouch to left. Capt. Eppingwell and Loraine Lisznayi have rejoined Mrs. Eppingwell.

Loraine Lisznayi says good-bye to them and starts to make exit to right, passing close to Freda and Sitka Charley. She pauses one or two paces away.

LORAINE: (*favoring Freda with a quick but sweeping, scornful glance*). Come here, Charley. I want to speak to you a moment.

Her conduct angers Sitka Charley, who grows stolid and refuses to move or reply.

FREDA: Speak with her, Charley.

SITKA CHARLEY: (*sullenly*). No speak.

Loraine Lisznayi, scornful expression on face, proceeds on her way and makes exit to right.

FREDA: Why didn't you, Charley?

SITKA CHARLEY: (*angrily*). What for she look at you that way?

FREDA: (*ignoring the question*). They say she is a rich woman in her own country. But I don't believe it. I think she is after Vanderlip's money.

SITKA CHARLEY: Lisznayi woman no got money. I know. I sell her dogs—eight hundred dollars. She pay me three hundred. Two weeks, three weeks, I no get other five hundred dollars. Um no got five hundred. I say, "My dogs, give me back." She give back. Me have fur robe. Good fur robe. She buy, two hundred dollar. Um no pay. Um have

good fur robe. Me no have nothing. Um have cabin. Um
no pay rent to Johnson. Um smile very nice, um Johnson
wait. I know, I see. Um dogs she got now, Vanderlip give,
make present. Um no pay firewood. Um no pay many
things.

FREDA: I thought so. And now to win the race. Dogs first of
all. Flossie must be brought in tonight. I want you here
in Dawson, Charley. So you must send some Indian up
the trail with a fresh team of dogs. Flossie camps at
Mooseback tonight. He is to let her think that Vanderlip
has sent the dogs and that Vanderlip wants her to come
right on tonight. Understand?

SITKA CHARLEY: Um. Sure.

FREDA: (*preparing to start toward door at right*). Start the
dogs right away with a man you can trust. And he must
be sure to let Flossie think that Vanderlip sent him. At the
best, Flossie can't arrive until late tonight. And there may
be delays. You keep on Vanderlip's trail so that you will
know always where he is. (*Freda and Sitka Charley start to
walk toward the door at right.*) When I send for him, you
must bring him to me, and I'll hold him till Flossie gets in.

SITKA CHARLEY: (*touching Freda's arm*). No very strong, Freda.

FREDA: (*tapping her forehead*). Vanderlip no very strong,
Charley.

Both cover ears, pull on mittens, and go out.

*Dave Harney, unobserved, has been squatting on hams
in front of counter to right, intently reading newspaper.
He is making dumb show of excited interest. One of the
miners discovers him, runs over to him, and starts to read
newspaper over his shoulder. Dave Harney folds newspaper
across, resting it on his knee, and looks up coolly into face
of Miner.*

MINER: (*in hurt voice*). Can't you give a fellow a squint at
your paper?

DAVE HARNEY: Got any sugar?

MINER: Sure.

DAVE HARNEY: Give me a whack at your sugar barrel?

MINER: (*surprised and shocked*). No.

DAVE HARNEY: Then nary squint at my noospaper.

In meantime other miners and clerks have surrounded him, all demanding to see his newspaper. Whereupon he puts paper in his pocket, rises to his feet, and starts toward door to right, miners and clerks following him and grumbling at his meanness.

DAVE HARNEY: (*pausing with his hand on door*). You think you're smart, don't you? Got a corner on sugar, eh? And poor Dave Harney left without no sweetenin' for his coffee an' mush. Well, poor Dave Harney's got a corner on noos. When you want noos, come an' see him, an' be sure an' bring your sugar along.

Goes out, followed by miners.

Mrs. Eppingwell and Capt. Eppingwell come forward to stove and warm their hands.

CAPT. EPPINGWELL: (*continuing conversation*). Perhaps Freda doesn't know about Flossie. I always thought her a good girl at heart.

MRS. EPPINGWELL: Why this haste, then? Why are they running away tonight instead of tomorrow, as they had planned? They must have received information somehow, even before the mail carrier arrived. (*Enter Mail Carrier from left.*) And look how she captured the mail carrier at once, and for one thing, I know, to learn Flossie's whereabouts.

CAPT. EPPINGWELL: Here he is now. Let's ask him. (*Beckons Mail Carrier over to him.*) You were talking with Freda a little while ago. What did she want to learn?

MAIL CARRIER: (*pausing only long enough to reply and then going on to make exit to right*). Same thing as your wife— where I passed that girl's outfit.

MRS. EPPINGWELL: (*quietly*). I knew it.

CAPT. EPPINGWELL: But why couldn't I go around, or you, and talk with Freda, explain the situation fully to her, and make an appeal to whatever good is in her?

MRS. EPPINGWELL: (*smiling*). You don't know women, Archie—(*adding as an afterthought*)—as well as women know women. No, she must be beaten at her own game. Flossie must arrive before midnight tonight.

CAPT. EPPINGWELL: But she camps at Mooseback.

MRS. EPPINGWELL: There are dogs in Dawson. Now, Archie, this is for you to do. Borrow a team of fresh dogs somewhere, put your Indian in charge of it—that one-eyed man, he's faithful—and start him up the trail to Flossie. Let her think Floyd Vanderlip has sent the dogs to bring her in right away.

CAPT. EPPINGWELL: (*smiling*). Ah, I see. The impatience of the ardent and long-denied lover.

MRS. EPPINGWELL: (*smiling in return*). And once Flossie is here and gets her arms around Floyd Vanderlip's neck, Freda Moloof will wait in vain at the water hole.

CAPT. EPPINGWELL: That will settle it. Freda's not the woman to stand knocking her feet around a water hole very long for any man.

MRS. EPPINGWELL: (*good-naturedly*). You seem to know a great deal about what kind of a woman this dancer is.

CAPT. EPPINGWELL: I know enough about her, when it comes to Vanderlip and Flossie, to think her the best of the boiling . . . and to have a sneaking regret for her being beaten this way.

MRS. EPPINGWELL: You may be kindhearted, Archie, but you are unwise.

CAPT. EPPINGWELL: (*sighing*). Oh, well, after the manner of civilized man I submit to my womenkind. All right, I'll send the dogs at once. (*Makes a movement to start toward door to right, and Mrs. Eppingwell starts with him. Mrs. Eppingwell, struck suddenly by a new idea, pauses. Capt.*

Eppingwell pauses a step in advance and looks at her.)
What's wrong now?

MRS. EPPINGWELL: Suppose there is some mischance, a delay, and Flossie doesn't get in by midnight?

CAPT. EPPINGWELL: Then Freda wins.

MRS. EPPINGWELL: (*decisively*). No, she doesn't. (*Thinks for a moment.*) Floyd Vanderlip is coming to the ball. I'll see that he comes. I'll be very nice to him and watch him closely so that he does not sneak away. If Flossie fails to arrive, say, by half past eleven, I'll be taken ill and I'll ask Vanderlip to take me home; and I'll hold him, no matter how terribly ill or terribly nice I have to be, until midnight is well past or until Flossie arrives.

CAPT. EPPINGWELL: Then it's my duty to disappear about the time you are taken ill.

MRS. EPPINGWELL: Archie, though I tell you for the thousandth time, you are a perfect dear. And I can be as terribly nice as I please to Floyd Vanderlip?
Capt. Eppingwell laughs and nods, and they continue toward door.

MRS. EPPINGWELL: (*while they are pulling on mittens, etc.*). And now the dogs. Don't delay a moment, Archie, please.

CAPT. EPPINGWELL: The one-eyed man and the six dogs start at once.
They go out.
Only clerks behind counter are left on the stage.
Nothing happens for a full minute, when Mrs. McFee appears at right, peeping through door, which she holds ajar. She peers cautiously about, enters, and sniffs the air several times. Then she smiles a sour smile of satisfaction.

MRS. MCFEE: And now a decent body can make her purchases.

CURTAIN

ACT II

Anteroom of Pioneer Hall. It is ten-thirty P.M. The room is large and bare. Its walls are of logs, stuffed between with brown moss. Street door to rear, in center. Doors, window frames, and sashes of rough, unstained pine boards. At one side of door is wisp broom for brushing snow from moccasins. On either side of door is an ordinary, small-paned window, and beneath either window is a rough wooden bench. Under benches are large outdoor moccasins, left there after the manner of overshoes, by their owners. In available space on rear wall, many wooden pegs, on which are hanging furs, parkas, hats, wraps, etc. Midway between front and rear, and at equal distances between center and sides, running at full blast, are two large wood-burning stoves. Alongside each stove is a wood box filled with firewood. On right, a window. On left, wide doorway, open, connecting with ballroom. Through doorway come occasional snatches of dance music, bursts of laughter and of voices.
Because it is very cold, street door is kept closed, and is opened by doorkeeper only when someone knocks, and then only long enough for that one to enter. All parleying is done on inside with door closed.

Prince, as doorkeeper, is standing at rear by street door. Men and women, in costume, are disappearing through door to left, from where come strains of a waltz.

PRINCE: (*drawing up his shoulders, as if cold*). B-r-r! (*Crosses rapidly to left and peers through doorway into ballroom, looking for somebody. Holds up his finger and beckons.*) Here, you, Billy! More fire! Hi yu skookum fire!

Enter Indian, who proceeds to fire up both stoves.

Prince stands looking into ballroom. A knock is heard at street door. He returns and opens door.

A Man enters, masked and in heavy fur overcoat.

PRINCE: (*hastily closing door*). Hello.

The Man hesitates, looks around, and starts to cross to left.

PRINCE: (*plucking him by the arm*). Well?

MAN: (*pausing, and then as if discovering reason for his detention*). Oh!

Sits down on bench and proceeds to remove moccasins.

PRINCE: Masks must be lifted at the door, you know.

MAN: (*in muffled voice*). And give myself away? Oh, no.

PRINCE: The doorkeeper's lips are sealed. I give nobody's identity away. Come on, let's see who you are. (*Reaches out and lifts mask.*) Jack Denison!

MAN: (*in clear voice*). Yours truly, Prince, my boy.

PRINCE: But you can't come in here, old man.

MAN: And why not?

PRINCE: (*stuttering and stammering*). Why—I—they're damned select—it's the women, you know—and I—they—well, they made me doorkeeper, and—(*breaking down*)—you know well enough yourself, Jack.

MAN: (*rising as though to go, and in angry tones*). By God, you can come down to Jack Denison's joint, all right, and buck Jack Denison's faro layout, all right, and have a social drink with him, all right; but when Jack Denison comes up to your doings, you turn'm down like he had smallpox.

PRINCE: It's not my fault. It's the women, I tell you. They're running the show.

MAN: (*wheedlingly*). You might let a fellow in just for a peep. Nobody'll know. I'll clear out before they unmask.

PRINCE: (*pleadingly*). I can't, really, old man, I— (*Catches sight of Mrs. McFee, who appears in doorway to left.*) Look at her! Get out quick!
Places hand on his shoulder in friendly way and starts to shove him out.

MAN: (*catching sight of Mrs. McFee*). Wow!
With bodily expression of fear, shrinks behind Prince and allows himself to be shoved out.

MRS. MCFEE: (*crossing over to Prince, and suspiciously*). Who might that body be?

PRINCE: (*wiping his brow*). One of the unelect, I am sorry to say, Mrs. McFee.

MRS. MCFEE: A gambler man, I take it? (*Prince nods.*) But I can no see, Mr. Prince, why you should conduct negotiations inside the door, contameenating the air with the bodily presence of the children of sin.

PRINCE: (*slight note of anger in his voice*). Do you know how cold it is, Mrs. McFee?

MRS. MCFEE: I have no given it a thought.

PRINCE: Well, it's seventy degrees below zero, and still going down. If that door is open one minute, a refrigerator would be comfortable alongside that ballroom. And if you don't like the way I'm doing things—
A knock is heard, and he opens door. Sitka Charley squeezes in.

PRINCE: (*very politely*). Can Sitka Charley come in, Mrs. McFee?

MRS. MCFEE: (*turning to go*). He is a good body. There is no reason why he should not bide a wee. (*To Sitka Charley.*) But you must go right away again, Charley.

SITKA CHARLEY: (*nods his head, and then to Prince*). Where um Vanderlip?

PRINCE: He's here somewhere. Go and find him.

Laughter and voices, and many couples enter from left, some in costume, several in hooded dominos.

SITKA CHARLEY: (*recoiling, startled and excited*). What that? (*Prince laughs.*) What for? Everybody crazy?

PRINCE: (*laughing*). Button, button, who's got the button. Go and find him.

Sitka Charley, walking stealthily, like a wild animal in dangerous territory, goes adventuring amongst the maskers. After some time, a domino takes Sitka Charley by the arm and leads him apart.

SITKA CHARLEY: (*dragging back and struggling to escape*). What for, crazymans?

VANDERLIP: Shut up! It's me, Vanderlip. Looking for me?

SITKA CHARLEY: (*with relief*). Um.

VANDERLIP: Anything wrong?

SITKA CHARLEY: (*shaking head*). No wrong. All right. Um Freda want you come right away.

VANDERLIP: (*surprised*). Freda! What's she want with me?

SITKA CHARLEY: Um no tell. Um say: "Charley, you go Pioneer Hall quick. All the same one big dance. You catch um Vanderlip. You make um come right away."

VANDERLIP: (*puzzled*). Where?

SITKA CHARLEY: Um Freda's cabin. You come now?

VANDERLIP: (*thinks for a minute, with a bothered air*). I'll come in a little while. You tell her. (*Turns to rejoin dancers and speaks over shoulder.*) Dogs all right?

SITKA CHARLEY: Um.

VANDERLIP: Be at the water hole at twelve o'clock?

SITKA CHARLEY: Um. Sure.

Sitka Charley gains street door and goes out.

A knock is heard at door. Enter Dave Harney, costumed as a Scotch minister. He passes Prince's inspection, removes street moccasins and parka, and walks to the front. His shambling, loose-jointed gait discovers him. There is hand clapping and

*laughter, and there are cries of "Harney! Harney!" "Dave
Harney!" Crowd sings, "For the sugar man will catch you if
you don't watch out." He accepts the discovery, goes over to
stove at right, pulls newspaper out of pocket, and begins to
read. The dancers crowd about him, demanding the news.
He makes to be offended by them and walks away, reading
paper. They follow behind him, still clamoring for the news.
He promenades about stage and then makes exit to left,
followed by the whole crew, with the exception of one domino
and a court lady of the time of Louis XVI, who linger by
stove to left.*

COURT LADY, MRS. EPPINGWELL: I haven't seen your makeup,
Archie.

DOMINO, CAPT. EPPINGWELL: (*in disguised voice, declaiming*).
Would that I might claim Archie for myself, there is such
affectionate possession in the way you say it. Who is this
Archie, sweet lady?

MRS. EPPINGWELL: Come, come, Archie, a truce to fooling.
Besides, you can't fool me anyway. Did you get the
dogs off?

CAPT. EPPINGWELL: (*in natural voice*). Promptly, and with the
one-eyed man. Also a spare man to come back posthaste
and let us know their progress.

MRS. EPPINGWELL: Then when should Flossie arrive?

CAPT. EPPINGWELL: We figured it out. Barring accidents or the
unusual, she'll be here by eleven-thirty—at any rate, not
later than midnight.

MRS. EPPINGWELL: (*considering*). Not later than midnight.

CAPT. EPPINGWELL: Of course, after all, one can't tell within
an hour.

MRS. EPPINGWELL: And she is to be brought here?

CAPT. EPPINGWELL: She'll ride the sled right up to the door. A
knock, and then, enter Flossie.

MRS. EPPINGWELL: (*with gratified smile*). And then all our

troubles will be over. And now for your makeup. I insist. *Capt. Eppingwell slips off domino and stands forth a faithful copy of Sitka Charley.*

MRS. EPPINGWELL: Sitka Charley!

CAPT. EPPINGWELL: (*imitating Sitka Charley's voice*). Um wantum dogs? I sell um dogs, much good dogs.

MRS. EPPINGWELL: (*clapping her hands*). Excellent! (*She catches sight of Sitka Charley, who is entering through street door at rear.*) Quick! (*Helps Capt. Eppingwell on with domino.*) Now let us return to the ballroom and find Floyd Vanderlip. I'm pretty sure of him. He's in a domino, too.

They start for exit to left. Sitka Charley, mistaking Capt. Eppingwell for Vanderlip, signals to him a desire to speak with him, but is ignored. Exit Mrs. Eppingwell and Capt. Eppingwell. Sitka Charley stands a moment, puzzled, watching them go, then follows after them. Makes exit, and a moment later enters with Vanderlip, who is still in domino.

VANDERLIP: (*testily*). What do you want now?

SITKA CHARLEY: Me no want. Freda want.

VANDERLIP: What's she want?

SITKA CHARLEY: Want you.

VANDERLIP: I haven't anything to do with her. She can keep on wanting. I'm busy.

SITKA CHARLEY: Um want you now, right away, quick.

VANDERLIP: (*angrily*). You go to the devil. And she can go, too, for all I care.

Enter Dave Harney from left, still reading newspaper and followed by the dancers.

SITKA CHARLEY: I tell Freda you say go to devil?

VANDERLIP: (*flinging away angrily*). Tell her! Tell her! Just as long as you quit bothering me. (*And then seriously.*) And when you've told her, you'd better go and see everything's in shape.

SITKA CHARLEY: (*starting for street door*). Dogs, sleds, everything all right.
Exit Sitka Charley.

DAVE HARNEY: (*in center of stage, turning suddenly upon rout at his heels*). Well? What d'ye want?
The rout gathers about him, facing him. There are cries of "The news! The news!" "What's happening down in God's country?" "Who won the championship?" "How'd the election turn out?" "Was Tammany downed?" "Is it true the United States is fighting Germany?" "Is war really declared?" etc.

DAVE HARNEY: Got any sugar?
Groans, catcalls, and laughter.

A VOICE: The meanest man in the Klondike.

DAVE HARNEY: So you'd be, dodgast you, if you hadn't no sweetenin' for your coffee and mush.

ANOTHER VOICE: Speech! Speech!

VOICES: Speech! Speech!

DAVE HARNEY: All right, consarn you, I'll speechify. (*Clears his throat.*) Ladies an' gentlemen—ahem—
Stops to clear throat.

A VOICE: Bring him some water. A glass of water, please, for the speaker.

ANOTHER VOICE: Get a box for him.
The firewood is dumped out of the wood box, which is placed before Dave Harney upside down. He is helped up on it.

A VOICE: Now he's going to read us all the news.
Cheers and hand clapping.

DAVE HARNEY: (*folding newspaper and putting it in his pocket*). My friend, you've got another guess comin'. I'm goin' to read you the riot act. An' here it is, short an' simple. You've got all the sugar, an' I've got all the noos. Nothin' to it but a dicker. We'll swop. That's what we'll do, we'll swop. (*Cheers.*) An' I say again, for them as is dull of

hearin', we'll swop. After the unmaskin', you all will
assemble here in this here room an' hear the noospaper
read, advertisements an' all. (*Cheers.*) An' in the meantime,
I'm open to subscriptions in the form of promissory notes.
Said notes shall be for the sum of one heapin', large tin
cup of sugar, white or brown, to be paid to party of the
first part—you all is party to the second part—to be paid
to party of the first part inside twenty-four hours after the
delivery of the goods, to wit, the noos. Said party of the
first part hereby agreein' to send a man with a sack
around to the cabins of said party of the second part an'
collect face value of promissory note, to wit, one heapin',
large tin cup of sugar, white or brown. Them that signs
notes hears the noospaper read, them that don't, don't.
Thankin' you kindly, one an' all, I remain, yours truly, an'
am ready to take promissory notes here an' now.
Cheers, laughter, and consent.

A VOICE: But we haven't any pen or ink, Dave.

DAVE HARNEY: You've got to sit up all night to get up earlier
than Dave Harney in the mornin'. Here you are. (*Draws
pen, inkstand, and paper pad from pockets.*) An' you might
as well sign first, young feller. (*The signing of notes begins,
Dave Harney, with ink and paper, passing from one to
another as the rout breaks up and starts back to ballroom
for next dance. Pausing in doorway to left.*) Just as easy—
like shooting fish in a bucket.
Goes out.

*Enter Mrs. Eppingwell on arm of Vanderlip, who is still in
domino. They promenade, talking, about room. They are
followed by Loraine Lisznayi, masked and magnificently
costumed, who keeps her eyes on them and betrays keen
interest in them.*

MRS. EPPINGWELL: Wasn't it funny I guessed you, Mr.
Vanderlip, in that first dance?

VANDERLIP: You have a good eye.

MRS. EPPINGWELL: And possibly I really wanted to find you, you know.

VANDERLIP: (*awkwardly, but pleased*). Hum, yes, I suppose so. And I was looking for you, too, hard as I could.

MRS. EPPINGWELL: You'd never guess how I guessed you. (*He shakes his head.*) It is very simple. You are the same height as Captain Eppingwell.

She laughs merrily.

VANDERLIP: (*looking at dance card*). Hello, I haven't the next dance with you!

MRS. EPPINGWELL: No, that's promised to—well, to somebody else.

VANDERLIP: But the next after is mine.

MRS. EPPINGWELL: (*looking at dance card*). And the next after that. I'm almost afraid I'm dancing too much with you. What will people say?

VANDERLIP: (*pleased, and eagerly*). Ah, but they don't know who we are.

MRS. EPPINGWELL: They will after the unmasking. Then they will remember us together so much.

VANDERLIP: (*as though struck by a thought of something else*). What time will they unmask?

MRS. EPPINGWELL: Two o'clock. And—(*looks at card*)—there is a waltz after that I should like. You do waltz so well, Mr. Vanderlip.

VANDERLIP: I won't be able to make that waltz, I— *Breaks off suddenly.*

MRS. EPPINGWELL: Why, you, of all men, are not going home early?

VANDERLIP: No—I—that is— (*Looks at card, studies it profoundly, as though it would get him out of his difficulty.*) Why, yes, of course we can have that waltz together. I thought it was already engaged, that was all.

Enter Capt. Eppingwell, who comes up to them, still in domino.

CAPT. EPPINGWELL: (*disguising voice*). The next is mine, I believe, fair lady. (*Vanderlip ranges up alongside of him and measures height of shoulders. Capt. Eppingwell curiously observes the action and speaks with gruff voice.*) Well, stranger, what's up?

VANDERLIP: We're both up.

CAPT. EPPINGWELL: Up to what?

VANDERLIP: Up to each other. We're the same height, and I've guessed you, Captain Eppingwell.

All laugh together, and Capt. Eppingwell bears Mrs. Eppingwell away. They make exit to left.

Loraine accosts Vanderlip.

LORAINE: (*in disguised voice*). A word in your ear, sir. (*Vanderlip is politely agreeable and listens.*) All is discovered. (*He starts.*) Your actions have betrayed you.

VANDERLIP: Who are you?

LORAINE: Never mind who I am. I know. (*Takes his hand and looks at palm.*) You are about to make a long journey. (*He starts.*) I see a water hole. (*He starts.*) I hear a clock strike twelve. (*He starts.*) She is a dark woman, a foreigner. (*He starts.*) And her name is—(*in natural voice, laughing*) —Loraine.

VANDERLIP: (*with relief in voice*). You fooled me all right, Loraine. You said you weren't coming to the ball.

LORAINE: I didn't intend to, but everything was packed and ready for the start, and I had nothing to do. So I came. (*A pause.*) Floyd, don't you think you've been dancing with that Mrs. Eppingwell rather frequently?

VANDERLIP: No, I don't.

LORAINE: You've danced every dance with her.

VANDERLIP: Somebody else is dancing with her now.

LORAINE: And, in consequence, you are not dancing at all.

VANDERLIP: (*making movement to take her into ballroom*).
Come, then, let us dance it together.

LORAINE: (*pouting*). No.

VANDERLIP: (*persuasively*). Aw, come on.

LORAINE: No.

VANDERLIP: All right, then don't.

He stands stolid and silent.

LORAINE: (*after a pause, softly, hesitatingly, tears in voice, etc.*).
Floyd—I—

Breaks down and weeps in feminine way.

*Vanderlip is soft as mush at once. His arm is around her,
and she is drawn close to him.*

VANDERLIP: There, there, dear. You know I love you.

LORAINE: (*still weeping*). I—I am jealous, Floyd. I know it, but
I can't help it. You are a man to touch women's hearts.
They can't help loving you, and—and—

VANDERLIP: (*showing that he is secretly pleased*). Oh, pshaw.
Anyway, you are the one woman, or I wouldn't be taking
you downriver tonight.

*Prince has gone to left and is looking into ballroom, so they
are unobserved.*

LORAINE: (*recovering*). Yes, yes, I know. Forgive me. And now
I must be going. (*They move to rear to street door. He helps
her on with moccasins and street wraps.*) Aren't you
coming, too?

VANDERLIP: (*opening door for her*). No, not yet. But I'll be
on time.

*She glances at Prince's back, lifts mask, and raises face for
kiss. He bends and kisses her.*

LORAINE: At the water hole.

VANDERLIP: At twelve sharp.

She kisses him again, clings to him, and goes out.

*At sound of door shutting, Prince turns around, then returns
to street door.*

PRINCE: Hello!

VANDERLIP: Hello. How d'ye like the job?

PRINCE: I wouldn't undertake it again for all the gold in Klondike.

VANDERLIP: Losing all your friends, eh?

PRINCE: Half of them. They will butt in, and I have to turn them away. Oh, it's hospitality, you bet. I've been with them on trail, I've eaten their food and slept in their blankets, and now I turn them away from the merrymaking of myself and my friends. (*A knock is heard at door.*) There's one now. (*Opens door.*) No, it's only Sitka Charley. *Enter Sitka Charley, who draws Vanderlip to one side.*

SITKA CHARLEY: You come?

VANDERLIP: No, I tell you. No.

SITKA CHARLEY: No come?

VANDERLIP: (*explosively*). No!

SITKA CHARLEY: Then um Freda come. She say, you no come, she come. Sure.

VANDERLIP: Come here? (*He shakes his head and laughs incredulously.*) Not on your life.

SITKA CHARLEY: (*starting toward street door*). No come?

VANDERLIP: (*explosively*). No!

Exit Sitka Charley.

Vanderlip goes to rear, takes off domino, disclosing himself as a cowboy. Hangs domino on wall. Takes down from wall a sombrero, which he puts on head. Makes exit to left.

Prince, who is now alone, walks over to stove at left, adjusts damper, and warms his hands.

The street door is cautiously opened, without knocking, and Sitka Charley puts head inside and peers around. Withdraws head.

Street door is again cautiously opened, this time the masked face of a woman appearing, and then Freda, in long cloak, enters. She removes street moccasins, revealing dancing slippers on her feet, and puts moccasins under bench close to door. She removes cloak and reveals herself in a striking evening gown. As she turns her back to hang cloak on wall, Prince happens to see her. She starts toward ballroom, but he steps in her way and stops her.

PRINCE: I beg your pardon. (*She waits silently.*) I am the doorkeeper, you know. (*A pause.*) The instructions are that all masks must be lifted at the door. (*Still silence on part of Freda. The situation is awkward for Prince, and he begins again.*) I don't know who you are, but the rules are imperative. I must see your face.

Steps forward and lifts his hand to raise mask.

FREDA: (*quickly stepping back and speaking in a slightly muffled voice*). You will be sorry if you see my face.

PRINCE: I have been made sorry by more than one face I've seen tonight and turned away from the door.

FREDA: But in my case you will be sorry for quite a different reason.

PRINCE: (*curiously*). For what reason, then, pray?

FREDA: Because, after seeing my face, you will not turn me away.

PRINCE: (*with certitude*). Then there will be no reason for me to turn you away.

FREDA: On the contrary, all the reason in the world. But you won't. (*Prince laughs incredulously. Mrs. McFee appears in doorway to left, looks suspiciously at them, and disappears.*) So it will be better, Stanley, if you let me in without seeing my face.

PRINCE: (*starting at her use of his given name*). You know me! —er—well!

FREDA: And you know me well. Now let me pass. Someday I will tell you about it, my reason for coming here, and you will be glad.

She starts as though to go to the ballroom.

PRINCE: (*springing in her way and seizing her arm*). No,
you don't, my lady! Enough fooling. Let me see
your face.

FREDA: There have been times when you treated me less
roughly. For the sake of those times, let me pass.

PRINCE: (*still retaining hold on her arm, and after hesitating for
a moment*). No, it's a bluff you're running on me. I don't
know who you are, but I'm going to find out.
He lifts free hand toward her mask.

FREDA: You will be sorry. (*He hesitates.*) Be in ignorance of
me, and let me pass. It will be better so.

PRINCE: If you have no right, I'll not let you pass anyway.
Now let me see you.
Still holding her by one arm, he tries to lift mask.
*Mrs. McFee appears in doorway to left and watches suspi-
ciously.*
*Sitka Charley knocks and then enters through street door,
Prince giving a quick glance in his direction and ascertaining
that it is all right for him to enter.*

FREDA: (*in natural voice*). Stanley!

PRINCE: (*releasing her and speaking with awe*). No! Not you!
(*Freda lifts her mask, her back to Mrs. McFee, and for
several seconds, her face serious with resolve, her eyes
flashing, she gazes upon him. She lowers mask and makes
as though to start toward door to left. He hesitates, stands
aside, then hesitates again.*) It is all my social standing in
Dawson is worth, to—to let you pass.

FREDA: (*mockingly*). I told you you would be sorry.
(*Seriously.*) There is Sitka Charley. I want to speak to him.
And there's that psalm singer in the doorway. Don't let her
suspect me.

PRINCE: I shall resign my post.

FREDA: Resign? You will be of more help to me if you
retain it.

PRINCE: I have been unfaithful to it. Pass, Freda, pass. Who am I to say you nay?

He leaves her and returns to street door. Freda goes over to Sitka Charley. Mrs. McFee disappears from doorway, but reappears one or two times to stare suspiciously.

FREDA: How is Vanderlip dressed? What does he look like?

SITKA CHARLEY: Um all the same long black dress, like um woman.

FREDA: Dressed as a woman!

SITKA CHARLEY: (*shaking his head*). No dress woman. Um like—um—um—like um priest man. (*Makes motion of hand around head to describe hood of domino, and motion down to his feet to describe length of domino.*) Um long black, like priest man. (*A domino, with lady on arm, appears in doorway, as though about to enter, then changing mind, disappears.*) Look see! Just like that. That um Vanderlip.

FREDA: All right, Charley. I understand. And now for you. Flossie can't get here too quickly. You must take dogs, fresh dogs, up the trail, and when you meet her, put her on your sled and race in with her as fast as you can. Tell her Vanderlip sent you and is waiting for her.

SITKA CHARLEY: (*dubiously*). Um dogs, fresh dogs, have not got.

FREDA: Take my dogs. You know them.

SITKA CHARLEY: (*enthusiastically*). Um best dogs in Klondike. Sure.

FREDA: And bring Flossie straight to my cabin. Don't stop anywhere else for anything. Right up to the door and in with her. Understand?

SITKA CHARLEY: Um Vanderlip there?

FREDA: Yes, Vanderlip will be there waiting for her. (*Starts him toward street door.*) Now hurry. (*Exit Sitka Charley. To Prince, who is standing forlornly at his post.*) I'm sorry,

Stanley, but I had to do this thing. Now I want to find
Floyd Vanderlip.

PRINCE: You'll find him in the ballroom. Black domino—you
know his height.

FREDA: (*resting one hand on his arm and laughing cheerily*).
There, there, don't look so glum. All is not lost. Nobody
will know me, and I'll be gone in five minutes.

*Mrs. McFee appears in doorway to left. Looks at them
standing together.*

*Freda crosses to left and goes out, Mrs. McFee standing aside
and looking at her closely.*

Mrs. McFee crosses to Prince.

MRS. MCFEE: Who might that woman be, Mr. Prince?

PRINCE: (*coldly*). The doorkeeper's lips are sealed. Those were
my instructions. The doorkeeper can disclose identities to
nobody.

MRS. MCFEE: But to me—

PRINCE: (*interrupting icily*). To nobody. You are made no
exception, Mrs. McFee. And, furthermore, I'm going to
resign.

MRS. MCFEE: Resign!

PRINCE: And right now. And whoever takes my place—you'd
better put a mask on him, or he'll lose all his friends, as
I have.

MRS. MCFEE: (*insinuatingly*). Your friends, the kind of men
and women you turned from this door?

PRINCE: (*angrily*). Yes, my friends, men and women, children
of sin, lost, hopeless wretches—my friends.

MRS. MCFEE: (*sniffing and tossing her head, and very frigidly*).
I believe it is just as well, Mr. Prince. I had my doots of
you all along. There is no telling what base creatures you
have admitted. I shall get an honorable man to guard the
door. I shall inform the committee—

PRINCE: (*interrupting*). Get him! Get him! Go get him! You
can't be any too quick for me!

MRS. MCFEE: (*beginning angrily*). You are a shame and a disgrace, and when I bring your conduct before the committee—

PRINCE: (*interrupting*). If you don't go right away and get someone to take my place, I'll throw open the door and call in the scum of the town.

Makes a motion to open door.

MRS. MCFEE: (*aghast, throwing up arms*). No! No! Dinna be rash!

She hastens away into ballroom.

Several couples have entered from ballroom and are promenading, among them Capt. Eppingwell, by himself, in domino.

Enter Sitka Charley through street door, looking for someone. He mistakes Capt. Eppingwell for Vanderlip.

SITKA CHARLEY: Hello, Vanderlip. You no come Freda's cabin, you catch um hell, sure.

CAPT. EPPINGWELL: (*starting, and in disguised voice*). Hello. What's Freda want with me.

SITKA CHARLEY: (*recognizing that it is not Vanderlip's voice, and surprised*). You no Vanderlip?

CAPT. EPPINGWELL: (*imitating Sitka Charley's voice*). No. Me Sitka Charley.

SITKA CHARLEY: What for, crazymans? Me Sitka Charley.

CAPT. EPPINGWELL: Me Sitka Charley.

SITKA CHARLEY: No, me.

CAPT. EPPINGWELL: No, me. (*He suddenly takes off domino, disclosing himself in makeup of Sitka Charley. Sitka Charley gazes at him dumbfounded. Rubs his eyes.*) You buy um dogs, good dogs, I sell.

SITKA CHARLEY: You me. Who me? (*Rubs his eyes.*) What for? Everybody crazy. Me crazy too.

CAPT. EPPINGWELL: (*struck by an idea, he puts on domino again and drags Sitka Charley by arm to back of room*). Come on, we'll have some fun. (*Feels in pocket of overcoat*

*hanging on wall and brings out a mask, which he puts on
Sitka Charley.)* Now for fun!

*Capt. Eppingwell takes Sitka Charley to left, thrusts him
into ballroom, and remains in doorway, watching.*

*Enter Freda. Capt. Eppingwell stands aside for her to pass.
But she stops and measures his height and build with
her eye.*

FREDA: *(softly).* At last I've found you, Floyd.

CAPT. EPPINGWELL: I like that, guessing me the first time. And
who are you?

FREDA: *(surprised).* Oh! It was a mistake.

Starts to leave him, but he follows her, detaining her.

CAPT. EPPINGWELL: Not so fast, fair lady. I've an idea you'll
dance—*(looks at his dance card)*—the next quadrille, let
us say.

FREDA: I think it's engaged. I've lost my program.

CAPT. EPPINGWELL: *(putting hand inside domino and bringing
forth a program).* I have a spare one. Allow me.

He writes on card.

*Enter Sitka Charley from left, running away from Clown,
who is striking him on back with bladder.*

FREDA: Thank you. The next quadrille, then. *(Looking at Sitka
Charley.)* There is somebody I wish to speak to. Good-bye.

CAPT. EPPINGWELL: *(standing aside).* Good-bye.

*Mrs. McFee enters from left with man, whom she takes to
street door and who relieves Prince, who makes exit to left.
Freda joins in pursuit of Sitka Charley and drives Clown
away.*

Mrs. McFee watches Freda and Sitka Charley.

FREDA: *(severely).* I thought you had started up the trail with
the dogs long ago. Anything the matter?

SITKA CHARLEY: Me come back speak to you. Me think, um
Lisznayi woman wait at water hole, no Vanderlip come,
maybe she make much trouble. Much better Lisznayi

woman go long way off. Maybe I think very good tell
Lisznayi woman lie. Maybe say Vanderlip meet her twenty
mile down trail. One Indian man take her on sled twenty
mile down trail, then she sure make no trouble.

FREDA: (*laughing*). A good idea. You hurry and fix it up quick
and then start after Flossie. (*Sitka Charley starts to go.*)
One moment, Charley. Ten miles downriver is Salmon
Stake. One missionary man lives at Salmon Stake. Tell
Indian man to take Lisznayi woman to missionary house
and knock on door. Missionary man gets out of bed and
lets them in. Indian man tells missionary man that Lisznayi
woman come to see him, come to be good woman. (*She
laughs merrily.*) Understand?

SITKA CHARLEY: (*laughing silently*). Very good. Dam good. All
right.

FREDA: (*turning to leave him*). And hurry as fast as you can.
*Freda, looking over one after another of couples and groups
and watched suspiciously by Mrs. McFee, continues search
for Vanderlip and goes to left.*
*Sitka Charley starts toward street door, but is interrupted by
Mrs. McFee.*

MRS. MCFEE: Who is that woman?

SITKA CHARLEY: Um crazy womans maybe.

MRS. MCFEE: But who is she?

SITKA CHARLEY: (*stirring the air with his hand to describe
general mix-up*). Everybody somebody; somebody nobody;
nobody anybody. What for? Sitka Charley no Sitka
Charley. Sitka Charley somebody else. Somebody else
Sitka Charley.

MRS. MCFEE: (*with a sour smile of appreciation*). You do it
very well. Allow me to congratulate you.

SITKA CHARLEY: What for long words? Sitka Charley don't
know long words.

MRS. MCFEE: Oh, I know you, Captain Eppingwell.

SITKA CHARLEY: Me no Captain Eppingwell. Me Sitka Charley.

MRS. MCFEE: You do it excellently. Even I would be almost deceived, I assure you, Captain Eppingwell.

SITKA CHARLEY: Me Captain Eppingwell?

MRS. MCFEE: Of course you are. I knew you at once.

SITKA CHARLEY: Mrs. Eppingwell my squaw?

MRS. MCFEE: Yes, and Mrs. Eppingwell is your wife. Now tell me who that woman was.

SITKA CHARLEY: (*after holding head in both hands*). Me no drink whiskey all day. Yet me all the same drunk. Me no me. Me Captain Eppingwell. Me have one fine squaw. Wow! (*Soberly, holding one hand to head and shaking head.*) Sitka Charley much sick. Sitka Charley go home.

Starts for street door, but Mrs. McFee detains him.

MRS. MCFEE: No, no, Captain, you are coming with me to see how the supper is being laid, and you are going to tell me who that woman is.

Sitka Charley does not want to go, but vainly protesting, is lugged off by Mrs. McFee through door to left.

Capt. Eppingwell, who has lingered about, watches them go, and when gone, he takes off domino, hangs same on wall, and discloses himself in makeup of Sitka Charley. He proceeds to put wood in stove to right.

Freda enters from left and sees Capt. Eppingwell bending over wood box. She crosses over to him in an angry, determined way.

FREDA: (*very severely*). Still here! When I asked you to hurry! (*Capt. Eppingwell straightens up abruptly.*) Shame on you, Charley. Now go, as fast as you can.

CAPT. EPPINGWELL: (*imitating Sitka Charley*). What for go? You buy dogs? I sell dogs, good dogs.

FREDA: (*with petulant dismay*). Oh! You again!

CAPT. EPPINGWELL: Me Sitka Charley.

FREDA: You are the man in the domino. I might have known you were not Sitka Charley. You are taller.

CAPT. EPPINGWELL: (*natural voice*). And in the domino you mistook me because of my height. (*Freda starts.*) Oh, I know. The man you seek is about my height, eh?

FREDA: Who are you?

CAPT. EPPINGWELL: Who are you?

FREDA: You don't know me. I am a new arrival in Dawson. I came in over the ice.

CAPT. EPPINGWELL: (*with sudden conviction*). Now I have you! I met you today.

FREDA: (*shaking head*). No, you didn't.

CAPT. EPPINGWELL: Yes, I did. You are the Lisznayi—I beg pardon—Miss—er—Miss Lisznayi.

FREDA: (*simulating surrender*). It's a shame to be found out so quickly. Mister—? Mister—?

CAPT. EPPINGWELL: Mr. Sitka Charley.

FREDA: Well, then, Mr. Sitka Charley, I am displeased with you. You are too cunning. I am really vexed, and for punishment I am going to leave you.
She curtsies deeply and walks away toward left.

CAPT. EPPINGWELL: (*to himself as he watches her*). That voice. That walk! That carriage! (*Scratches head, then suddenly.*) Fooled! Fooled! That's not the Lisznayi! (*He springs after her. A voice offstage is heard calling, "Take partners for a quadrille!"*) I beg pardon, but this dance is ours.

FREDA: (*drawing watch and looking at it*). Yes, it is, but really, I must beg off. I—I don't like quadrilles. (*Looks at dance card.*) There's a waltz two dances down. I'll give you that.
A man in costume appears in doorway to left and shouts: "One more couple needed! Here, you! One more couple!"

CAPT. EPPINGWELL: (*offering his arm*). There! We're needed.
Man in doorway, who has turned around and surveyed ballroom, turns back and calls: "Too late! Sets are full!"

Opening bars of dance are heard.

CAPT. EPPINGWELL: (*seizing Freda in his arms and starting to waltz*). We'll make a waltz of it here.

They waltz a few steps, Freda abandoning herself to it, when she suddenly stops and withdraws herself from his arms.

FREDA: Please let me go. You may have that waltz later.

She looks at watch and betrays her need for haste.

CAPT. EPPINGWELL: (*very deliberately*). There is something familiar about you. I have seen you before. I have danced with you before. And—well, I have never danced with the Lisznayi.

FREDA: No, you don't know me.

CAPT. EPPINGWELL: Let me tell you the occasion.

FREDA: (*very restless and desiring to go*). There has been no occasion.

CAPT. EPPINGWELL: (*firmly*). Nevertheless, let me tell you. It may interest you. (*Makes appropriate gestures.*) Here was the stove, here the piano. Three-fingered Jack played the fiddle. It was Old Dan Tucker that we danced. Remember? (*She shakes her head.*) There was the doorway to the front, always open. Through it came the clatter of chips, the rattle of roulette balls, the calls of the gamekeepers. And there was the rear door. It opened upon the street. When it opened, the frost came through in a cloud of vapor, rolling along the floor and hiding the feet and legs of the dancers to the knees. And we danced, you and I, we danced Old Dan Tucker.

FREDA: (*innocently*). How interesting! Tell me, that—that what you described, it is a—a dance hall? Am I right?

CAPT. EPPINGWELL: (*with firm conviction*). I remember when you came in through the door. The frost rolled in with you, and you wore the most magnificent furs in all the Klondike. And you danced in moccasins, in little red moccasins. Remember?

FREDA: (*still innocently*). Ah, those furs! Is there a woman in the land who has not heard of them and envied their possessor, this woman you take me for—and I know who you mean—this—this dance-hall artist, this—this Freda Moloof. And how often have you danced with her?—with me, I mean.

CAPT. EPPINGWELL: (*shaken for the moment*). Once. That one night. But I have seen her several times. Who has not?

FREDA: Her? Me, you mean.

CAPT. EPPINGWELL: (*with renewed and emphatic conviction*). Yes, and one other thing. That accent! (*Gripping her by the arm.*) Freda, it is you!

FREDA: At last I am discovered. Confess, sir, it took you some time.

CAPT. EPPINGWELL: I do confess you puzzled me not a little. But what are you doing here? It's daring, to say the least.

FREDA: (*nonchalantly*). Oh, I was weary for a change. I was yawning my head off. So I thought I'd come up and see if you and your select friends danced Old Dan Tucker as well as we danced it that—that night.

CAPT. EPPINGWELL: But if you are discovered?

FREDA: Only you could discover me.

CAPT. EPPINGWELL: (*with due hesitancy*). There is trouble brewing, Freda. Frankly, I believe it would be better for you to go. (*Freda laughs long, a mocking, silvery laughter, which perplexes and bewilders him.*) Come, come. What's the matter? (*Freda continues to laugh.*) What's struck you so funny?

FREDA: (*quieting down, but holding hand to side*). It is better than I dreamed.

CAPT. EPPINGWELL: What is better?

FREDA: My makeup.

CAPT. EPPINGWELL: (*in doubt*). Makeup?

FREDA: The makeup under my makeup, if you please.

CAPT. EPPINGWELL: (*with a faint glimmer of conviction this time*). But the accent! You can't get away from it.

FREDA: Far be it from me to get away from it. On the contrary, I sought after it, and I flatter myself that I got it pretty close to the original. I'd like to meet this Freda. I'll wager my accent is nearer hers than her own is.

CAPT. EPPINGWELL: (*completely beaten, slowly*). Then who the deuce are you? Where could you have learned that accent?

FREDA: (*as one will tell a story*). Why, I was caught in a storm over on Indian River. We were compelled to seek shelter in a little cabin, and whom should we find there, likewise driven in by the storm, but this Freda Moloof. There was no standing on ceremony nor conventionality. It was life or death, and in I went. We were stormbound two days. And she was very kind to me. (*A pause, then, voice tender and sympathetic.*) I felt so sorry for her.

A pause.

CAPT. EPPINGWELL: (*impatiently*). Well?

FREDA: Well, I studied her, that is all.

CAPT. EPPINGWELL: (*triumphantly*). Now I have you! You are the woman reporter of the *Kansas City Star*!

FREDA: (*mockingly*). Think so? Think so? (*She laughs.*) Now I am really going to leave you. I must. But don't forget that waltz.

She walks away and makes exit to left.

CAPT. EPPINGWELL: (*in utter bewilderment, watching her till she disappears*). Well, I'll be damned.

He puts on domino and follows after her, still intent on discovering her identity, and makes exit to left.

The quadrille is over, and as he passes out, couples begin to enter from left.

Mrs. McFee and Sitka Charley enter from left. She still holds him captive, hanging on his arm.

MRS. MCFEE: (*ingratiatingly, making as near a simper as her sour mouth and age will permit*). You might have asked me to dance, Captain.

SITKA CHARLEY: (*rolling his head*). Me no dance. Me much sick. Me crazy. Me drunk. Me go home.
Strives to get to street door, but she clings to his arm and holds him back.

MRS. MCFEE: Dinna you think by now, Captain, that you've convinced me what a fine actor you are?

SITKA CHARLEY: (*striving for street door, but being held back, in final breakdown of patience*). What for, dam fool woman you?

MRS. MCFEE: (*dropping his arm and recoiling*). Oh!

SITKA CHARLEY: (*in a rage, dancing about*). Crazy! Fool! Dam! What for?

MRS. MCFEE: Oh! Oh! And I thought you were a gentleman! You have insulted me!

SITKA CHARLEY: (*raging*). Sure! Me insult. Much insult. Dam! Dam! Dam!

MRS. MCFEE: Oh! This cannot be Captain Eppingwell. 'Tis some base creature from the town. I am contameenated! (*Sticks fingers in ears and screams shrilly. Many come running from ballroom at sound of screams. Sitka Charley still rages, shouting, "Dam! Dam! Dam!" Capt. Eppingwell comes in with some lady on arm and joins an onlooking group near stove to right. He still wears domino. To onlookers.*) This vile creature has insulted me. Where is the doorkeeper? (*Turns and beckons Doorkeeper.*) Come you, Mr. McFarline, and eject this beast.
Doorkeeper starts forward. Clown startles Sitka Charley by unexpectedly hitting him a resounding blow with bladder between the shoulders. Sitka Charley runs in and out amongst people, pursued by Doorkeeper and Clown. The Doorkeeper is slow and ponderous, and falls down. At the moment he

falls, Sitka Charley dashes into group where stands Capt.
Eppingwell, whom he strips, with one rush, of domino. Sitka
Charley swiftly puts domino on himself and dashes on, still
pursued by Clown, who is striking him with bladder. Both
make exit to left. Doorkeeper, getting up, mistakes Capt.
Eppingwell for Sitka Charley and proceeds to eject him.
Capt. Eppingwell resists. Mrs. McFee urges on the Doorkeeper.
In struggle Capt. Eppingwell's mask comes off. Doorkeeper,
in amazement, lets go of him. Capt. Eppingwell is angry,
Mrs. McFee dumbfounded, everybody excited. —Tableau.
Sitka Charley dashes in from left, pursued by Clown. Sitka
Charley races madly across stage, like a dog with a tin
can to its tail, and jerks open street door. Doorkeeper tries
to stop him, clutches domino, but Sitka Charley plunges
through and slams door after him, leaving domino in hands
of Doorkeeper, who is nonplussed for a moment, then walks
over and presents it to Capt. Eppingwell.
Excitement quiets down. Groups break up and begin to pass
off stage to left.
Capt. Eppingwell, having lingered in order to recover his
breath, goes to left rear and hangs up domino on wall.
Vanderlip, in costume of cowboy, and Mrs. Eppingwell are
standing talking by stove to right front.
Freda enters alone from left and looks about. Recognizes
Capt. Eppingwell and goes up to him.

CAPT. EPPINGWELL: (*gallantly*). Ah, mysterious fair one!

FREDA: (*lightly*). Surely you have guessed me by now.

CAPT. EPPINGWELL: (*shaking head sadly*). I was never so
befooled in my life. I could swear I know you, but to
save me, I can't put my finger on you.

FREDA: You may if you wish.

CAPT. EPPINGWELL: (*surprised*). What?

FREDA: (*seriously*). I say you may know me if you wish.

CAPT. EPPINGWELL: (*eagerly*). How?—when?

FREDA: Now. (*He eagerly makes to lift mask and learn her identity. She steps back quickly, with one hand holding him off.*) No, no, there are certain stipulations.

CAPT. EPPINGWELL: (*displaying in advance a willingness to consent*). Yes, yes.

FREDA: (*deliberately*). First, you must ask no questions. (*He nods head.*) Second, you must tell nobody. (*He nods.*) And third, you must point out to me Floyd Vanderlip.

CAPT. EPPINGWELL: (*nodding head*). I agree. Now, who are you?

FREDA: (*laughing*). But you haven't pointed out Floyd Vanderlip.

CAPT. EPPINGWELL: (*briskly, indicating with his head*). There he is.

FREDA: (*looking*). And with whom is he talking?

CAPT. EPPINGWELL: (*starting as though to answer, then changing his mind*). That was not in the bond. Now, who are you?

FREDA: (*mockingly*). Guess.

CAPT. EPPINGWELL: I call that cruel. I've exhausted my guesses.
Freda lifts mask and gazes at him for several seconds, her face serious, her eyes flashing.

CAPT. EPPINGWELL: (*giving a long whistle of comprehension*). Freda!

FREDA: Even so, Freda. And I thank you. And I shall have yet more to thank you for. That waltz—you must let me off.

CAPT. EPPINGWELL: There is no reason. Let me have it.

FREDA: Impossible. I shall be gone. (*Looks at watch.*) Why, it is half past eleven! I am going now, in a minute.

CAPT. EPPINGWELL: With Vanderlip?

FREDA: With Vanderlip.

CAPT. EPPINGWELL: (*earnestly*). Freda, do you know all the

circumstances of this—er—affair? Do you know what you are doing?

FREDA: (*lightly*). You are asking questions, sir. It is not in the bond.

CAPT. EPPINGWELL: (*giving in*). Right. I beg your pardon.
A knock is heard at street door. Doorkeeper opens. Enter messenger, an Indian, in parka and trail costume. He appears tired. He looks about hesitatingly, dazzled by the lights.

CAPT. EPPINGWELL: (*recognizing messenger, to Freda*). Pardon me, please, a moment. I must speak to that man. (*Walks over to Indian.*) How soon she come?

INDIAN: Come soon. Much dogs. Come fast. One hour maybe. Maybe half hour.

CAPT. EPPINGWELL: All right. Come along. (*Walks to Mrs. Eppingwell and Vanderlip at stove at right front, Indian at his heels.*) Here's that man I told you of, Maud. You had better speak with him—I beg your pardon, Vanderlip.

VANDERLIP: (*jovially*). That's all right. Business is business.

MRS. EPPINGWELL: (*sweetly*). Oh, Mr. Vanderlip, I left my program on the piano, and I really don't know with whom I have the next dance. Please.
She steps aside with Indian to talk.
Vanderlip starts toward exit to left.
Capt. Eppingwell starts to rejoin Freda.
Freda starts to cut off Vanderlip, crossing Capt. Eppingwell.

CAPT. EPPINGWELL: (*softly*). Oh, Freda! That waltz.

FREDA: One moment, please.
Passes on to Vanderlip.
Capt. Eppingwell stands gazing.
A dance has finished, and couples begin to stray in.
Clown and a lady accost Capt. Eppingwell, and the three move along together.
Mrs. McFee enters. As she passes by, she looks hard and suspiciously at Freda.

FREDA: Come with me, Floyd. I want you now.

VANDERLIP: (*with mock politeness*). And who are you, may I ask?

FREDA: Freda.

VANDERLIP: (*beginning explosively*). What the— (*Then breaking down.*) My God, Freda, what have you come here for?

FREDA: For you.

VANDERLIP: (*hesitatingly*). I don't understand. You are nothing to me.

FREDA: And never have been anything, remember that, Floyd. (*Conveying the impression that she may be something to him in the immediate future.*) But I want you now.

VANDERLIP: And never will be anything, I assure you. (*Getting back his courage.*) Faugh! What have you come here for, anyway?

FREDA: For you. And, moreover, you are going to come with me. You are going to let me take your arm, and you see that door there—you are going to take me out through it.

VANDERLIP: (*bellicosely*). I see myself doing it.

FREDA: Yes, and I see you going on to my cabin.

VANDERLIP: (*interested, curiously*). To your cabin?

FREDA: Yes, to my cabin. I want to talk with you.

VANDERLIP: This is a good place right here. Talk away.

FREDA: No, you must come with me.

VANDERLIP: (*obstinately*). Not on your life, Freda. Right here I stay.

FREDA: You have seen a little of me, Floyd, but you have heard more of me.

VANDERLIP: (*interrupting*). Oh, yes, I have heard that you play with men as a child plays with bubbles. It is a saying in the country. Well—(*planting himself firmly*)—I am no bubble.

FREDA: (*quietly*). What time is it, Floyd?

VANDERLIP: (*looking at watch, startled*). Twenty-five to twelve! Gee! I've got to get out of this! (*Makes a hasty movement,*

as though to start toward street door. Freda takes his arm.)
What's this?

FREDA: Nothing. Come along. I am in a hurry.

VANDERLIP: Now, look here, Freda, I'm not going with you because you're making me. I've got to go anyway. I've got to be elsewhere, and pretty quick.

FREDA: Oh, far from it. I never make anybody do anything. They just—do it.

VANDERLIP: All right, I'll let you come with me, but only outside. I'm not going to your cabin.

FREDA: That is for you to determine. Let us start.

Mrs. Eppingwell talks with Indian. Mrs. Eppingwell now and again glances anxiously at Freda and Vanderlip; Mrs. McFee is more suspicious than ever, her hands involuntarily clutching and unclutching, as though with desire to spring upon Freda and held back only by doubt.

VANDERLIP: (*absently*). I'll have to rush. Got to change my clothes—

FREDA: (*interrupting*). Not for my cabin. Those clothes are good enough.

VANDERLIP: (*angrily*). But I tell you I am not going to your cabin.

FREDA: Oh, well, never mind. The first thing is to get out of here. After that we'll see.

VANDERLIP: (*defiantly*). You bet we'll see.

They start toward street door, Freda on his arm.

MRS. EPPINGWELL: (*hurriedly, to Capt. Eppingwell*). Who is that woman?

CAPT. EPPINGWELL: (*awkwardly*). How should I know?

MRS. EPPINGWELL: (*reproachfully and hurriedly*). Archie! I saw her lift her mask to you a moment ago.

CAPT. EPPINGWELL: I can't tell—I—she—

Mrs. Eppingwell does not listen further, but hastens to cut off Freda and Vanderlip.

FREDA: (*seeing Mrs. Eppingwell approaching*). If anybody stops me, Floyd, I shall quarrel, I know.

VANDERLIP: (*frightened*). For goodness' sake, don't make a scene.

FREDA: Then get me out of here quick. Don't stop.

But Vanderlip stops when cut off by Mrs. Eppingwell.

MRS. EPPINGWELL: I beg pardon. You are not going, Mr. Vanderlip?

VANDERLIP: (*awkwardly*). I—yes, I'm going.

MRS. EPPINGWELL: But those dances?

VANDERLIP: (*hiding embarrassment behind brusqueness*). I've suddenly recollected something. I'm in a hurry. Please excuse me, Mrs. Eppingwell.

Freda starts at mention of name.

MRS. EPPINGWELL: (*reproachfully*). And you promised to take me in to supper.

VANDERLIP: Of course, of course. And I will. I'll come back.

MRS. EPPINGWELL: I'd rather you didn't go—Floyd. The next dance—(*looking at his card*)—is ours. It will begin in a minute.

Vanderlip does not know what to say. Freda urges him to continue toward door by tugging privily on his arm. Also, she glances apprehensively at Mrs. McFee, who, with a set expression on face, has drawn nearer.

VANDERLIP: (*hesitatingly*). Really, Mrs. Eppingwell, I—

FREDA: (*interrupting, urging him by arm to start toward door*). We'll be late. We must go.

Vanderlip half starts to go with her toward door.

MRS. EPPINGWELL: (*to Freda*). I beg pardon, but you scarcely understand.

FREDA: (*sharply, overwrought, nervously*). It would be better, Mrs. Eppingwell, did your husband understand as well as I.

Mrs. Eppingwell is visibly hurt and for the moment shocked into silence.

VANDERLIP: Now, look here, I'm not going to have any quarreling between you women.

MRS. EPPINGWELL: (*with sudden suspicion, ignoring Vanderlip*). Who are you?

FREDA: (*coldly*). One whose existence would scarcely interest you, Mrs. Eppingwell.

VANDERLIP: (*whose efforts to make peace are ignored*). Oh, I say—

Mrs. McFee has drawn nearer. Everybody on stage is interested.

MRS. EPPINGWELL: I have the right to know.

FREDA: (*scathingly*). As custodian of the community's morals?

MRS. EPPINGWELL: And why not?

FREDA: (*mockingly*). Ah, and why not?

MRS. EPPINGWELL: (*with energy, but coolly and collectedly*). You have the advantage. You know who I am. Who are you? I demand to know.

Freda laughs lightly and mockingly.

MRS. MCFEE: (*entering group with a very determined air and pausing an instant*). We'll settle that, Mrs. Eppingwell. *Mrs. McFee suddenly springs upon Freda, tearing mask from face. Freda is startled and frightened. Vanderlip, the situation beyond him, stares helplessly back and forth between Freda and Mrs. Eppingwell. Everybody on the stage stares at Freda, forming a wide and irregular circle of onlookers, who are too polite to crowd closer, but who, nevertheless, cannot resist staring, one and all, from a distance.*

MRS. MCFEE: (*sarcastically, shrilly*). Mrs. Eppingwell, it is with great pleasure I make you acquainted with Freda Moloof —*Miss* Freda Moloof, as I understand. (*Mrs. Eppingwell makes a gesture to silence Mrs. McFee, who pauses for a moment.*) Mayhap you dinna know the lady. Let me tell you—

VANDERLIP: (*interrupting*). Now, here, I say, what's the good—

MRS. MCFEE: (*interrupting, and withering him with a look*). Child of perdition! (*She continues.*) As I was saying, this woman's antecedents—a dancing girl, a destroyer of men's souls, a bold, brazen hussy, a servant of Satan, a—

MRS. EPPINGWELL: (*interrupting*). That will do, Mrs. McFee. Will you please leave me to talk with her?

Mrs. McFee, still holding mask, snorts and withdraws a step from group.

FREDA: (*quickly, excitedly, eyes flashing*). I do not want you to talk with me. What more can you say than that woman— (*indicating Mrs. McFee, who snorts*)—has said? I want to go. Come on, Floyd.

MRS. EPPINGWELL: (*gently*). I do not wish to be harsh.

FREDA: (*on verge of tears, yet dry-eyed and resolute*). Be anything but kind. That I will not bear.

MRS. EPPINGWELL: (*beginning gently*). I—

FREDA: (*interrupting, excitedly*). It is you that have the advantage now, hiding behind that mask. Your face is clothed. I am as naked before you—(*glancing around masked circle and shrinking as a naked woman might shrink*)—before all of you.

MRS. EPPINGWELL: But you should not have come here.

FREDA: I had reason to come.

MRS. EPPINGWELL: An evil reason, I fear. However—

She calmly removes her own mask.

For a long moment they regard each other with fixed gaze, Freda aggressive, meteoric, at bay; Mrs. Eppingwell calm-eyed, serene, dispassionate. Freda begins to soften.

FREDA: (*softly*). You *are* kind.

MRS. EPPINGWELL: No, it is merely fair play.

MRS. MCFEE: (*bursting out wrathfully*). Why dinna you tell the hussy to go?

MRS. EPPINGWELL: (*masterfully*). Be quiet.

FREDA: (*breaking down, seeming to droop for an instant, with one short, dry sob or catch in the throat).* Yes, I will go, Mrs. Eppingwell. (*Turning to Vanderlip.*) Will you come, Floyd?

Vanderlip looks to Mrs. Eppingwell for consent.

MRS. EPPINGWELL: Mr. Vanderlip will stay.

Freda, broken down, beaten, but with no tears, no wringing of hands, nor customary signs of feminine weakness, with head up, mechanically resolute and defiant, ordinary carriage and speed of walk, goes toward street door. Silence. Everybody watches her. Doorkeeper does not assist her when she gropes blindly under bench for street moccasins.

What is emphasized is her isolation. She is not one of them, and they regard her as they would regard a strange animal which had strayed in out of the night.

She sits down on bench to put on street moccasins. Just as she lifts one foot to put on first moccasin, she pauses, thinks, then puts foot down again. She puts down moccasins, stands up, pauses irresolutely a moment, then walks forward to Mrs. Eppingwell and Vanderlip.

FREDA: (*quietly*). Mrs. Eppingwell, pardon me, but I had forgotten for the moment what I came for.

MRS. EPPINGWELL: And that is—?

FREDA: Floyd Vanderlip.

VANDERLIP: (*angrily*). Now, look here, Freda, I tell you I won't stand for this.

Freda ignores him.

MRS. EPPINGWELL: I trust, Miss Moloof—

FREDA: (*interrupting*). Call me Freda. (*Bitterly.*) Everybody calls me Freda.

MRS. EPPINGWELL: Well, Freda, then. Have you thought what you are doing? It is an awkward thing to play with souls. What right have you?

FREDA: (*laughing harshly*). Right? I have no rights. Only privileges.

MRS. EPPINGWELL: (*with touch of anger*). Licenses, I should say.
Mrs. McFee snorts and approaches.

FREDA: Thank you, licenses. I have licenses which you have
not, for, you see, you are the wife of a captain.

MRS. EPPINGWELL: What do you want with this man?

FREDA: I might ask what you want with him. You have your
husband.

MRS. EPPINGWELL: And you?

FREDA: (*wearily*). Men, just men.

MRS. EPPINGWELL: (*anger growing*). You are all that has been
said of you, a destroyer of men.

FREDA: (*nodding her head in assent*). Come on, Floyd. I want
you. And be warned by Mrs. Eppingwell, I want to destroy
you. (*Imperiously.*) Come.
*Vanderlip has by now been reduced to the helplessness of a
puppet. He makes to start.*

MRS. EPPINGWELL: (*imperiously*). Floyd Vanderlip, you remain
where you are.
He stops.

FREDA: (*almost whispering*). Come.
He makes to start.

MRS. EPPINGWELL: (*warningly, imperiously*). Floyd!
He stops.

MRS. MCFEE: (*to Vanderlip, witheringly, imitating his hesitancy
by bobbing her body*). You weak and sinful creature,
bobbing here and bobbing there, like a chicken with its
head cut off!

VANDERLIP: (*stirred to sudden flame of anger*). Once for all,
Freda, I'm not going with you.

FREDA: (*quietly*). What time is it, Floyd?

VANDERLIP: (*looking at watch, startled*). Quarter to twelve! I
must go, Mrs. Eppingwell. Good-bye.
*He starts toward door at heels of Freda, who leads him by a
couple of steps.*

MRS. EPPINGWELL: Shame on you, Freda Moloof.
Freda glances back and smiles a hard smile.

MRS. EPPINGWELL: (*calling softly*). Floyd!
Vanderlip hesitates. Freda turns her face, blazingly imperious, upon him, and he slinks on after her. Dead silence.

FREDA: (*when they reach door*). Help me on with my moccasins, Floyd. (*He hesitates, with a last faint spark of rebellion. She looks at him, blazingly imperious.*) There they are.
He is beaten. Stoops for moccasins. She sits down on bench. He puts moccasins on her feet. They stand up. He helps her on with her cloak. While he is putting on his own moccasins and a big bearskin overcoat, she pulls hood of cloak over her head and covers her ears. Then she puts on her mittens. Then she waits for him. He puts on cap and mittens and opens street door.

FREDA: (*recollecting and turning toward Mrs. McFee*). Go, get my mask.
He obeys amid dead silence. Mrs. McFee mechanically surrenders mask to him. He returns. Opens door. Freda passes out. He follows.

CURTAIN

ACT III

*Freda Moloof's cabin. It is eleven forty-five at night. The
room is large and luxuriously furnished. Its walls are of logs,
stuffed between with brown moss. Doors of rough, unstained
pine boards, also window frames and sashes. Street door
to rear, in center. On either side of door is an ordinary,
small-paned window. To left of door a plain chair. On rear
wall, near door, are wooden pegs, from which hang cloaks,
wraps, furs, etc., also wisp brooms for brushing snow from
moccasins.*

*The luxury of furnishing is of the solid order. No gimcracks,
no bric-a-brac. Furniture is rough, made in the Klondike.
Tables, chairs, etc., are unpolished; they are made from pine
lumber, are unstained, rough, massive. There is no carpet.
Bearskins, etc., litter the floor. Strange juxtaposition of
rough pine furniture, costly rugs, etc.; and, strangest of all,
a grand piano. The cheapest and simplest and ugliest of
kerosene lamps are used for lighting purposes, also candles.
On walls are magnificent moose horns and other appropriate
trophies and weapons of the Northland (such as great
ivory-headed spears and a pair of tusks of the mammoth);
but there are no framed paintings.*

Midway between front and rear, and midway between center and right, a large wood-burning stove. Beside it a wood box. On stove a teakettle is simmering. To left of stove, and near it, table with table cover on it, a few books and magazines, and a cheap kerosene lamp; around table several pine chairs. Between table and stove two easy chairs of rough pine, massive, thrown over with furs. On right, at front, against wall, a large, comfortable lounging couch with many cushions. On left, at front, a grand piano. On piano a small, gilt French clock is ticking.

The room is luxurious, comfortable, picturesque, emphasizing the contact of civilization and the wilderness. In short, it is the best possible living apartment that money can purchase in the Klondike.

A Maid is in easy chair, reading magazine and yawning. Door opens on right. Indian enters with armful of firewood, which he carries to stove and dumps in wood box. He proceeds to put several sticks of wood into stove and to adjust damper. His entrance rouses Maid, who looks up, yawns, lays magazine facedown on lap, yawns again, at same time stretching arms behind head, and glances at clock. It is quite a distance to clock. She rubs eyes and looks again.

MAID: Ten minutes to twelve.

Yawns.

INDIAN: What time come?

MAID: (*shaking head*). I don't know. (*Yawning.*) I never know.

INDIAN: Me go to bed.

MAID: You'd better not. She said we were to stay up.

INDIAN: What for? Much trouble, you think? What she do? Where she go?

MAID: (*yawning*). How should I know?

INDIAN: Sitka Charley take dogs. Sitka Charley big hurry. What for?

MAID: (*listening*). There she comes now.

> *Maid rises to her feet, like a soldier coming to attention, hastily puts magazine on table, and brushes down front of skirt. Indian puts another stick of wood into stove and busies himself with raking ashes level in ash box of stove.*
>
> *Street door opens. Freda enters, leading Vanderlip by the hand. Both are mittened and in same wraps, coats, etc., with which they left anteroom of Pioneer Hall.*
>
> *Indian finishes with stove and goes out slowly to right. Maid goes to rear and helps Freda off with wraps, moccasins, etc. Vanderlip, who has come in reluctantly, does not remove mittens or cap, and stands sullenly inside the door, though he cannot forbear glancing curiously around.*

FREDA: (*seeming in high spirits, while Maid is taking off her street moccasins*). And now for a toddy! You've never tasted Minnie's. She makes them—(*holding up hands*)— oh, to the king's taste, and to a Klondike king's at that.

VANDERLIP: (*brusquely*). Sorry. Won't have time. What did you want me for?

FREDA: My! There's the man of it! (*Imitating his voice and manner.*) What did you want me for? (*Natural voice.*) Can't let the poor woman catch her breath. Won't sit down for a moment in the warm. (*Motions to Maid to help him off with his bearskin overcoat.*) Must know what he's wanted for. Must know right away. Must go right away. Oh, my! Oh, my!

> *Maid starts to help him off with overcoat. He jerks away from her.*

VANDERLIP: (*sullenly*). What do you want to say to me? Fire away.

FREDA: (*laying hand on his arm*). Floyd—(*hesitating*)—dear Floyd . . . You are big and strong. I know, too, that you are kind. Be kind now, just a little kind, a very little. I can't talk with you here, this way. It would be ridiculous.

(*Beginning to help him take off coat, in which operation his assistance is restricted to nonresistance.*) Come and sit by the fire a moment. (*Hands overcoat to Maid, who hangs it up on wall.*) Just for a moment.

Untying earflaps and removing his cap, which Maid hangs up. She pushes him onto chair and lifts one foot to remove street moccasins.

VANDERLIP: (*helplessly expostulating*). Now here, I say—(*she persists*)—I won't have a woman doing that for me. (*Pushes her away and removes moccasins himself. He stands up.*) I said I wasn't coming to your cabin, Freda, and I can't stay anyway—only for that one moment, that's all.

FREDA: (*taking his hand and starting to lead him forward*). That is all I wanted, just the moment. And it is sweet of you to give it to me.

Vanderlip pauses and looks around room with interest. Freda pauses with him. Maid remains in rear, putting moccasins away, etc.

VANDERLIP: (*more genially, forgetting to be sullen*). I say, Freda, you're fixed comfortably.

FREDA: Think so?

VANDERLIP: It's grand style, I must say. Nothing like it in the land. You're the only person that has three rooms.

FREDA: Four—counting the kitchen.

VANDERLIP: And my cabin is one room.

FREDA: And you a millionaire.

VANDERLIP: But this is the Klondike—

FREDA: (*laughing and interrupting*). Where even millionaires —(*imitating Dave Harney*)—can't buy sweetenin' for their coffee an' mush. Dodgast the luck anyway.

Vanderlip laughs appreciatively. They start on again to front, but he sees piano and stops again.

VANDERLIP: If there ain't a piano! It cost you a pretty penny, I'll bet.

FREDA: (*leading him toward piano, half singing, lightly*). "You

cannot pack a Broadwood half a mile." (*Looking at him.*)
Don't you know it? (*He shakes head.*) Don't know your
Kipling! (*Sitting down at piano.*) Here's the way it goes—
(*Plays and sings.*)

> You couldn't pack a Broadwood half a mile,
> You mustn't leave a fiddle in the damp,
> You couldn't raft an organ up the Nile
> And play it in an equatorial swamp—

VANDERLIP: (*who had first gazed admiringly at her, then gazed
curiously around until, by clock on piano, he sees what time
it is, interrupting by bringing hand heavily down on keys of
piano*). I can't wait another second. What do you want
with me?

FREDA: (*ceasing the song, looking up quite calmly, and placing
hand over face of clock*). I want you to stop looking at that
clock. And—(*rising, taking him by hand, and leading him
toward stove*)—I want you to come right over here and be
good. (*Turning to Maid.*) Minnie.
*Maid, who has been waiting in rear, comes forward and
again waits.*
*Freda pushes Vanderlip into easy chair near stove, runs to
couch at right for cushion, which she puts behind his head,
pressing his shoulders and head back upon it. She places
fur-covered footstool under his feet. He has not relaxed
himself and, in his stiff acceptance of comforts, makes a
ridiculous appearance.*

FREDA: (*giving cushion behind head a last pat*). And now you
may smoke.
Maid goes out to right.
*Vanderlip rolls head back and forth on cushion. His hand
searches for watch, which he draws forth from pocket.
But before he can look at it, Freda's hand covers the face
of it.*

FREDA: Oh my! My! What a busy man it is!

Maid enters with cigar box on tray. Vanderlip takes a cigar, and while he examines it critically, Freda puts watch back in his pocket.

VANDERLIP: (*biting off end of cigar*). Real Havana. And you can't buy them for love nor money. How do you manage it?

FREDA: (*striking match and holding it up to him*). Oh, I just do. I could have offered you worse, I assure you.

Vanderlip puffs on cigar—long, slow, appreciative puffs. His face loses its sullen expression. He sighs contentedly. He relaxes his body, sinks back, and for the first time looks really comfortable.

FREDA: And now, Minnie, you have your reputation to live up to.

MAID: (*hesitating an instant*). The Scotch?

Freda nods head, and Maid goes out to right.

VANDERLIP: (*taking cigar from mouth and looking at it*). I say, Freda, you *can* make a fellow comfortable.

FREDA: (*smiling*). Think so?

VANDERLIP: (*the sullenness returning into his face*). And you know how to make him uncomfortable.

FREDA: (*smiling*). Think so?

VANDERLIP: You are, by long odds, the most brutal woman I ever met.

FREDA: (*incredulously and innocently aghast*). I?

VANDERLIP: (*harshly*). I wouldn't treat a dog the way you treated me. (*Growing angry.*) You treated me like a cur, the way you lugged me away from the dance.

FREDA: Think so?

VANDERLIP: I'd sooner a man beat me with a club than take what I took from you. It was just as much as if you took a club to me. You beat me into submission, in front of everybody, until I followed at your heels—that's what you did.

FREDA: (*with mock solemnity*). Whom the Lord loveth he chasteneth.

VANDERLIP: But you are not the Lord. You are Freda—

FREDA: (*laughing and interrupting*). And whom Freda chasteneth—

VANDERLIP: (*interrupting*). She—

FREDA: (*interrupting*). Not at all. The Lord is the Lord, but Freda is only a woman. . . .

A pause.

VANDERLIP: (*impatiently*). And?

FREDA: Her ways are different from the Lord's. (*She pulls her chair alongside of his and rests one hand for a moment, caressingly, on his. Speaks softly.*) And aren't you glad? *The caress has its effect. He is soothed and puffs away at cigar with half-closed eyes.*

Freda, unobserved, throws a swift glance at clock, listens intently, as for sounds from without of an approaching sled, and betrays to the audience her anxiety and restlessness. Maid enters with two glasses on a tray. Freda, observed by Vanderlip, sips from one glass, nods head approvingly, and passes it to him. Takes other glass herself.

FREDA: Minnie. Candles.

Maid moves about room, putting out lamps and lighting candles, which latter, with tissue-paper shades, shed softer light.

Vanderlip suddenly recollects himself and draws watch. Freda tries to cover watch with hand, but fails. Vanderlip sees watch and starts to rise from chair. Freda half rises and presses him back.

VANDERLIP: (*with note of real regret in his voice, glancing from cigar in one hand, and glass in other hand, to the stove, about the room, and then at Freda*). It's a darn shame to leave all this, but I've really got to, Freda. I don't think I was ever so comfortable in my life.

FREDA: (*softly, almost whispering*). Then why leave it, Floyd?

VANDERLIP: I've got to hit the trail tonight, right away. And I've got to get my trail clothes. That bearskin overcoat's too warm. Can't travel in it. (*Starts to rise.*)

FREDA: (*pressing him back gently*). Wait a minute. Let me think. (*Thinks a moment. Her face brightens.*) Ah, the very thing. Why not send my Indian for your things? He can bring them here. That will give you a few minutes more of the warm—

VANDERLIP: (*interrupting, putting his arm out and around her waist*). And of you, Freda.
Freda lets his arm linger for a moment; then, warning him, by a look, of presence of Maid, gently disengages arm. Takes her time about disengaging it. Vanderlip sinks back comfortably on cushion.

FREDA: (*turning to Maid*). Minnie. (*Maid, who has finished lighting candles, approaches.*) Send Joe here. Tell him to put on his mittens and parka.
Maid goes out to right.
Freda resumes seat and lays one hand on Vanderlip's hand. Neither speaks.
Maid enters, followed by Indian, who, as he comes, is putting on parka and mittens.

FREDA: You know Mr. Vanderlip's cabin?

INDIAN: (*nodding*). Um.

FREDA: Give him the key, Floyd. (*Vanderlip reaches in pocket and gives key to Indian.*) You go Mr. Vanderlip's cabin and get parka—

VANDERLIP: (*interrupting*). Dog whip, fur cap, all together with parka.

FREDA: Dog whip, fur cap, all together with parka.
Indian nods.

VANDERLIP: And flask of whiskey on table.

FREDA: And flask of whiskey on table.

Indian nods.

VANDERLIP: And go quick.

FREDA: And go quick. (*Indian nods and starts toward door to rear. Makes exit. Freda rises, as though recollecting something.*) Excuse me, Floyd. (*Passes behind Vanderlip's back toward door to right and, unobserved, beckons Maid. They pause at door to right.*) Run quick, out the kitchen door, and catch Joe. Tell him not to come back. Tell him I said so—to go get drunk, anything, but not to come back. (*Vanderlip lifts head, turns head around, and is watching and listening. Freda continues in slightly louder voice.*) And then, Cupid's stew.

Maid makes exit to right.

Freda returns to chair, passing hand caressingly through Vanderlip's hair before she sits down.

VANDERLIP: (*gruffly, suspiciously*). What were you gassing about?

FREDA: (*mysteriously*). Cupid's stew.

VANDERLIP: I heard it, but what is it?

FREDA: (*pausing and considering*). Well, first you take the chafing dish—

VANDERLIP: (*interrupting*). What's the chafing dish? Use them in churches, don't they? Burn incense in them, or something or other.

FREDA: (*laughing*). A chafing dish, silly, is a very pretty something you cook things in.

VANDERLIP: Oh, I see. A highfalutin frying pan.

FREDA: (*nodding*). First you put some butter in it; and then, when the butter is melted, you stir in—oh, say, a tablespoon of flour. (*Vanderlip is listening closely.*) When it is stirred smooth—

VANDERLIP: (*interrupting*). Do you brown the flour?

FREDA: No, of course not.

VANDERLIP: (*with comprehension*). Oh.

FREDA: Then you stir in a cup of milk—Minnie's fixing it now,

out in the kitchen—and in her case it will have to be
condensed milk—

VANDERLIP: (*interrupting*). St. Anthony's Cream's the best
brand I know of. (*Regretfully.*) But you can't get it in this
country.

FREDA: I've got some.

VANDERLIP: (*in joyful amazement*). No!

FREDA: (*nodding head*). I have. Then you put in some
boneless chicken—tinned—

VANDERLIP: (*interrupting*). You got some of that, too?

FREDA: Yes. And then some mushrooms—tinned—

VANDERLIP: (*interrupting ecstatically*). Freda, you're a wonder!

FREDA: Then season to taste—(*rising to climax*)—and there
you are!

*Freda half rises, leaning toward him. He half rises to meet
her, reaching for her with both arms, to put around her
waist, but she catches his hands and very gently and slowly
disengages herself. Her very manner of disengaging herself
is caressing and seducing. They sink back slowly into their
respective chairs.*

*Freda listens intently, as for the sound of a sled without.
Glances anxiously at clock on piano. Vanderlip does not
notice, for he is drawing his watch and looking at it.*

VANDERLIP: It's ten after twelve. (*Looks anxiously at door to
right.*) Gee! I hate to go without having a crack at that
Cupid's stew. (*He looks at Freda. She is gazing at him
absently, apparently lost in meditation over him.*) Well?

FREDA: (*startled, as though discovered, in pretty embarrassment*). Oh!

VANDERLIP: I was just wondering what you wanted to see me
about. (*He draws his chair snugly against hers. She looks at
him, studying him, as though trying to make up her mind to
speak.*) Well, what is it?

FREDA: (*with steadiness and determination*). Floyd, I am tired

of the whole business. I want to go away—over the ice—
anywhere—away. I can't live it out here till the river
breaks next spring. I'll die. I know it. I want to quit it
all and go away. And I want to go at once. (*She lays her
hand in appeal on the back of his. His hand turns over and
captures hers. He does not know what to say.*) Well?

VANDERLIP: (*hastily*). I don't know what to say. Nothing I'd
like better, Freda. You know that well enough. (*He presses
her hand, and she nods.*) But you see, I'm—(*blurting it
out*)—I'm engaged. Of course you know that. Everybody
knows it. The girl's coming in over the ice to marry me.
(*Meditatively.*) Don't know what was up with me when
I asked her, but it was a long while back, and I was
all-fired young.

FREDA: And you intend to wait for her? (*He nods.*) And to
marry her? (*He nods.*) Men sometimes make mistakes, you
know, when they are young.

VANDERLIP: (*warmly*). And this is one of them. What did I
know about women then?

FREDA: (*slyly*). Nothing to what you know about them now.

VANDERLIP: I should say so.

FREDA: But, Floyd, by persisting in the mistake, do you mend
matters? (*He shakes his head dubiously.*) Will you be
happy? Will she be happy? She is sure to find out the
mistake; then it will be tragedy.

VANDERLIP: (*in despair*). I don't know. Women keep bothering
me so. There are so many of them, and I like them all.
Seems to me I like best the one I'm with at the time.

FREDA: Mrs. Eppingwell, let us say.

VANDERLIP: (*with positiveness*). Yes, Mrs. Eppingwell. Why,
when I'm with her, I think there's nothing like her under
the sun. I feel like going out and killing her husband just
to get her.

FREDA: (*seductively*). And when you are with me, Floyd?

Vanderlip reaches out impulsively and draws her to him. Her head rests on his shoulder. She snuggles into him in a contented way, her hand petting his. He buries his face in her hair. The scent of her hair gets into his brain and maddens him. He disengages hand from hers and slips it gradually up her bare arm. His other arm, about waist and shoulder, draws her closely against him. All the while, however, they are occupying their respective chairs. They remain this way for a long moment or so, his hand still progressing up her bare arm.

FREDA: (*tearing herself suddenly loose from him and holding him from her at arm's length, tragically*). Floyd! Floyd! I want to go away—out of the land—anywhere!—anywhere!

VANDERLIP: (*soothingly*). Dear Freda.

FREDA: I am tired, tired, so tired of it all. I—I—(*voice breaking*)—I think I shall cry.

VANDERLIP: (*gently and soothingly drawing her to him*). There, there, little woman. Brace up, buck up, don't give in.

FREDA: (*slowly disengaging herself and gently holding him off at arm's length*). I've been running over in my mind the men I know, and reached the conclusion that . . . that . . .

VANDERLIP: (*beaming with self-complacency*). I was the likeliest of the lot.

FREDA: (*quickly*). No, not that, but . . . but . . . that I liked you best of all.

VANDERLIP: (*drawing her to him*). Dear Freda.

FREDA: Dear Floyd.

Door on right opens. They break away from each other and assume a more decorous position. Maid enters, bearing tray, on which are chafing dish, dishes, napkins, etc., and a quart bottle of champagne. She sets tray on table. Freda serves Cupid's stew to Vanderlip, while Maid, a little to rear, is wrestling with champagne bottle.

VANDERLIP: (*who has not noticed champagne bottle, aroused by popping of cork and turning around quickly, simulating a person roused from sleep, rubbing his eyes, etc.*). Wake me up, somebody. I'm dreaming. Pinch me. (*Takes hold of bottle, Maid still retaining her hold, and looks at it.*) The real thing. (*Releases bottle and looks admiringly at Freda.*) Freda, you're a peach. There isn't another bottle in the Klondike.

FREDA: Oh, yes, there is.

VANDERLIP: (*incredulously*). You've got to show *me*.

FREDA: I've three dozen in the storeroom— (*Turning to Maid.*) Isn't that right, Minnie?

MAID: And two over. I counted them this afternoon.

VANDERLIP: (*awestricken*). Gosh!

FREDA: All right, Minnie. You may go now.

Maid goes out to right.

Vanderlip begins eating Cupid's stew. Shows that he is pleased with it. Freda watches him, herself eating. Glances at clock and listens. She seems to hear something. Puts down her plate on table. A knock is heard on door at rear. Freda rises, goes swiftly to rear, and opens door.

An Indian enters. He is dazzled by the light and pulls ice from lips. Freda shuts door. Vanderlip, after one glance around, goes on eating and drinking.

INDIAN: Hello.

FREDA: (*not knowing his errand*). Hello.

INDIAN: Brrr! Much cold.

FREDA: Very cold.

INDIAN: Me come Sitka Charley.

FREDA: Oh, you are the man.

INDIAN: Sitka Charley say him come quick.

FREDA: How quick?

INDIAN: Maybe ten minutes. What time now?

FREDA: Fifteen minutes after twelve.

INDIAN: Him come twenty-five minutes after twelve. Ten minutes more him come, I think.

FREDA: How is the girl?

INDIAN: Much tired. Ride on sled. Plenty tired, cry little bit, like baby. She say must camp right away. Sitka Charley say make Dawson. She say no camp right away she die. Sitka Charley say don't care, make Dawson anyway. I go now. Good-bye.

FREDA: Don't you want to go out in the kitchen and get warm?

INDIAN: No. Good-bye.

FREDA: Good-bye.

Indian opens door and goes out. Freda returns to chair at stove.

FREDA: (*sitting down*). You haven't told me how you like it.

VANDERLIP: (*turning plate upside down*). Actions speak louder than words. (*She helps him to some more.*) Let me see, Cupid's slumgullion, eh?

FREDA: (*laughing*). Cupid's stew.

VANDERLIP: (*thrusting fork into stew on his plate*). What's in a name, so long as it's in your plate anyway?

Eats silently for a space.

FREDA: (*softly*). Floyd. (*He is absorbed in eating.*) Floyd.

VANDERLIP: (*looking at her*). Unh-hunh.

FREDA: (*still softly*). I've been thinking. Why couldn't we go downriver?

VANDERLIP: (*dropping fork and looking at her blankly, then around room, then at plate, and holding up glass of champagne—pathetically*). And leave all this?

FREDA: Why not? We'd soon be down in the world, where we could swim in wine and all kinds of good things.

VANDERLIP: (*seriously*). I don't know, Freda. I almost believe you've got to be in a place like this to get the value out of things. I tell you, champagne on tap is not all it's cracked up to be. It never bites in and lays hold the way this does. Down in the world it's all wine and no thirst—

FREDA: (*interrupting*). And up here it's all thirst and no wine.

VANDERLIP: (*enthusiastically*). But when you *do* get hold of the wine—Lord! Lord! (*Tilts back head and empties glass, his face beaming like to the full moon. He regards Freda thoughtfully as she fills his glass, and speaks with sudden suspicion.*) You don't happen to care for palaces, do you?

FREDA: (*shaking her head*). Why, what put that into your head?

VANDERLIP: Well, I had a hankering after them myself till I got to thinking a while back, and I've about sized it up that one gets fat living in palaces, and soft and lazy. No, sir, no champagne on tap and soft summer skies for me.

FREDA: I suppose it's nice in palaces—for a time. But one would soon tire. The world is good, but life should be many-sided. The way we'll do it will be to rough and knock about for a while and then rest up somewhere. (*Vanderlip begins to lean forward, interested.*) Off to the South Seas on a yacht, then, say, a nibble of Paris.

VANDERLIP: (*gleefully*). Paris!

FREDA: Then a winter in South America, and a summer in Norway—

VANDERLIP: (*interrupting*). I always wanted a look-see at South America.

FREDA: A few months in England—

VANDERLIP: (*interrupting*). Good society?

FREDA: Certainly. And then, heigh-ho for the dogs and the sleds and the Hudson Bay country!

VANDERLIP: (*half rising, enthusiastically*). Freda, you were made for me! It's just the life I want. I couldn't have hit it off better myself if I'd tried. The way you put it—a bit of this and a bit of that—variety, you know—that's me.

FREDA: That's it, variety, change. A strong man like you, full of vitality and go, could not possibly stand a palace for a year. (*He shakes his head.*) It's all very well for effeminate men, but you weren't made for such a life. You are masculine, intensely masculine.

VANDERLIP: (*taking her hand and beginning to draw her toward him*). Do you think so?

FREDA: (*yielding herself*). It doesn't require thinking. I know. Have you ever noticed that it was easy to make women care for you?

VANDERLIP: (*superbly innocent, yet showing by his expression that he agrees with her*). Oh, I don't know.

FREDA: You know it is so.

VANDERLIP: Well, for the sake of argument, yes.

FREDA: It is very easy. And why?

VANDERLIP: (*still playing innocent*). Darned if I know.

FREDA: (*impressively*). Because you are masculine. You strike the deepest chords of a woman's heart. Woman is weak. You are a wall of strength to her. You are something to cling to—big-muscled, strong, and brave. In short, because you are a *man*. (*He folds her to him.*) Dear, dear Floyd! *She lies in his arms a long moment, both still on their respective chairs. Then she slowly and gently disengages herself, at the same time stealing a glance at the clock.*

VANDERLIP: (*holding up her arm and studying it for a moment*). How much do you weigh, Freda?

FREDA: (*smiling*). What now?

VANDERLIP: I just wanted to know.

FREDA: But why?

VANDERLIP: Oh, nothing, I was just thinking you were not the kind to put on fat.

FREDA: (*decisively*). Well, I think not!

VANDERLIP: (*suddenly, by her hands, lifts her to her feet and thrusts her several steps away from him, then sinking back in chair and running his eyes critically over her*). Your lines *are* good.

FREDA: (*lightly*). Think so?

VANDERLIP: You just bet I do. (*Jubilantly.*) *You'll* never get fat!

FREDA: (*coming to his chair and rumpling his hair*). No, thank goodness, I wasn't born that way.

VANDERLIP: (*beginning pompously*). Now, some women—

FREDA: (*interrupting*). The Lisznayi, for example.

VANDERLIP: (*spontaneously, positively*). She'll never get fat, Freda.

FREDA: Oh, she won't, eh? How do you know? You'd never have guessed it all of yourself. She must have told you. (*Vanderlip shows confusion.*) Why, she's started already. She's carrying twenty pounds more than she ought. It spoils her figure. And—my!—now that she's started, won't she just put it on!

VANDERLIP: (*anxiously*). But how do you know?

FREDA: I've my eyes. So have you. Surely you've noticed it?

VANDERLIP: (*slowly*). Honest, now, I've had my suspicions that way. (*He remains silent for a moment or so. Freda rumples his hair.*) I like that.

FREDA: What?

VANDERLIP: That what you are doing.

FREDA: Oh!

Slaps his arm playfully and sits down in her chair. Listens intently for sounds from without while Vanderlip sips from glass.

VANDERLIP: (*after a pause, setting down glass and looking amorously at Freda*). Say, Freda, do you know . . . ? (*A pause. Freda glances at clock.*) Do you know what I'd like?

FREDA: Not in the slightest.

VANDERLIP: Well, I'll tell you. I'd like to see you with your hair down.

FREDA: (*change in whole manner beginning here, but beginning slightly*). Think so?

VANDERLIP: You just bet I would.

FREDA: (*rising*). Wait a moment.

Passes behind him to door at right.

Vanderlip rests under the idea that she has gone to take down hair, fills glass, and leans complacently back in chair and sips from glass.

Freda opens door to right and beckons. Closes door, listens for a moment on way back to chair, and sits down.

VANDERLIP: (*looking at her hair, still up, surprised and grieved*). Why, I thought all the time you were taking it down.

Freda laughs her silvery, scornful laughter. Vanderlip is puzzled, thinks she is teasing him.

Maid enters, unobserved by Vanderlip. Freda issues her order with her eyes, glancing at Vanderlip's bearskin overcoat hanging on wall to rear. Maid goes and gets coat and returns, still unobserved by Vanderlip, at the rear of whom she stands waiting.

VANDERLIP: (*expostulating*). Now I say, Freda. (*Freda still laughs.*) What's the matter, anyway?

FREDA: I have just recollected.

VANDERLIP: (*puzzled*). What?

FREDA: That you had an engagement at twelve sharp.

VANDERLIP: I did. But it will keep.

FREDA: It is now half past twelve.

VANDERLIP: Well, and what of it?

FREDA: Nothing, only . . .

Pauses and considers.

VANDERLIP: Only what?

FREDA: Only isn't it rather cold down at the water hole? (*Vanderlip is stunned for a moment and can only stare at her in a bewildered way. Her laughter, at his bewilderment, becomes wholly mirthful.*) Minnie, help Mr. Vanderlip on with his overcoat.

Vanderlip glances swiftly around and sees Maid holding coat. He looks at his watch very slowly and puts it away very slowly. Slowly empties glass of champagne and carefully puts empty glass on table. Just as slowly drags himself out of chair and to his feet. Maid offers to help on with overcoat, but he ignores her.

FREDA: (*who has ceased laughing, showing that she is a bit frightened by his preternatural calmness, but still keeping her nerve).* Let me thank you for your kindness, Floyd. I wanted half an hour or so of your time, and you have given it. The turning to the left, as you leave the cabin, leads quickest to the water hole. Good night. I'm going to bed. *(Starts to go toward door at left.)* Minnie, see Mr. Vanderlip out, please. *(Turning head over shoulder, looking back at Vanderlip, and beginning again her silvery laughter. Vanderlip has not spoken a word. He springs, lionlike, after her, seizing her by the arm and whirling her fiercely about, face to face, and still keeping his clutch.)* Don't be rough. *(He glares at her. She still keeps her nerve, speaks lightly.)* On second thought—*(looks at his detaining hand)*—I've decided not to go to bed. Don't be ridiculous, Floyd. *(He growls inarticulately.)* Tragedy doesn't at all become you. Do sit down and be comfortable. *(To Maid, who has remained composed and holding coat.)* Mr. Vanderlip doesn't want his coat yet a while.

Maid goes to rear, hangs up coat, and remains at rear, waiting.

VANDERLIP: *(speaking with slow, clear enunciation).* What do you know about the water hole? *(Freda laughs. He closes his grip on her arm till she winces.)* What do you know about the water hole?

FREDA: *(lightly).* More than you know.

VANDERLIP: *(again closing grip).* Then tell me. I want to know.

FREDA: *(wincing, but still lightly).* I know that the fair lady waiting there has flown away a good half hour ago.

VANDERLIP: Where?

FREDA: Down the river.

VANDERLIP: How do you know it?

FREDA: I arranged it.

VANDERLIP: *(softening for a moment).* Tell me, it was because you wanted me?

FREDA: *(defiantly).* No.

VANDERLIP: (*hardening again*). Then you didn't want me? (*She shakes her head.*) You don't want me? (*She shakes head.*) Well, then, will you have me?—now? (*She shakes head.*) Then this was a game you worked on me?

FREDA: Yes.

VANDERLIP: You didn't mean a word of it?

FREDA: Not a word of it. I was playing.

VANDERLIP: (*grimly*). Well, I wasn't, that's the difference.

FREDA: Do let go of my arm. You are hurting me.

VANDERLIP: (*ignoring her protest, dragging her roughly by her arm to the front and just to left of table, holding her face to face with him and beginning to speak faster*). Look here, Freda, I'm a fool. I know it. I was a fool there in that chair. You put it all over me. You women all make a fool of me. I don't think quick. I'm not used to it, I guess. My tongue is awkward. I can't think of bright things to say, or the right things to say. And I believe what is said to me. And then I like women, too. I can't help it. I was born that way. I just like them, and they take advantage of me—

FREDA: (*interrupting*). Won't you let go of me and sit down?

VANDERLIP: (*ignoring her*). Why do they take advantage of me? (*Freda shrugs her shoulders.*) Because I am a fool. Because I am playing their game and don't know how to play it. They know how to play it. They ought to know—it is their game. A man's a fool to buck another man's game. The percentage is all in favor of the house. And a man is a bigger fool to buck a woman's game. And I've been dead soft and easy. I know it. I've played your game and you've tied knots in me. . . .

He pauses, as though debating the next thing to say.

FREDA: (*lightly*). I must say you are untying the knots fast.

VANDERLIP: (*with touch of anger*). I'm untying nothing. I'm going to begin tying. What I'm going to do is to play my game, and you're going to play it with me, my lady. (*His speech grows slow and clear again.*) Do you know what my game is? (*Freda shakes her head.*) It's not palavering, and being society monkey, and ducking, and bowing, and scraping, and giving crooked talk, and saying smart things, and that sort of stuff. It's just this— (*He takes hold of her other arm with other hand and puts the pressure on with both hands. At first she merely winces, but he grips until she cries aloud in pain. Maid shows alarm for first time and starts hastily forward.*) That's it. Muscle's my game—the only game I can play, and I've been a fool to go out of my class.

MAID: (*interrupting, to Freda*). What shall I do?

FREDA: Nothing. It is all right.

MAID: Shall I go for help?

FREDA: No, no. (*To Vanderlip.*) Let go of me, Floyd. You are crushing my arms.

VANDERLIP: (*laughing savagely*). Did you let go when you crushed me?

FREDA: (*with blaze of defiance*). You coward!

VANDERLIP: (*savagely*). Were you less coward when you beat me down to my knees with your woman's wit, your woman's beauty, your woman's weapons? Your face is beautiful. Your body is beautiful. With these have you drawn me to you, making yourself soft and yielding so that at a distance the very feel of you was soft and yielding—(*with scorn*)—a play actress, you! Your mind is quick. Your tongue is crooked. You lied to me. When you let me hold your hand, you lied to me. When you looked softly at me, or passed your hand through my hair, you lied to me. When you came against me and rested your head on my breast so that the scent of your hair got into my brain and maddened me, you lied to me. You knew all the time that my blood was pounding up hot within me, you knew all the time that I was honest and playing fair, and all the time you were lying to me.

He pauses and debates upon what next to say.

MAID: (*calmly, to Freda*). Shall I go for help?

VANDERLIP: (*ferociously*). Shut up, you! (*Continuing, to Freda.*) Well, I've taken your medicine. Now you take mine. Here it is. I want you. I'm pretty sure I'd sooner have you than Loraine. You can marry me if you want, but marry or no marry, you're mine. Downriver you go with me tonight, my lady, so you'd better tell that girl of yours to pack your duds.

FREDA: (*laughing defiantly in his face*). Think so?

VANDERLIP: (*maddened by desire of her*). I know so—and here's a foretaste of my game. Tell me how you like it. (*Bends her back, face upturned; gets proper grips so that she is helpless; and deliberately and passionately kisses her several times on the lips. Maid springs upon him, but he flings her off and away with one arm. Holds Freda by one arm again.*) How do you like it, eh? How do you like it?

FREDA: (*almost suffocating with rage, wiping lips with back of free hand*). You beast! You beast! You beast! (*Maid is starting to spring at him again.*) No, no, Minnie! Stop! I can deal with him.

VANDERLIP: Not in a man's game, Freda.

FREDA: (*all defiance*). In a man's game, Floyd Vanderlip.

She no longer winces nor struggles to free herself, but confronts him, head erect, expression of cold anger on face.

VANDERLIP: (*looking at her admiringly for a moment*). Ah, you beauty! You've made me mad for you. I'll crush you into submission as you crushed me into submission at the dance tonight. You beat me down to my knees, but I'll bring you down on your knees to me till you're glad to kiss the toe of my moccasin. (*He surveys her again.*) And now, you beauty, you beauty, I am thirsty for your lips again. (*He starts to bend her back again, but she refuses to struggle, holding her face up to him defiantly. He pauses.*) Well, why don't you fight and scratch and claw around some?

FREDA: Because I won't give you the chance to pull and haul and maul me around, that is all.

VANDERLIP: (*who, as usual, is baffled by a change of attitude*). Then I'll kiss you.

FREDA: You may pollute me with your lips, but you shall not master me with your strength.

VANDERLIP: (*gaily*). Nay, nay, not pollute. You should call it— (*imitating Mrs. McFee*)—"contameenate." That's right. Blaze away at me with those eyes of yours. You may keep quiet with your body, but you can't take the fight out of your eyes. I tell you that blaze gives value to your kisses, and now I'm going to— (*Leans forward to kiss her, while she remains motionless and passive. He pauses with lips close to hers.*) Nothing like prolonging anticipation, eh? You know you said I was masculine, intensely masculine. How do you like it? How do you like leaning up against the wall of my strength? Ah, you beauty! You beauty!

FREDA: (*suddenly listening*). Minnie! Open the door!
A jingling of dog bells is heard without, and a man's voice crying "Haw!" Maid runs toward the door. Vanderlip listens, still holding Freda close in his arms. A knock at door. Maid throws open door.

FREDA: (*in triumphant voice as door is thrown open*). Now will you let go of me?
Enter Mrs. Eppingwell, followed by Capt. Eppingwell and a Northwest mounted Policeman.
Mrs. Eppingwell, looking at Policeman, points at Vanderlip. Policeman hesitates, embarrassed at interrupting such a scene. Vanderlip and Freda in consternation, he still holding her. He releases her abruptly and is himself all awkwardness and

confusion. Freda separates from him, moving away uncon-
sciously several steps, her eyes fixed upon Mrs. Eppingwell.

FREDA: (*surprise, awe, etc.*). You!

MRS. EPPINGWELL: (*sharp and businesslike*). Yes, I. And I am
glad I am not too late.

FREDA: (*striving to recover her poise, speaking automatically in
artificial manner*). Delighted, I assure you. (*With sudden
break in manner, becoming candid.*) No, I am not delighted
at all.

MRS. EPPINGWELL: I should scarcely think so.

FREDA: It is intrusion.

MRS. EPPINGWELL: It is intrusion, I know, but—

FREDA: (*interrupting, again artificial manner*). Oh, not at all.
(*Starting toward Mrs. Eppingwell.*) Won't you take off your
wraps? (*To Maid.*) Minnie!
Maid offers to help Mrs. Eppingwell off with wraps.

MRS. EPPINGWELL: (*declining Maid's offer*). No, it is not necessary.
We shall stop only a moment.

FREDA: (*artificial manner*). I hope you'll pardon my curiosity,
but—(*hesitates an instant*)—why didn't you come sooner?
What was the delay?

MRS. EPPINGWELL: (*indicating Policeman, who bows*). I had to
get this gentleman. It took time—

POLICEMAN: (*interrupting, bowing*). Sorry.

MRS. EPPINGWELL: And then I went to the wrong water hole.
(*Freda and Vanderlip both start, Mrs. Eppingwell observing
Vanderlip's start.*) Good morning, Mr. Vanderlip.

VANDERLIP: (*awkwardly*). Hum, yes. How do you do? Good
morning.

FREDA: (*the real state of affairs dawning on her*). I see. You
expected to find me at the water hole. (*Mrs. Eppingwell
nods.*) And you didn't.

MRS. EPPINGWELL: No. Then I went to the other water hole.

FREDA: Expecting to find me?

MRS. EPPINGWELL: Yes. Then I came here.

FREDA: (*with mock admiration*). Unerring instinct.

MRS. EPPINGWELL: (*replying in kind*). Yes, wasn't it?

FREDA: Er—by the way, didn't you find anybody at the second water hole?

MRS. EPPINGWELL: A strange woman. I thought she was you at first. She seemed restless enough.

VANDERLIP: (*starts at mention of strange woman, suddenly moving toward the street door*). I've fooled around here long enough. I'm going.

FREDA: Good luck, Floyd.

POLICEMAN: (*stepping forward, meeting and stopping Vanderlip*). Sorry.

VANDERLIP: (*irritated*). What's the matter now?

POLICEMAN: (*drawing document from pocket*). I've got a warrant for you. Forgery. Sorry.

VANDERLIP: (*astounded*). What in hell—
Breaks off.

POLICEMAN: Sorry.

VANDERLIP: (*expostulating*). Now, look here, I say, whose game is this?
Freda laughs her silvery laughter; it is laughter of amusement only.

FREDA: (*to Mrs. Eppingwell, still laughing, accusingly*). You did this.

MRS. EPPINGWELL: (*nodding*). I had tried everything else to stop him from running away.

FREDA: (*laughing merrily and shaking her head*). Poor Floyd! Poor, poor Floyd!

VANDERLIP: (*wrathfully*). Look here, Mrs. Eppingwell. This is your work. You'd better call it off. I'm done with bucking other people's games. (*Starts toward door, but Policeman lays hand on his arm.*) Get out of my way, you whippersnapper!

POLICEMAN: (*not backing down a bit*). Sorry.

VANDERLIP: (*flinging off hand, but remaining where he is*). You'd better call him off, Mrs. Eppingwell, or there'll be the almightiest ruction round here you ever saw.

FREDA: (*lightly*). Don't be in a hurry, Floyd. She's gone.

VANDERLIP: No, she isn't.

FREDA: Ask Mrs. Eppingwell.

MRS. EPPINGWELL: Whom do you mean?

FREDA: The strange, restless lady at the water hole.

MRS. EPPINGWELL: Why, yes. She went away on a sled down the river.

VANDERLIP: Who'd she go with?

MRS. EPPINGWELL: With nobody. She had an Indian dog driver, though.

Vanderlip makes gesture of despair, signifying that he has been completely beaten. Freda laughs merrily.

VANDERLIP: (*wrathfully*). Oh, you women!

MRS. EPPINGWELL: (*to Freda*). Who is this strange lady?

FREDA: (*indicating Vanderlip*). Ask him.

Mrs. Eppingwell looks inquiringly at Vanderlip.

VANDERLIP: (*wrathfully*). None of your business, you and your games! I quit. I've bucked myself broke against you— (*whirling on Freda*)—against all of you. (*To Policeman.*) Go ahead, arrest me. It's a fake, and you know it. But go ahead.

POLICEMAN: I've only got my orders. Sorry. You'll come along peaceably?

Vanderlip grunts savage assent.

VANDERLIP: You know it's a fake.

POLICEMAN: I know only my orders. Sorry.

General movement of preparation to leave.

FREDA: (*to Mrs. Eppingwell*). It's too bad you can't stop longer, but—

Suddenly breaks off and listens intently.

A jingling of dog bells is heard without, and shouts of men.

A knock on street door. Maid opens door. Flossie appears in doorway and enters. Sitka Charley enters at her heels and closes door. Flossie is dazzled by the lights and looks about hesitatingly. She is well frosted up. A nose strap is across her nose. She removes nose strap. Looks about and sees Vanderlip. Freda starts toward her, impulsively, to receive her.

FLOSSIE: (*making a weak little lame run toward Vanderlip, with infinite relief in her voice*). Floyd!

VANDERLIP: (*dazed*). Flossie!

He opens his arms, and she staggers and falls into them. Her head lies on his breast for a space while he holds her and stares helplessly around. Then she lifts her head, inviting the kiss, and perforce he bends head and kisses her.

FLOSSIE: (*infinite gladness*). Oh, Floyd! Floyd!

VANDERLIP: Dear, dear Flossie!

FLOSSIE: (*still in his arms, but throwing her head back to look at him, in playful manner*). You big, impatient man! (*Vanderlip is puzzled and only awkwardly pats her shoulder with one arm that is around her.*) You cruel, cruel man! (*He is still puzzled.*) Couldn't wait. Couldn't let me have my night's rest and arrive in the morning fresh.

VANDERLIP: Ah—hum—yes.

She puts her lips up to him, and he again kisses her.
Sitka Charley remains inside street door. Capt. Eppingwell is restless, betraying a feeling that it is time to go. Policeman is restless. Mrs. Eppingwell and Freda, now near to each other, are looking on.

FLOSSIE: My! What lots of dogs you must have!

VANDERLIP: (*more puzzled than ever*). Hum, yes.

FLOSSIE: First came an Indian with six dogs. You know, the Indian with one eye. (*Mrs. Eppingwell and Capt. Eppingwell look at each other significantly. Vanderlip, after a moment's hesitancy, nods.*) Then came the second Indian with eight dogs. (*Mrs. Eppingwell looks inquiringly at Capt. Eppingwell, who shakes head, then each looks with bepuzzlement at the*

other. Vanderlip, again hesitating, nods.) And then came
Sitka Charley with seven of the most magnificent dogs I
ever saw. Oh, Floyd, they were just grand! (*Mrs. Eppingwell
and Capt. Eppingwell look more bepuzzled than ever.
Vanderlip looks across at Freda with comprehension, by his
look as much as saying, "You are responsible for this." Freda
smiles. Mrs. Eppingwell and Capt. Eppingwell observe the
proceeding and look at each other significantly.*) We just
flew along—like the wind!

VANDERLIP: (*seeing the whole situation and lying up to it*). I
just bet you did. I knew they'd bring you in on the jump. I
told them I didn't want any loafing, and . . . well, from
the looks of it, I guess there wasn't any.

FLOSSIE: (*snuggling in against him*). Couldn't wait a bit longer,
could you, dear?

VANDERLIP: (*holding her closely*). You just bet I couldn't.

POLICEMAN: (*unobserved by Flossie, whose back is toward him,
stepping forward toward Vanderlip, the warrant still in his
hand*). Sorry—

MRS. EPPINGWELL: (*interrupting, stepping toward him*). Give it
to me. (*Policeman hands warrant to her.*) It will be all
right. You understand.

POLICEMAN: (*nodding, pulling on mittens, and bowing very
politely*). Then I will wish you good night.
Makes exit with final bow.

CAPT. EPPINGWELL: (*to Mrs. Eppingwell, indicating desire to go*).
We're scarcely needed here, I think.

MRS. EPPINGWELL: One moment, Archie. I'm all in a daze, and
I'm curious. (*Turning to Sitka Charley.*) Charley, the team
of dogs you drove, whose were they?

FREDA: (*who, now that the fight is over and won, is on the
verge of breaking down, interrupts Sitka Charley and speaks
herself*). Now I wish you would all go home and leave me
alone. I want to go to bed.

MRS. EPPINGWELL: (*gently*). But I am curious, Freda, as you were curious. I want to know. I insist.

FREDA: (*choking, on the verge of tears*). Please, please go.

FLOSSIE: (*who has lifted head and been regarding Freda, to Vanderlip. Loud enough for all to hear, but not too loud.*) Who is that woman?

VANDERLIP: (*painfully embarrassed, hesitatingly*). Well . . . you see, Flossie . . . it's like this.

FLOSSIE: (*with asperity*). She is not a friend of yours?

VANDERLIP: No, no, of course not. You see, this is the Klondike. Things are different here than from what you've been used to, and . . . and . . .

FLOSSIE: (*interrupting, showing in voice and demeanor comprehension of Freda's status*). Oh, I understand. It will be better for us to go, I think.

They start toward street door, Vanderlip supporting Flossie around waist. She is very tired and leans heavily against him. He puts on bearskin coat, mittens, etc. He does not speak, though he nods awkwardly. As they make exit, he glances back at Freda.

FREDA: (*to Mrs. Eppingwell, harshly*). Now will you go?

MRS. EPPINGWELL: (*gently*). No, I insist. There has been a misunderstanding.

Freda, tears imminent, makes nervous exclamation and with both hands makes nervous gesture. Turns her back, walks rapidly to front, and throws herself into easy chair, where she sits, face up, facing audience.

MRS. EPPINGWELL: (*to Sitka Charley*). Those dogs you drove, Charley. Whose were they?

SITKA CHARLEY: (*hesitating, shifting weight from one leg to the other and back again, looking appealingly at back of chair in which Freda is seated*). Me no know.

MRS. EPPINGWELL: (*impatiently*). Of course you know.

SITKA CHARLEY: (*still hesitatingly, still shifting weight back and forth, still looking appealingly at back of chair occupied by Freda*). Maybe know, maybe not know.

MRS. EPPINGWELL: (*imperatively*). Tell me.

SITKA CHARLEY: (*angrily*). What for, all you womans? Make Sitka Charley much tired. All the time—(*imitating their manner*)—"Charley, tell me this, Charley, tell me that." All the time, "Charley, no tell this, Charley, no tell that." Sitka Charley tired. Sitka Charley much tired. Sitka Charley dam tired. Now Sitka Charley tell. (*He pauses, while Mrs. Eppingwell waits expectantly and Freda, with expressionless face, faces audience.*) Sitka Charley big fool, too. Him think you love Vanderlip. Him think Freda love Vanderlip. (*Shaking head.*) No love. All the same make Vanderlip big fool. All the time all womans make all mans big fool. You say, no tell Freda. Freda say, no tell you. All right. Sitka Charley no tell. Now Sitka Charley much tired. Now him tell. Um, him drive Freda's dogs. Freda say, "Charley, bring Flossie girl much quick." (*Looking at Mrs. Eppingwell with expression of pride, boastfully.*) Sitka Charley bring Flossie girl much quick.

MRS. EPPINGWELL: Who was the woman at the water hole?

SITKA CHARLEY: Um Lisznayi woman.

Mrs. Eppingwell is surprised. Capt. Eppingwell makes dumb show of delight.

MRS. EPPINGWELL: (*beaten, pathetically*). Archie, will you ever have faith in me again?

SITKA CHARLEY: (*moving toward door, turning toward back of Freda's chair*). Dogs much hungry. (*Stops and waits, looking at Freda's chair.*) Um, me go feed dogs. (*After regarding chair for a moment, starts on toward street door. Again stops and looks at chair.*) I go now, Freda.

FREDA: (*not turning head, expressionless face and voice*). Good night, Charley.

Sitka Charley makes exit. Door slams.

Mrs. Eppingwell looks toward Freda's chair, starts as though

to go to Freda, hesitates, and stops. Turns upon Capt. Epping-
well and shoves him toward street door. Capt. Eppingwell
makes exit. Door slams. Mrs. Eppingwell remains standing
on one side of door, looking toward Freda's chair. Maid
stands on other side of door, looking at Mrs. Eppingwell.
When door slams, Freda rises to her feet. The breakdown
has come.

FREDA: Thank God!

Without looking toward street door, or becoming aware that
Mrs. Eppingwell still remains, Freda goes rapidly to right, to
couch, sobs struggling up, her breast heaving. She sinks to
floor, resting arms on couch, face buried in arms and couch,
and sobs convulsively.

Mrs. Eppingwell comes forward and touches Freda on shoulder.

FREDA: (*starting, but not looking up*). It is all right, Minnie.
You may go to bed.

Goes on sobbing.

Mrs. Eppingwell waits a moment, sits down on couch, and
rests hand on Freda's head.

MRS. EPPINGWELL: (*very gently*). Freda.

FREDA: (*starting with violent surprise and looking up*). You!

MRS. EPPINGWELL: (*gently*). Yes, I.

FREDA: (*trying to be harsh, but succeeding in being only*
reproachful). I asked you to go.

Turns face away from Mrs. Eppingwell and looks straight
forward toward audience.

MRS. EPPINGWELL: (*gently*). Freda.

Freda turns head and looks into Mrs. Eppingwell's face. Mrs.
Eppingwell puts her arm around Freda's shoulder and draws
her close. Freda bursts into tears and buries face in Mrs.
Eppingwell's lap. Mrs. Eppingwell bends over her, soothing her.

CURTAIN

THE SCORN OF WOMEN

SHORT STORY (1901)

Once Freda and Mrs. Eppingwell clashed. Now, Freda was a Greek girl and a dancer. At least she purported to be Greek; but this was doubted by many, for her classic face had over-much strength in it and the tides of hell which rose in her eyes made at rare moments her ethnology the more dubious. To a few—men—this sight had been vouchsafed, and though long years may have passed, they have not forgotten, nor will they ever forget. She never talked of herself, so that it were well to let it go down that when in repose, expurgated, Greek she certainly was. Her furs were the most magnificent in all the country from Chilcoot to St. Michael's, and her name was common on the lips of men. But Mrs. Eppingwell was the wife of a captain; also a social constellation of the first magnitude, the path of her orbit marking the most select coterie in Dawson—a coterie captioned by the profane as the "official clique." Sitka Charley had traveled trail with her once, when famine drew tight and a man's life was less than a cup of flour, and his judgment placed her above all women. Sitka Charley was an Indian; his criteria were primitive; but his word was fiat and his verdict a hallmark in every camp under the circle.

These two women were man-conquering, man-subduing

134

machines, each in her own way, and their ways were different. Mrs. Eppingwell ruled in her own house and at the Barracks, where were younger sons galore, to say nothing of the chiefs of the police, the executive, and the judiciary. Freda ruled down in the town; but the men she ruled were the same who functioned socially at the Barracks or were fed tea and canned preserves at the hand of Mrs. Eppingwell in her hillside cabin of rough-hewn logs. Each knew the other existed; but their lives were apart as the poles, and while they must have heard stray bits of news and were curious, they were never known to ask a question. And there would have been no trouble had not a free lance in the shape of the model-woman come into the land on the first ice, with a spanking dog team and a cosmopolitan reputation. Loraine Lisznayi—alliterative, dramatic, and Hungarian—precipitated the strife, and because of her Mrs. Eppingwell left her hillside and invaded Freda's domain, and Freda likewise went up from the town to spread confusion and embarrassment at the Governor's ball.

All of which may be ancient history so far as the Klondike is concerned, but very few, even in Dawson, know the inner truth of the matter; nor beyond those few are there any fit to measure the wife of the captain or the Greek dancer. And that all are now permitted to understand, let honor be accorded Sitka Charley. From his lips fell the main facts in the screed herewith presented. It ill befits that Freda herself should have waxed confidential to a mere scribbler of words, or that Mrs. Eppingwell made mention of the things which happened. They may have spoken, but it is unlikely.

II

Floyd Vanderlip was a strong man, apparently. Hard work and hard grub had no terrors for him, as his early history in the country attested. In danger he was a lion, and when he held in check half a thousand starving men, as he once did, it was remarked that no cooler eye ever took the glint of sunshine on a rifle sight. He had but one weakness, and even that, rising from out his strength, was of a negative sort. His parts were strong, but they lacked coordination. Now it happened that while his center of amativeness was pronounced, it had lain mute and passive during the years he lived on moose and salmon and chased glowing Eldorados over chill divides. But when he finally blazed the corner post and center stakes on one of the richest Klondike claims, it began to quicken; and when he took his place in society, a full-fledged Bonanza King, it awoke and took charge of him. He suddenly recollected a girl in the States, and it came to him quite forcibly, not only that she might be waiting for him, but that a wife was a very pleasant acquisition for a man who lived some several degrees north of 53. So he wrote an appropriate note, enclosed a letter of credit generous enough to cover all expenses, including trousseau and chaperon, and addressed it to one Flossie. Flossie? One could imagine the rest. However, after that he built a comfortable cabin on his claim, bought another in Dawson, and broke the news to his friends.

And just here is where the lack of coordination came into play. The waiting was tedious, and having been long denied, the amative element could not brook further delay. Flossie was coming, but Loraine Lisznayi was here. And not only was Loraine Lisznayi here, but her cosmopolitan reputation was somewhat the worse for wear, and she was not exactly so young as when she posed in the studios of artist queens and received at her door the cards of cardinals and princes. Also, her finances were unhealthy. Having run the gamut in her time, she was now not averse to trying conclusions with a Bonanza King whose wealth was such that he could not guess it within six figures. Like a wise soldier casting about, after years of service, for a comfortable billet, she had come into the Northland to be married. So one day her eyes flashed up into Floyd Vanderlip's as he was buying table linen for Flossie in the P.C. Company's store, and the thing was settled out of hand.

When a man is free, much may go unquestioned, which, should he be rash enough to cumber himself with domestic ties, society will instantly challenge. Thus it was with Floyd Vanderlip. Flossie was coming, and a low buzz went up when Loraine Lisznayi rode down the main street behind his wolf dogs. She accompanied the lady reporter of the *Kansas City Star* when photographs were taken of his Bonanza properties, and watched the genesis of a six-column article. At that time they were dined royally in Flossie's cabin, on Flossie's table linen. Likewise there were comings and goings, and junketings, all perfectly proper, by the way, which caused the men to say sharp things and the women to be spiteful. Only Mrs. Eppingwell did not hear. The distant hum of wagging tongues rose faintly, but she was prone to believe good of people and to close her ears to evil; so she paid no heed.

Not so with Freda. She had no cause to love men, but by some strange alchemy of her nature, her heart went out to women—to women whom she had less cause to love. And her heart went out to Flossie, even then traveling the Long Trail and facing into the bitter North to meet a man who might not wait for her. A shrinking, clinging sort of a girl, Freda pictured her, with weak mouth and pretty pouting lips, blow-away, sun-kissed hair, and eyes full of the merry shallows and the lesser joys of life. But she also pictured Flossie, face nose-strapped and frost-rimed, stumbling wearily behind the dogs. Wherefore she smiled, dancing one night, upon Floyd Vanderlip.

Few men are so constituted that they may receive the smile of Freda unmoved; nor among them can Floyd Vanderlip be accounted. The grace he had found with the model-woman had caused him to remeasure himself, and by the favor in which he now stood with the Greek dancer, he felt himself doubly a man. There were unknown qualities and depths in him, evidently, which they perceived. He did not know exactly what those qualities and depths were, but he had a hazy idea that they were there somewhere, and of them was bred a great pride in himself. A man who could force two women such as these to look upon him a second time was certainly a most remarkable man. Someday, when he had the time, he would sit down and analyze his strength; but now, just now, he would take what the gods had given him. And a thin little thought began to lift itself, and he fell to wondering whatever under the sun he had seen in Flossie, and to regret exceedingly that he had sent for her. Of course Freda was out of the running. His dumps were the richest on Bonanza Creek, and they were many, while he was a man of responsibility and position. But Loraine Lisznayi—she was just the woman. Her life had been large; she could do the honors of his establishment and give tone to his dollars.

But Freda smiled, and continued to smile, till he came to spend much time with her. When she, too, rode down the street behind his wolf dogs, the model-woman found food for thought and, the next time they were together, dazzled him with her princes and cardinals and personal little anecdotes of courts and kings. She also showed him dainty missives, superscribed "My dear Loraine," and ended "Most affectionately yours," and signed by the given name of a real live queen on a throne. And he marveled in his heart that the great woman should deign to waste so much as a moment upon him. But she played him cleverly, making flattering contrasts and comparisons between him and the noble phantoms she drew mainly from her fancy, till he went away dizzy with self-delight and sorrowing for the world which had been denied him so long. Freda was a more masterful woman. If she flat-

tered, no one knew it. Should she stoop, the stoop were unobserved. If a man felt she thought well of him, so subtly was the
feeling conveyed that he could not for the life of him say why
or how. So she tightened her grip upon Floyd Vanderlip and
rode daily behind his dogs.

And just here is where the mistake occurred. The buzz rose
loudly and more definitely, coupled now with the name of the
dancer, and Mrs. Eppingwell heard. She, too, thought of
Flossie lifting her moccasined feet through the endless hours,
and Floyd Vanderlip was invited up the hillside to tea, and invited often. This quite took his breath away, and he became
drunken with appreciation of himself. Never was man so mal-
treated. His soul had become a thing for which three women
struggled, while a fourth was on the way to claim it. And
three such women!

But Mrs. Eppingwell and the mistake she made. She spoke
of the affair, tentatively, to Sitka Charley, who had sold dogs
to the Greek girl. But no names were mentioned. The nearest
approach to it was when Mrs. Eppingwell said, "This—er—
horrid woman," and Sitka Charley, with the model-woman
strong in his thoughts, had echoed, "This—er—horrid woman."
And he agreed with her that it was a wicked thing for a
woman to come between a man and the girl he was to marry.
"A mere girl, Charley," she said, "I am sure she is. And she is
coming into a strange country without a friend when she gets
here. We must do something." Sitka Charley promised his help
and went away thinking what a wicked woman this Loraine
Lisznayi must be, also what noble women Mrs. Eppingwell
and Freda were to interest themselves in the welfare of the
unknown Flossie.

Now, Mrs. Eppingwell was open as the day. To Sitka
Charley, who took her once past the Hills of Silence, belongs
the glory of having memorialized her clear-searching eyes, her
clear-ringing voice, and her utter downright frankness. Her

lips had a way of stiffening to command, and she was used to coming straight to the point. Having taken Floyd Vanderlip's measurement, she did not dare this with him, but she was not afraid to go down into the town to Freda. And down she went, in the bright light of day, to the house of the dancer. She was above silly tongues, as was her husband, the captain. She wished to see this woman and to speak with her, nor was she aware of any reason why she should not. So she stood in the snow at the Greek girl's door, with the frost at sixty below, and parleyed with the waiting maid for a full five minutes. She had also the pleasure of being turned away from that door, and of going back up the hill, wroth at heart for the indignity which had been put upon her. "Who was this woman that she should refuse to see me?" she asked herself. One would think it the other way around, and she herself but a dancing girl denied at the door of the wife of a captain. As it was, she knew, had Freda come up the hill to her—no matter what the errand—she would have made her welcome at her fire, and they would have sat there as two women, and talked merely as two women. She had overstepped convention and lowered herself, but she had thought it different with the women down in the town. And she was ashamed that she had laid herself open to such dishonor, and her thoughts of Freda were unkind.

Not that Freda deserved this. Mrs. Eppingwell had descended to meet her who was without caste, while she, strong in the traditions of her own earlier status, had not permitted it. She could worship such a woman, and she would have asked no greater joy than to have had her into the cabin and sat with her, just sat with her, for an hour. But her respect for Mrs. Eppingwell, and her respect for herself, who was beyond respect, had prevented her doing that which she most desired. Though not quite recovered from the recent visit of Mrs. McFee, the wife of the minister, who had descended upon her in a whirlwind of exhortation and brimstone, she could not imagine what had prompted the present visit. She was not aware of any particular wrong she had done, and surely this woman who waited at the door was not concerned with the welfare of her soul. Why had she come? For all the curiosity she could not help but feel, she steeled herself in the pride of those who are without pride, and trembled in the inner room like a maid on the first caress of a lover. If Mrs. Eppingwell suffered going up the hill, she too suffered, lying face downward on the bed, dry-eyed, dry-mouthed, dumb.

Mrs. Eppingwell's knowledge of human nature was great. She aimed at universality. She had found it easy to step from the civilized and contemplate things from the barbaric aspect. She could comprehend certain primal and analogous characteristics in a hungry wolf dog or a starving man and predicate lines of action to be pursued by either under like conditions. To her, a woman was a woman, whether garbed in purple or the rags of the gutter; Freda was a woman. She would not have been surprised had she been taken into the dancer's cabin and encountered on common ground; nor surprised had she been taken in and flaunted in prideless arrogance. But to be treated as she had been treated was unexpected and disappointing. Ergo, she had not caught Freda's point of view. And this was good. There are some points of view which cannot be gained save through much travail and personal crucifixion, and it were well for the world that its Mrs. Eppingwells should, in certain ways, fall short of universality. One cannot understand defilement without laying hands to pitch, which is very sticky, while there be plenty willing to undertake the experiment. All of which is of small concern, beyond the fact that it gave Mrs. Eppingwell ground for grievance and bred for her a greater love in the Greek girl's heart.

III

And in this way things went along for a month—Mrs. Eppingwell striving to withhold the man from the Greek dancer's blandishments against the time of Flossie's coming; Flossie lessening the miles each day on the dreary trail; Freda pitting her strength against the model-woman; the model-woman straining every nerve to land the prize; and the man moving through it all like a flying shuttle, very proud of himself, whom he believed to be a second Don Juan.

It was nobody's fault except the man's that Loraine Lisznayi at last landed him. The way of a man with a maid may be too wonderful to know, but the way of a woman with a man passeth all conception; whence the prophet were indeed unwise who would dare forecast Floyd Vanderlip's course twenty-four hours in advance. Perhaps the model-woman's attraction lay in that to the eye she was a handsome animal; perhaps she fascinated him with her Old World talk of palaces and princes; leastwise she dazzled him whose life had been worked out in uncultured roughness, and he at last agreed to her suggestion of a run down the river and a marriage at Forty Mile. In token of his intention he bought dogs from Sitka Charley— more than one sled is necessary when a woman like Loraine Lisznayi takes to the trail—and then went up the creek to give orders for the superintendence of his Bonanza mines during his absence.

He had given it out, rather vaguely, that he needed the animals for sledding lumber from the mill to his sluices, and right here is where Sitka Charley demonstrated his fitness. He agreed to furnish dogs on a given date, but no sooner had Floyd Vanderlip turned his toes up-creek, than Charley hied himself away in perturbation to Loraine Lisznayi. Did she know where Mr. Vanderlip had gone? He had agreed to supply that gentleman with a big string of dogs by a certain time;

but that shameless one, the German trader Meyers, had been buying up the brutes and skimped the market. It was very necessary he should see Mr. Vanderlip; because of the shameless one he would be all of a week behindhand in filling the contract. She did know where he had gone? Up-creek? Good! He would strike out after him at once and inform him of the unhappy delay. Did he understand her to say that Mr. Vanderlip needed the dogs on Friday night? That he must have them by that time? It was too bad, but it was the fault of the shameless one who had bid up the prices. They had jumped fifty dollars per head, and should he buy on the rising market, he would lose by the contract. He wondered if Mr. Vanderlip would be willing to meet the advance. She knew he would? Being Mr. Vanderlip's friend, she would even meet the difference herself? And he was to say nothing about it? She was kind to so look to his interests. Friday night, did she say? Good! The dogs would be on hand. An hour later, Freda knew the elopement was to be pulled off on Friday night; also, that Floyd Vanderlip had gone up-creek, and her hands were tied. On Friday morning, Devereaux, the official courier, bearing dispatches from the Governor, arrived over the ice. Besides the dispatches, he brought news of Flossie. He had passed her camp at Sixty Mile; humans and dogs were in good condition; and she would doubtless be in on the morrow. Mrs. Eppingwell experienced a great relief on hearing this; Floyd Vanderlip was safe up-creek, and ere the Greek girl could again lay hands upon him, his bride would be on the ground. But that afternoon her big St. Bernard, valiantly defending her front stoop, was downed by a foraging party of trail-starved malamutes. He was buried beneath the hirsute mass for about thirty seconds, when rescued by a couple of axes and as many stout men. Had he remained down two minutes, the chances were large that he would have been roughly apportioned and carried away in the respective bellies of the attacking party; but as it was, it was a mere case of neat and expeditious mangling. Sitka Charley came to repair the damages, especially a right fore-paw which had inadvertently been left a fraction of a second too long in some other dog's mouth. As he put on his mittens to go, the talk turned upon Flossie and in natural sequence passed on to the "—er horrid woman." Sitka Charley remarked incidentally that she intended jumping out downriver that night with Floyd Vanderlip, and further ventured the informa-tion that accidents were very likely at that time of year.

So Mrs. Eppingwell's thoughts of Freda were unkinder than ever. She wrote a note, addressed it to the man in question, and entrusted it to a messenger who lay in wait at the mouth of Bonanza Creek. Another man, bearing a note from Freda, also waited at that strategic point. So it happened that Floyd Vanderlip, riding his sled merrily down with the last daylight, received the notes together. He tore Freda's across. No, he would not go to see her. There were greater things afoot that night. Besides, she was out of the running. But Mrs. Epping-well! He would observe her last wish—or rather, the last wish it would be possible for him to observe—and meet her at the Governor's ball to hear what she had to say. From the tone of the writing it was evidently important; perhaps— He smiled fondly, but failed to shape the thought. Confound it all, what a lucky fellow he was with the women, anyway! Scattering her letter to the frost, he mushed the dogs into a swinging lope and headed for his cabin. It was to be a masquerade, and he had to dig up the costume used at the Opera House a couple of months before. Also, he had to shave and to eat. Thus it was that he, alone of all interested, was unaware of Flossie's proximity.

"Have them down to the water hole off the hospital, at mid-night, sharp. Don't fail me," he said to Sitka Charley, who dropped in with the advice that only one dog was lacking to fill the bill and that that one would be forthcoming in an hour or so. "Here's the sack. There's the scales. Weigh out your own dust and don't bother me. I've got to get ready for the ball."

Sitka Charley weighed out his pay and departed, carrying with him a letter to Loraine Lisznayi, the contents of which he correctly imagined to refer to a meeting at the water hole off the hospital, at midnight, sharp.

IV

Twice Freda sent messengers up to the Barracks, where the dance was in full swing, and as often they came back without answers. Then she did what only Freda could do—put on her furs, masked her face, and went up herself to the Governor's ball. Now, there happened to be a custom—not an original one by any means—to which the official clique had long since become addicted. It was a very wise custom, for it furnished protection to the womankind of the officials and gave greater selectness to their revels. Whenever a masquerade was given, a committee was chosen, the sole function of which was to stand by the door and peep beneath each and every mask. Most men did not clamor to be placed upon this committee, while the very ones who least desired the honor were the ones whose services were most required. The chaplain was not well enough acquainted with the faces and places of the towns-people to know whom to admit and whom to turn away. In like condition were the several other worthy gentlemen who would have asked nothing better than to so serve. To fill the coveted place, Mrs. McFee would have risked her chance of salvation, and did one night, when a certain trio passed in under her guns and muddled things considerably before their identity was discovered. Thereafter only the fit were chosen, and very ungracefully did they respond.

On this particular night Prince was at the door. Pressure

had been brought to bear, and he had not yet recovered from amaze at his having consented to undertake a task which bid fair to lose him half his friends, merely for the sake of pleasing the other half. Three or four of the men he had refused were men whom he had known on creek and trail—good comrades, but not exactly eligible for so select an affair. He was canvassing the expediency of resigning the post there and then, when a woman tripped in under the light. Freda! He could swear it by the furs, did he not know that poise of head so well. The last one to expect in all the world. He had given her better judgment than to thus venture the ignominy of refusal, or, if she passed, the scorn of women. He shook his head, without scrutiny; he knew her too well to be mistaken. But she pressed closer. She lifted the black silk ribbon and as quickly lowered it again. For one flashing, eternal second he looked upon her face. It was not for nothing, the saying which had arisen in the country, that Freda played with men as a child with bubbles. Not a word was spoken. Prince stepped aside, and a few moments later might have been seen resigning, with warm incoherence, the post to which he had been unfaithful.

A woman, flexible of form, slender, yet rhythmic of strength in every movement, now pausing with this group, now scanning that, urged a restless and devious course among the revelers. Men recognized the furs and marveled—men who should have served upon the door committee; but they were not prone to speech. Not so with the women. They had better eyes for the lines of figure and tricks of carriage, and they knew this form to be one with which they were unfamiliar; likewise the furs. Mrs. McFee, emerging from the supper room, where all was in readiness, caught one flash of the blazing, questing eyes through the silken mask slits and received a start. She tried to recollect where she had seen the like, and a vivid picture was recalled of a certain proud and rebellious sinner whom she had once encountered on a fruitless errand for the Lord.

So it was that the good woman took the trail in hot and righteous wrath, a trail which brought her ultimately into the company of Mrs. Eppingwell and Floyd Vanderlip. Mrs. Eppingwell had just found the opportunity to talk with the man. She had determined, now that Flossie was so near at hand, to proceed directly to the point, and an incisive little ethical discourse was titillating on the end of her tongue, when the couple became three. She noted, and pleasurably, the faintly foreign accent of the "beg pardon" with which the furred woman prefaced her immediate appropriation of Floyd Vanderlip; and she courteously bowed her permission for them to draw a little apart.

Then it was that Mrs. McFee's righteous hand descended, and accompanying it in its descent was a black mask torn from a startled woman. A wonderful face and brilliant eyes were exposed to the quiet curiosity of those who looked that way, and they were everybody. Floyd Vanderlip was rather confused. The situation demanded instant action on the part of a man who was not beyond his depth, while *he* hardly knew where he was. He stared helplessly about him. Mrs. Eppingwell was perplexed. She could not comprehend. An explanation was forthcoming somewhere, and Mrs. McFee was equal to it.

"Mrs. Eppingwell," and her Celtic voice rose shrilly, "it is with great pleasure I make you acquainted with Freda Moloof, *Miss* Freda Moloof, as I understand."

Freda involuntarily turned. With her own face bared, she felt as in a dream, naked; upon her turned the clothed features and gleaming eyes of the masked circle. It seemed almost as though a hungry wolf pack girdled her, ready to drag her down. It might chance that some felt pity for her, she thought, and at the thought, hardened. She would by far prefer their scorn. Strong of heart was she, this woman, and though she had hunted the prey into the midst of the pack, Mrs. Eppingwell or no Mrs. Eppingwell, she could not forgo the kill.

But here Mrs. Eppingwell did a strange thing. So this, at last, was Freda, she mused, the dancer and the destroyer of men; the woman from whose door she had been turned. And she, too, felt the imperious creature's nakedness as though it were her own. Perhaps it was this, her Saxon disinclination to meet a disadvantaged foe, perhaps, forsooth, that it might give her greater strength in the struggle for the man, and it might have been a little of both; but be that as it may, she did do this strange thing. When Mrs. McFee's thin voice, vibrant with malice, had raised and Freda turned involuntarily, Mrs. Eppingwell also turned, removed her mask, and inclined her head in acknowledgment.

It was another flashing, eternal second, during which these two women regarded each other. The one, eyes blazing, meteoric; at bay, aggressive; suffering in advance and resenting in advance the scorn and ridicule and insult she had thrown herself open to; a beautiful, burning, bubbling lava cone of flesh and spirit. And the other, calm-eyed, cool-browed, serene; strong in her own integrity, with faith in herself, thoroughly at ease; dispassionate, imperturbable; a figure chiseled from some cold marble quarry. Whatever gulf there might exist, she recognized it not. No bridging, no descending; her attitude was that of perfect equality. She stood tranquilly on the ground of their common womanhood. And this maddened Freda. Not so, had she been of lesser breed; but her soul's plummet knew not the bottomless, and she could follow the other into the deeps of her deepest depths and read her aright. "Why do you not draw back your garment's hem?" she was fain to cry out, all in that flashing, dazzling second. "Spit upon me, revile me, and it were greater mercy than this!" She trembled. Her nostrils distended and quivered. But she drew herself in check, returned the inclination of head, and turned to the man.

"Come with me, Floyd," she said simply. "I want you now."

"What the—" he began explosively, and quit as suddenly, discreet enough to not round it off. Where the deuce had his wits gone, anyway? Was ever a man more foolishly placed? He gurgled deep down in his throat and high up in the roof of his mouth, heaved as one his big shoulders and his indecision, and glared appealingly at the two women.

"I beg pardon, just a moment, but may I speak first with Mr. Vanderlip?" Mrs. Eppingwell's voice, though flutelike and low, predicated will in its every cadence.

The man looked his gratitude. He, at least, was willing enough.

"I am very sorry," from Freda. "There isn't time. He must come at once." The conventional phrases dropped easily from her lips, but she could not forbear to smile inwardly at their inadequacy and weakness. She would much rather have shrieked.

"But, Miss Moloof, who are you that you may possess yourself of Mr. Vanderlip and command his actions?"

Whereupon relief brightened his face, and the man beamed his approval. Trust Mrs. Eppingwell to drag him clear. Freda had met her match this time.

"I—I—" Freda hesitated, and then, her feminine mind putting on its harness, "—and who are you to ask this question?"

"I? I am Mrs. Eppingwell, and—"

"There!" the other broke in sharply. "You are the wife of a captain, who is therefore your husband. I am only a dancing girl. What do you want with this man?"

"Such unprecedented behavior!" Mrs. McFee ruffled herself and cleared for action, but Mrs. Eppingwell shut her mouth with a look and developed a new attack.

"Since Miss Moloof appears to hold claims upon you, Mr. Vanderlip, and is in too great haste to grant me a few seconds of your time, I am forced to appeal directly to you. May I speak with you alone, and now?"

Mrs. McFee's jaws brought together with a snap. That settled the disgraceful situation.

"Why, er—that is, certainly," the man stammered. "Of course, of course," growing more effusive at the prospect of deliverance.

Men are only gregarious vertebrates, domesticated and evolved, and the chances are large that it was because the Greek girl had in her time dealt with wilder masculine beasts of the human sort; for she turned upon the man with hell's tides aflood in her blazing eyes, much as a bespangled lady upon a lion which has suddenly imbibed the pernicious theory that he is a free agent. The beast in him fawned to the lash.

"That is to say, ah, afterward. Tomorrow, Mrs. Eppingwell; yes, tomorrow. That is what I meant." He solaced himself with the fact, should he remain, that more embarrassment awaited. Also, he had an engagement which he must keep shortly, down by the water hole off the hospital. Ye gods, he had never given Freda credit! Wasn't she magnificent!

"I'll thank you for my mask, Mrs. McFee."

That lady, for the nonce speechless, turned over the article in question.

"Good night, Miss Moloof." Mrs. Eppingwell was royal even in defeat.

Freda reciprocated, though barely downing the impulse to clasp the other's knees and beg forgiveness—no, not forgiveness, but something, she knew not what, but which she nonetheless greatly desired.

The man was for her taking his arm; but she had made her kill in the midst of the pack, and that which led kings to drag their vanquished at the chariot tail led her toward the door alone, Floyd Vanderlip close at heel and striving to reestablish his mental equilibrium.

V

It was bitter cold. As the trail wound, a quarter of a mile brought them to the dancer's cabin, by which time her moist breath had coated her face frostily, while his had massed his heavy mustache till conversation was painful. By the greenish light of the aurora borealis, the quicksilver showed itself frozen hard in the bulb of the thermometer which hung outside the door. A thousand dogs, in pitiful chorus, wailed their ancient wrongs and claimed mercy from the unheeding stars. Not a breath of air was moving. For them there was no shelter from the cold, no shrewd crawling to leeward in snug nooks. The frost was everywhere, and they lay in the open, ever and anon stretching their trail-stiffened muscles and lifting the long wolf howl.

They did not talk at first, the man and the woman. While the maid helped Freda off with her wraps, Floyd Vanderlip replenished the fire; and by the time the maid had withdrawn to an inner room, his head over the stove, he was busily thawing out his burdened upper lip. After that he rolled a cigarette and watched her lazily through the fragrant eddies. She stole a glance at the clock. It lacked half an hour of midnight. How was she to hold him? Was he angry for that which she had done? What was his mood? What mood of hers could meet his best? Not that she doubted herself. No, no. Hold him she could, if need be at pistol point, till Sitka Charley's work was done, and Devereaux's too.

There were many ways, and with her knowledge of this her contempt for the man increased. As she leaned her head on her hand, a fleeting vision of her own girlhood, with its mournful climacteric and tragic ebb, was vouchsafed her, and for the moment she was minded to read him a lesson from it. God, it must be less than human brute who could not be held by such a tale, told as she could tell it, but—bah! He was not worth it, nor worth the pain to her. The candle was positioned just right, and even as she thought of these things sacredly shameful to her, he was pleasuring in the transparent pinkiness of her ear. She noted his eye, took the cue, and turned her head till the clean profile of the face was presented. Not the least was that profile among her virtues. She could not help the lines upon which she had been built, and they were very good; but she had long since learned those lines and, though little they needed, was not above advantaging them to the best of her ability. The candle began to flicker. She could not do anything ungracefully, but that did not prevent her improving upon nature a bit when she reached forth and deftly snuffed the red wick from the midst of the yellow flame. Again she rested head on hand, this time regarding the man thoughtfully, and any man is pleased when thus regarded by a pretty woman.

She was in little haste to begin. If dalliance were to his liking, it was to hers. To him it was very comfortable, soothing his lungs with nicotine and gazing upon her. It was snug and warm here, while down by the water hole began a trail which he would soon be hitting through the chilly hours. He felt he ought to be angry with Freda for the scene she had created, but somehow he didn't feel a bit wrathful. Like as not, there wouldn't have been any scene if it hadn't been for that McFee woman. If he were the Governor, he would put a poll tax of a hundred ounces a quarter upon her and her kind and all gospel sharks and sky pilots. And certainly Freda had behaved very ladylike—held her own with Mrs. Eppingwell besides. Never gave the girl credit for the grit. He looked lingeringly over her, coming back now and again to the eyes, behind the deep earnestness of which he could not guess lay concealed a deeper sneer. And Jove, wasn't she well put up! Wonder why she looked at him so? Did she want to marry him, too? Like as not; but she wasn't the only one. Her looks were in her favor, weren't they? And young—younger than Loraine Lisznayi. She couldn't be more than twenty-three or -four, twenty-five at most. And she'd never get stout. Anybody could guess that the first time. He couldn't say it of Loraine, though. *She* certainly had put on flesh since the day she served as model. Huh! Once he got her on trail, he'd take it off. Put her on the snowshoes to break ahead of the dogs. Never knew it to fail yet. But his thought leaped ahead to the palace under the lazy Mediterranean sky—and how would it be with Loraine then? No frost, no trail, no famine now and again to cheer the monotony, and she getting older and piling it on with every sunrise. While this girl Freda—he sighed his unconscious regret that he had missed being born under the flag of the Turk, and came back to Alaska.

"Well?" Both hands of the clock pointed perpendicularly to midnight, and it was high time he was getting down to the water hole.

"Oh!" Freda started, and she did it prettily, delighting him as his fellows have ever been delighted by their womenkind. When a man is made to believe that a woman, looking upon him thoughtfully, has lost herself in meditation over him, that man needs be an extremely cold-blooded individual in order to trim his sheets, set a lookout, and steer clear.

"I was just wondering what you wanted to see me about," he explained, drawing his chair up to hers by the table.

"Floyd," she looked him steadily in the eyes, "I am tired of the whole business. I want to go away. I can't live it out here till the river breaks. If I try, I'll die. I am sure of it. I want to quit it all and go away, and I want to do it at once."

She laid her hand in mute appeal upon the back of his,

which turned over and became a prison. Another one, he thought, just throwing herself at him. Guess it wouldn't hurt Loraine to cool her feet by the water hole a little longer.

"Well?" This time from Freda, but softly and anxiously.

"I don't know what to say," he hastened to answer, adding to himself that it was coming along quicker than he had expected. "Nothing I'd like better, Freda. You know that well enough." He pressed her hand, palm to palm.

She nodded. Could she wonder that she despised the breed?

"But you see, I—I'm engaged. Of course you know that. And the girl's coming into the country to marry me. Don't know what was up with me when I asked her, but it was a long while back, and I was all-fired young."

"I want to go away, out of the land, anywhere," she went on, disregarding the obstacle he had reared up and apologized for. "I have been running over the men I know and reached the conclusion that—that—"

"I was the likeliest of the lot?"

She smiled her gratitude for his having saved her the embarrassment of confession. He drew her head against his shoulder with the free hand, and somehow the scent of her hair got into his nostrils. Then he discovered that a common pulse throbbed, throbbed, throbbed, where their palms were in contact. This phenomenon is easily comprehensible from a physiological standpoint, but to the man who makes the discovery for the first time, it is a most wonderful thing. Floyd Vanderlip had caressed more shovel handles than women's hands in his time, so this was an experience quite new and delightfully strange. And when Freda turned her head against his shoulder, her hair brushing his cheek till his eyes met hers, full and at close range, luminously soft, ay, and tender—why, whose fault was it that he lost his grip utterly? False to Flossie, why not to Loraine? Even if the women did keep bothering him, that was no reason he should make up his mind in a hurry. Why, he had slathers of money, and Freda was just the girl to grace it. A wife she'd make him for other men to envy. But go slow. He must be cautious.

"You don't happen to care for palaces, do you?" he asked.

She shook her head.

"Well, I had a hankering after them myself till I got to thinking a while back, and I've about sized it up that one'd get fat living in palaces, and soft and lazy."

"Yes, it's nice for a time, but you soon grow tired of it, I imagine," she hastened to reassure him. "The world is good, but life should be many-sided. Rough and knock about for a while and then rest up somewhere. Off to the South Seas on a yacht, then a nibble of Paris; a winter in South America and a summer in Norway; a few months in England—"

"Good society?"

"Most certainly—the best; and then, heigh-ho for the dogs and sleds and the Hudson Bay country. Change, you know. A strong man like you, full of vitality and go, could not possibly stand a palace for a year. It is all very well for effeminate men, but you weren't made for such a life. You are masculine, intensely masculine."

"Think so?"

"It does not require thinking. I know. Have you ever noticed that it was easy to make women care for you?"

His dubious innocence was superb.

"It is very easy. And why? Because you are masculine. You strike the deepest chords of a woman's heart. You are something to cling to—big-muscled, strong, and brave. In short, because you *are* a man."

She shot a glance at the clock. It was half after the hour. She had given a margin of thirty minutes to Sitka Charley; and it did not matter now when Devereaux arrived. Her work was done. She lifted her head, laughed her genuine mirth, slipped her hand clear, and, rising to her feet, called the maid.

"Alice, help Mr. Vanderlip on with his parka. His mittens are on the sill by the stove."

The man could not understand.

"Let me thank you for your kindness, Floyd. Your time was invaluable to me, and it was indeed good of you. The turning to the left, as you leave the cabin, leads the quickest to the water hole. Good night. I am going to bed."

Floyd Vanderlip employed strong words to express his perplexity and disappointment. Alice did not like to hear men swear, so dropped his parka on the floor and tossed his mittens on top of it. Then he made a break for Freda, and she ruined her retreat to the inner room by tripping over the parka. He brought her upstanding with a rude grip on the wrist. But she only laughed. She was not afraid of men. Had they not wrought their worst with her, and did she not still endure?

"Don't be rough," she said finally. "On second thought," here she looked at his detaining hand, "I've decided not to go to bed yet a while. Do sit down and be comfortable instead of ridiculous. Any questions?"

"Yes, my lady, and reckoning, too." He still kept his hold. "What do you know about the water hole? What did you mean by—no, never mind. One question at a time."

"Oh, nothing much. Sitka Charley had an appointment there with somebody you may know, and not being anxious for a man of your known charm to be present, fell back upon me to kindly help him. That's all. They're off now, and a good half hour ago."

"Where? Downriver and without me? And he an Indian!"

"There's no accounting for taste, you know, especially in a woman."

"But how do I stand in this deal? I've lost four thousand dollars' worth of dogs and a tidy bit of a woman, and nothing to show for it. Except you," he added as an afterthought, "and cheap you are at the price."

Freda shrugged her shoulders.

"You might as well get ready. I'm going out to borrow a couple of teams of dogs, and we'll start in as many hours."

"I am very sorry, but I'm going to bed."

"You'll pack if you know what's good for you. Go to bed or not, when I get my dogs outside, so help me, onto the sled you go. Mebbe you fooled with me, but I'll just see your bluff and take you in earnest. Hear me?"

He closed on her wrist till it hurt, but on her lips a smile was growing, and she seemed to listen intently to some outside sound. There was a jingle of dog bells, and a man's voice crying "Haw!" as a sled took the turning and drew up at the cabin.

"*Now* will you let me go to bed?"

As Freda spoke she threw open the door. Into the warm room rushed the frost, and on the threshold, garbed in trail-worn furs, knee-deep in the swirling vapor, against a background of flaming borealis, a woman hesitated. She removed her nose strap and stood blinking blindly in the white candle-light. Floyd Vanderlip stumbled forward.

"Floyd!" she cried, relieved and glad, and met him with a tired bound.

What could he but kiss the armful of furs? And a pretty armful it was, nestling against him wearily, but happy.

"It was good of you," spoke the armful, "to send Mr. Devereaux with fresh dogs after me, else I would not have been in till tomorrow."

The man looked blankly across at Freda, then the light breaking in upon him: "And wasn't it good of Devereaux to go?"

"Couldn't wait a bit longer, could you, dear?" Flossie snuggled closer.

"Well, I was getting sort of impatient," he confessed glibly, at the same time drawing her up till her feet left the floor, and getting outside the door.

That same night an inexplicable thing happened to the Reverend James Brown, missionary, who lived among the natives several miles down the Yukon and saw to it that the trails they trod led to the white man's paradise. He was roused from his sleep by a strange Indian, who gave into his charge not only the soul but the body of a woman and, having done this, drove quickly away. This woman was heavy and handsome and angry, and in her wrath unclean words fell from her mouth. This shocked the worthy man, but he was yet young and her presence would have been pernicious (in the simple eyes of his flock), had she not struck out on foot for Dawson with the first gray of dawn.

The shock to Dawson came many days later, when the summer had come and the population honored a certain royal lady at Windsor by lining the Yukon's bank and watching Sitka Charley rise up with flashing paddle and drive the first canoe across the line. On this day of the races, Mrs. Eppingwell, who had learned and unlearned numerous things, saw Freda for the first time since the night of the ball. "Publicly, mind you," as Mrs. McFee expressed it, "without regard or respect for the morals of the community," she went up to the dancer and held out her hand. At first, it is remembered by those who saw, the girl shrank back, then words passed between the two, and Freda, great Freda, broke down and wept on the shoulder of the captain's wife. It was not given to Dawson to know why Mrs. Eppingwell should crave forgiveness of a Greek dancing girl, but she did it publicly, and it was unseemly.

It were well not to forget Mrs. McFee. She took a cabin passage on the first steamer going out. She also took with her a theory which she had achieved in the silent watches of the long dark nights; and it is her conviction that the Northland is unregenerate because it is so cold there. Fear of hellfire cannot be bred in an icebox. This may appear dogmatic, but it is Mrs. McFee's theory.

THEFT

ACT I

A Room in the House of Senator Chalmers

ACT II

Rooms of Howard Knox at Hotel Waltham

ACT III

A Room in the Washington House of Anthony Starkweather

ACT IV

Same as Act I

Time of play, today, Washington, D.C.
It occurs in twenty hours.

CHARACTERS

MARGARET CHALMERS: Wife of Senator Chalmers.

HOWARD KNOX: A Congressman from Oregon.

THOMAS CHALMERS: A United States Senator and several times millionaire.

MASTER THOMAS CHALMERS: Son of Margaret and Senator Chalmers.

ELLERY JACKSON HUBBARD: A journalist.

ANTHONY STARKWEATHER: A great magnate, and father of Margaret Chalmers.

MRS. STARKWEATHER: His wife.

CONNIE STARKWEATHER: Their younger daughter.

FELIX DOBLEMAN: Secretary to Anthony Starkweather.

LINDA DAVIS: Maid to Margaret Chalmers.

JULIUS RUTLAND: Episcopalian minister.

JOHN GIFFORD: Labor agitator.

MATSU SAKARI: Secretary of Japanese Embassy.

DOLORES ORTEGA: Wife of Peruvian Minister.

SENATOR DOWSETT

MRS. DOWSETT

Housekeeper, servants, agents, etc.

ACTORS' DESCRIPTION OF CHARACTERS

MARGARET CHALMERS: Twenty-seven years of age; a strong, mature woman, but quite feminine where her heart or sense of beauty are concerned. Her eyes are wide apart. Has a dazzling smile, which she knows how to use on occasion. Also, on occasion, she can be firm and hard, even cynical. An intellectual woman, and at the same time a very womanly woman, capable of sudden tendernesses, flashes of emotion, and abrupt actions. She is a finished product of high culture and refinement and at the same time possesses robust vitality and instinctive right promptings that augur well for the future of the race

HOWARD KNOX: He might have been a poet, but was turned politician. Inflamed with love for humanity. Thirty-five years of age. He has his vision and must follow it. He has suffered ostracism because of it and has followed his vision in spite of abuse and ridicule. Physically a well-built, powerful man. Strong-featured rather than handsome. Very much in earnest and, despite his university training, a trifle awkward in carriage and demeanor, lacking in social ease. He has been elected to Congress on a reform ticket and is almost alone in the fight he is making. He has no party to

back him, though he has a following of a few independents
and insurgents.

THOMAS CHALMERS: Forty-five to fifty years of age. Iron-gray
mustache. Slightly stout. A good liver, much given to
Scotch and soda, with a weak heart. Is liable to collapse
anytime. If anything, slightly lazy or lethargic in his emo-
tional life. One of the "owned" senators representing a
decadent New England state, himself master of the state
political machine. Also, he is nobody's fool. He possesses
the brain and strength of character to play his part. His
most distinctive feature is his temperamental opportunism.

MASTER THOMAS CHALMERS: Six years of age. Sturdy and
healthy despite his grandmother's belief to the contrary.

ELLERY JACKSON HUBBARD: Thirty-eight to forty years of age.
Smooth-shaven. A star journalist with a national reputation; a large, heavyset man, with large head, large hands—
everything about him is large. A man radiating prosperity,
optimism, and selfishness. Has no morality whatever. Is a
conscious individualist, cold-blooded, pitiless, working only
for himself and believing in nothing but himself.

ANTHONY STARKWEATHER: An elderly, well-preserved gentleman, slenderly built, showing all the signs of a man who
has lived clean and has been almost an ascetic. One to
whom the joys of the flesh have had little meaning. A cold,
controlled man whose one passion is for power. Distinc-
tively a man of power. An eaglelike man, who, by keenness
of brain and force of character, has carved out a fortune of
hundreds of millions. In short, an industrial and financial
magnate of the first water and of the finest type to be
found in the United States. Essentially a moral man, his
rigid New England morality has suffered a sea change and
developed into the morality of the master man of affairs,
equally rigid, equally uncompromising, but essentially Jesuitical in that he believes in doing wrong that right may

come of it. He is absolutely certain that civilization and progress rest on his shoulders and upon the shoulders of the small group of men like him.

MRS. STARKWEATHER: Of the helpless, comfortably stout, elderly type. She has not followed her husband in his moral evolution. She is the creature of old customs, old prejudices, old New England ethics. She is rather confused by the modern rush of life.

CONNIE STARKWEATHER: Margaret's younger sister, twenty years old. She is nothing that Margaret is, and everything that Margaret is not. No essential evil in her, but has no mind of her own—hopelessly a creature of convention. Gay, laughing, healthy, buxom—a natural product of her carefree environment.

FELIX DOBLEMAN: Private secretary to Anthony Starkweather. A young man of correct social deportment, thoroughly and in all things just the sort of private secretary a man like Anthony Starkweather would have. He is a weak-souled creature, timorous, almost effeminate.

LINDA DAVIS: Maid to Margaret. A young woman of twenty-five or so, blond, Scandinavian, though American-born. A cold woman, almost featureless because of her long years of training, but with a hot heart deep down, and characterized by an intense devotion to her mistress. Wild horses could drag nothing from her where her mistress is concerned.

JULIUS RUTLAND: Having no strong features about him, the type realizes itself.

JOHN GIFFORD: A labor agitator. A man of the people, rough-hewn, narrow as a labor leader may well be, earnest and sincere. He is a proper, better type of labor leader.

MATSU SAKARI: Secretary of the Japanese Embassy. He is the perfection of politeness and talks classical book English. He bows a great deal.

DOLORES ORTEGA: Wife of the Peruvian Minister; bright and vivacious, and uses her hands a great deal as she talks, in the Latin American fashion.

SENATOR DOWSETT: Fifty years of age; well preserved.

MRS. DOWSETT: Stout and middle-aged.

ACT I

*In Senator Chalmers's home. It is four o'clock in the afternoon,
in a modern living room with appropriate furnishings. In
particular, in front, on left, a table prepared for the serving
of tea, all excepting the tea urn itself. At rear, right of center,
is main entrance to the room. Also, doorways at sides, on
left and right.*
*Curtain discloses Chalmers and Hubbard seated loungingly
at the right front.*

HUBBARD: (*after an apparent pause for cogitation*). I can't
understand why an old wheelhorse like Elsworth should
kick over the traces that way.

CHALMERS: Disgruntled. Thinks he didn't get his fair share of
plums out of the Tariff Committee. Besides, it's his last
term. He's announced that he's going to retire.

HUBBARD: (*snorting contemptuously, mimicking an old man's
pompous enunciation*). "A Resolution to Investigate the
High Cost of Living!"—old Senator Elsworth introducing a
measure like that! The old buck! . . . How are you going
to handle it?

CHALMERS: It's already handled.

HUBBARD: Yes?

169

CHALMERS: (*pulling his mustache*). Turned it over to the Committee to Audit and Control the Contingent Expenses of the Senate.

HUBBARD: (*grinning his appreciation*). And you're chairman. Poor old Elsworth. This way to the lethal chamber, and the bill's on its way.

CHALMERS: Elsworth will be retired before it's ever reported. In the meantime, say, after a decent interval, Senator Hodge will introduce another resolution to investigate the high cost of living. It will be like Elsworth's, only it won't.

HUBBARD: (*nodding his head and anticipating*). And it will go to the Committee on Finance and come back for action inside of twenty-four hours.

CHALMERS: By the way, I see *Cartwright's Magazine* has ceased muckraking.

HUBBARD: *Cartwright's* never did muckrake—that is, not the big Interests—only the small independent businesses that didn't advertise.

CHALMERS: Yes, it deftly concealed its reactionary tendencies.

HUBBARD: And from now on the concealment will be still more deft. I've gone into it myself. I have a majority of the stock right now.

CHALMERS: I thought I had noticed a subtle change in the last two numbers.

HUBBARD: (*nodding*). We're still going on muckraking. We have a splendid series on aged paupers, demanding better treatment and more sanitary conditions. Also, we are going to run "Barbarous Venezuela" and show up thoroughly the rotten political management of that benighted country.

CHALMERS: (*nods approvingly, and after a pause*). And now concerning Knox. That's what I sent for you about. His speech comes off tomorrow per schedule. At last we've got him where we want him.

HUBBARD: I have the ins and outs of it pretty well. Everything's arranged. The boys have their cue, though they don't know just what's going to be pulled off; and this time tomorrow afternoon their dispatches will be singing along the wires.

CHALMERS: (*firmly and harshly*). This man Knox must be covered with ridicule, swamped with ridicule, annihilated with ridicule.

HUBBARD: It is to laugh. Trust the great American people for that. We'll make those little western editors sit up. They've been swearing by Knox, like a little tin god. Roars of laughter for them.

CHALMERS: Do you do anything yourself?

HUBBARD: Trust me. I have my own article for *Cartwright's* blocked out. They're holding the presses for it. I shall wire it along hotfooted tomorrow evening. Say . . . ?

CHALMERS: (*after a pause*). Well?

HUBBARD: Wasn't it a risky thing to give him his chance with that speech?

CHALMERS: It was the only feasible thing. He never has given us an opening. Our service men have camped on his trail night and day. Private life as unimpeachable as his public life. But now is our chance. The gods have given him into our hands. That speech will do more to break his influence—

HUBBARD: (*interrupting*). —than a Fairbanks cocktail. (*Both laugh.*) But don't forget that this Knox is a live wire. Somebody might get stung. Are you sure, when he gets up to make that speech, that he won't be able to back it up?

CHALMERS: No danger at all.

HUBBARD: But there are hooks and crooks by which facts are sometimes obtained.

CHALMERS: (*positively*). Knox has nothing to go on but suspicions and hints, and unfounded assertions from the yellow press. (*Manservant enters, goes to tea table, looks it over, and makes slight rearrangements. Lowering his voice.*) He will make himself a laughingstock. His charges will turn into boomerangs. His speech will be like a sheet from a Sunday supplement, with not a fact to back it up. (*Glances at Servant.*) We'd better be getting out of here. They're going to have tea. (*The Servant, however, makes exit.*) Come to the library and have a highball.

They pause as Hubbard speaks.

HUBBARD: (*with quiet glee*). And tomorrow Ali Baba gets his.

CHALMERS: Ali Baba?

HUBBARD: That's what your wife calls him—Knox.

CHALMERS: Oh, yes, I believe I've heard it before. It's about time he hanged himself, and now we've given him the rope.

HUBBARD: (*sinking voice and becoming deprecatingly confidential*). Oh, by the way, just a little friendly warning, Senator Chalmers. Not so fast and loose up New York way. That certain lady, not to be mentioned—there's gossip about it in the New York newspaper offices. Of course all such stories are killed. But be discreet, be discreet. If Gherst gets hold of it, he'll play it up against the Administration in all his papers.

Chalmers, who throughout this speech is showing a growing resentment, is about to speak when voices are heard without, and he checks himself.

Enter Mrs. Starkweather, rather flustered and imminently in danger of a collapse, followed by Connie Starkweather, fresh, radiant, and joyous.

MRS. STARKWEATHER: (*with appeal and relief*). Oh, Tom!

Chalmers takes her hand sympathetically and protectingly.

CONNIE: (*who is an exuberant young woman, bursts forth*). Oh, brother-in-law! Such excitement! That's what's the matter with Mother. We ran into a go-cart. Our chauffeur was not to blame. It was the woman's fault. She tried to cross just as we were turning the corner. But we hardly grazed it. Fortunately the baby was not hurt—only spilled. It *was* ridiculous. (*Catching sight of Hubbard.*) Oh, there you are, Mr. Hubbard. How de do.

Steps halfway to meet him and shakes hands with him. Mrs. Starkweather looks around helplessly for a chair, and Chalmers conducts her to one soothingly.

MRS. STARKWEATHER: Oh, it was terrible! The little child might have been killed. And such persons love their babies, I know.

CONNIE: (*to Chalmers*). Has Father come? We were to pick him up here. Where's Madge?

MRS. STARKWEATHER: (*espying Hubbard, faintly*). Oh, there is Mr. Hubbard. (*Hubbard comes to her and shakes hands.*) I simply can't get used to these rapid ways of modern life. The motorcar is the invention of the devil. Everything is *too* quick. When I was a girl, we lived sedately, decorously. There was time for meditation and repose. But in this age there is time for nothing. How Anthony keeps his head is more than I can understand. But, then, Anthony is a wonderful man.

HUBBARD: I am sure Mr. Starkweather never lost his head in his life.

CHALMERS: Unless when he was courting you, Mother.

MRS. STARKWEATHER: (*a trifle grimly*). I'm not so sure about that.

CONNIE: (*imitating a grave, businesslike enunciation*). Father probably conferred first with his associates, then turned the affair over for consideration by his corporation lawyers, and, when they reported no flaws, checked the first spare half hour in his notebook to ask Mother if she would have him. (*They laugh.*) And looked at his watch at least twice while he was proposing.

MRS. STARKWEATHER: Anthony was not so busy then as all that.

HUBBARD: He hadn't yet taken up the job of running the United States.

MRS. STARKWEATHER: I'm sure I don't know what he is running, but he is a very busy man—business, politics, and madness; madness, politics, and business. (*She stops breathlessly and glances at tea table.*) Tea. I should like a cup of tea. Connie, I shall stay for a cup of tea, and then, if your father hasn't come, we'll go home. (*To Chalmers.*) Where is Tommy?

CHALMERS: Out in the car with Madge. (*Glances at tea table and consults watch.*) She should be back now.

CONNIE: Mother, you mustn't stay long. I have to dress.

CHALMERS: Oh, yes, that dinner. (*Yawns.*) I wish I could loaf tonight.

CONNIE: (*explaining to Hubbard*). The Turkish Chargé d'Affaires—I never can remember his name. But he's great fun—a positive joy. He's giving the dinner to the British Ambassador.

MRS. STARKWEATHER: (*starting forward in her chair and listening intently*). There's Tommy, now.

Voices of Margaret Chalmers and of Tommy heard from without. Hers is laughingly protesting, while Tommy's is gleefully insistent.

Margaret and Tommy appear and pause just outside door, holding each other's hands, facing each other, too immersed in each other to be aware of the presence of those inside the room. Margaret and Tommy are in street costume.

TOMMY: (*laughing*). But Mama.

MARGARET: (*herself laughing, but shaking her head*). No.

TOMMY: First—

MARGARET: No, you must run along to Linda, now, mother's boy. And we'll talk about that some other time.

Tommy notices for the first time that there are persons in the room. He peeps in around the door and espies Mrs. Stark-

*weather. At the same moment, impulsively he withdraws his
hands and runs in to Mrs. Starkweather.*

TOMMY: (*who is evidently fond of his grandmother*). Grandma!
They embrace and make much of each other.
*Margaret enters, appropriately greeting the others—a kiss
(maybe) to Connie and a slightly cold handshake to Hubbard.*

MARGARET: (*to Chalmers*). Now that you're here, Tom, you
mustn't run away.
Greets Mrs. Starkweather.

MRS. STARKWEATHER: (*turning Tommy's face to the light and
looking at it anxiously*). A trifle thin, Margaret.

MARGARET: On the contrary, Mother—

MRS. STARKWEATHER: (*to Chalmers*). Don't you think so, Tom?

CONNIE: (*aside to Hubbard*). Mother continually worries about
his health.

HUBBARD: A sturdy youngster, I should say.

TOMMY: (*to Chalmers*). I'm an Indian, aren't I, Daddy?

CHALMERS: (*nodding his head emphatically*). And the stoutest-
hearted in the tribe. (*Linda appears in doorway, evidently
looking for Tommy, and Chalmers notices her.*) There's
Linda looking for you, young stout heart.

MARGARET: Take Tommy, Linda. Run along, mother's boy.

TOMMY: Come along, Grandma. I want to show you
something. (*He catches Mrs. Starkweather by the hand.
Protesting, but highly pleased, she allows him to lead her to
the door, where he extends his other hand to Linda. Thus,
pausing in doorway, leading a woman by either hand, he
looks back at Margaret. Roguishly.*) Remember, Mama,
we're going to scout in a little while.

MARGARET: (*going to Tommy and bending down with her arms
around him*). No, Tommy. Mama has to go to that horrid
dinner tonight. But tomorrow we'll play. (*Tommy is cast
down and looks as if he might pout.*) Where is my little
Indian now?

HUBBARD: Be an Indian, Tommy.

TOMMY: (*brightening up*). All right, Mama. Tomorrow . . . if you can't find time today.

Margaret kisses him.

Exit Tommy, Mrs. Starkweather, and Linda, Tommy leading them by a hand in each of theirs.

CHALMERS: (*nodding to Hubbard, in low voice to Hubbard and starting to make exit to right*). That highball.

Hubbard disengages himself from proximity of Connie and starts to follow.

CONNIE: (*reproachfully*). If you run away, I won't stop for tea.

MARGARET: Do stop, Tom. Father will be here in a few minutes.

CONNIE: A regular family party.

CHALMERS: All right. We'll be back. We're just going to have a little talk.

Chalmers and Hubbard make exit to right.

Margaret puts her arm impulsively around Connie—a sheerly spontaneous act of affection—kisses her, and at same time evinces preparation to leave.

MARGARET: I've got to get my things off. Won't you wait here, dear, in case anybody comes? It's nearly time.

Starts toward exit to rear, but is stopped by Connie.

CONNIE: Madge. (*Margaret immediately pauses and waits expectantly, smiling, while Connie is hesitant.*) I want to speak to you about something, Madge. You don't mind? (*Margaret, still smiling, shakes her head.*) Just a warning. Not that anybody could believe for a moment there is anything wrong, but . . .

MARGARET: (*dispelling a shadow of irritation that has crossed her face*). If it concerns Tom, don't tell me, please. You know he does do ridiculous things at times. But I don't let him worry me anymore; so don't worry me about him. (*Connie remains silent, and Margaret grows curious.*) Well?

CONNIE: It's not about Tom— (*Pauses.*) It's about you.

MARGARET: Oh.

CONNIE: I don't know how to begin.

MARGARET: By coming right out with it, the worst of it, all at once, first.

CONNIE: It isn't serious at all, but—well, Mother is worrying about it. You know how old-fashioned she is. And when you consider our position—Father's and Tom's, I mean—it doesn't seem just right for you to be seeing so much of such an enemy of theirs. He has abused them dreadfully, you know. And there's that dreadful speech he is going to give tomorrow. You haven't seen the afternoon papers. He has made the most terrible charges against everybody—all of us, our friends, everybody.

MARGARET: You mean Mr. Knox, of course. But he wouldn't harm anybody, Connie dear.

CONNIE: (bridling). Oh, he wouldn't? He as good as publicly called Father a thief.

MARGARET: When did that happen? I never heard of it.

CONNIE: Well, he said that the money magnates had grown so unprincipled, sunk so low, that they would steal a mouse from a blind kitten.

MARGARET: I don't see what Father has to do with that.

CONNIE: He meant him just the same.

MARGARET: You silly goose. He couldn't have meant Father. Father? Why, Father wouldn't look at anything less than fifty or a hundred million.

CONNIE: And you speak to him and make much of him when you meet him places. You talked with him for half an hour at that Dugdale reception. You have him here in your own house—Tom's house—when he's such a bitter enemy of Tom's.

During the foregoing speech, Anthony Starkweather makes entrance from rear. His face is grave, and he is in a brown study, as if pondering weighty problems. At sight of the two women he pauses and surveys them. They are unaware of his presence.

MARGARET: You are wrong, Connie. He is nobody's enemy.

He is the truest, cleanest, most right-seeking man I have ever seen.

CONNIE: (*interrupting*). He is a troublemaker, a disturber of the public peace, a shallow-pated demagogue—

MARGARET: (*reprovingly*). Now you're quoting somebody— Father, I suppose. To think of him being so abused—poor, dear Ali Baba—

STARKWEATHER: (*clearing his throat in advertisement of his presence*). A-hem.

Margaret and Connie turn around abruptly and discover him.

MARGARET and CONNIE: Father!

Both come forward to greet him, Margaret leading.

STARKWEATHER: (*anticipating, showing the deliberate method of the busy man saving time by eliminating the superfluous*). Fine, thank you. Quite well in every particular. This Ali Baba? Who is Ali Baba?

Margaret looks amused reproach at Connie.

CONNIE: Mr. Howard Knox.

STARKWEATHER: And why is he called Ali Baba?

MARGARET: That is my nickname for him. In the den of thieves, you know. You remember your Arabian Nights.

STARKWEATHER: (*severely*). I have been wanting to speak to you for some time, Margaret, about that man. You know that I have never interfered with your way of life since your marriage, nor with your and Tom's housekeeping arrangements. But this man Knox. I understand that you have even had him here in your house—

MARGARET: (*interrupting*). He is very liable to be here this afternoon, anytime now.

Connie displays irritation at Margaret.

STARKWEATHER: (*continuing imperturbably*). *Your* house—*you*, my daughter, and the wife of Senator Chalmers. As I said, I have not interfered with you since your marriage. But

this Knox affair transcends household arrangements. It is
of political importance. The man is an enemy to our class,
a firebrand. Why do you have him here?

MARGARET: Because I like him. Because he is a man I am
proud to call friend. Because I wish there were more
men like him, many more men like him, in the world.
Because I have ever seen in him nothing but the best and
highest. And besides, it's such good fun to see how one
virtuous man can so disconcert you captains of industry
and arbiters of destiny. Confess that you are very much
disconcerted, Father, right now. He will be here in a few
minutes, and you will be more disconcerted. Why? Because
it is an affair that transcends family arrangements. And it
is your affair, not mine.

STARKWEATHER: This man Knox is a dangerous character—one
that I am not pleased to see any of my family take up
with. He is not a gentleman.

MARGARET: He is a self-made man, if that is what you mean,
and he certainly hasn't any money.

CONNIE: (*interrupting*). He says that money is theft—at least
when it is in the hands of a wealthy person.

STARKWEATHER: He is uncouth—ignorant.

MARGARET: I happen to know that he is a graduate of the
University of Oregon.

STARKWEATHER: (*sneeringly*). A cow college. But that is not
what I mean. He is a demagogue, stirring up the wild-
beast passions of the people.

MARGARET: Surely you would not call his advocacy of that
child labor bill and of the conservation of the forest and
coal lands stirring up the wild-beast passions of the
people?

STARKWEATHER: (*wearily*). You don't understand. When I say
he is dangerous it is because he threatens all the stabilities,
because he threatens us who have made this country and

upon whom this country and its prosperity rest.
Connie, scenting trouble, walks across stage away from them.

MARGARET: The captains of industry—the banking magnates and the mergers?

STARKWEATHER: Call it so. Call it what you will. Without us the country falls into the hands of scoundrels like that man Knox and smashes to ruin.

MARGARET: (*reprovingly*). Not a scoundrel, Father.

STARKWEATHER: He is a sentimental dreamer, a harebrained enthusiast. It is the foolish utterances of men like him that place the bomb and the knife in the hand of the assassin.

MARGARET: He is at least a good man, even if he does disagree with you on political and industrial problems. And heaven knows that good men are rare enough these days.

STARKWEATHER: I impugn neither his morality nor his motives —only his rationality. Really, Margaret, there is nothing inherently vicious about him. I grant that. And it is precisely that which makes him such a power for evil.

MARGARET: When I think of all the misery and pain which he is trying to remedy—I can see in him only a power for good. He is not working for himself but for the many. That is why he has no money. You have heaven alone knows how many millions—you don't; you have worked for yourself.

STARKWEATHER: I, too, work for the many. I give work to the many. I make life possible for the many. I am only too keenly alive to the responsibilities of my stewardship of wealth.

MARGARET: But what of the child laborers working at the machines? Is that necessary, O steward of wealth? How my heart has ached for them! How I have longed to do something for them—to change conditions so that it will no longer be necessary for the children to toil, to have the playtime of childhood stolen away from them. Theft—that is what it is, the playtime of the children coined into profits. That is why I like Howard Knox. He calls theft theft. He is trying to do something for those children. What are you trying to do for them?

STARKWEATHER: Sentiment. Sentiment. The question is too vast and complicated, and you cannot understand. No woman can understand. That is why you run to sentiment. That is what is the matter with this Knox—sentiment. You can't run a government of ninety millions of people on sentiment, nor on abstract ideas of justice and right.

MARGARET: But if you eliminate justice and right, what remains?

STARKWEATHER: This is a practical world, and it must be managed by practical men—by thinkers, not by near-thinkers whose heads are addled with the half-digested ideas of the French Encyclopedists and Revolutionists of a century and a half ago. (*Margaret shows signs of impatience —she is not particularly perturbed by this passage at arms with her father—and is anxious to get off her street things.*) Don't forget, my daughter, that your father knows the books as well as any cow-college graduate from Oregon. I, too, in my student days, dabbled in theories of universal happiness and righteousness, saw my vision and dreamed my dream. I did not know then the weakness, and frailty, and grossness of the human clay. But I grew out of that and into a man. Some men never grow out of that stage. That is what is the trouble with Knox. He is still a dreamer, and a dangerous one. (*He pauses a moment, and then his thin lips shut grimly.*) But he has just about shot his bolt.

MARGARET: What do you mean?

STARKWEATHER: He has let himself in to give a speech tomorrow, wherein he will be called upon to deliver the proofs of all the lurid charges he has made against the Administration—against us, the stewards of wealth, if you please. He will be unable to deliver the proofs, and the nation will laugh. And that will be the political end of Mr. Ali Baba and his dream.

MARGARET: It is a beautiful dream. Were there more like him, the dream would come true. After all, it is the dreamers that build and that never die. Perhaps you will find that he is not so easily to be destroyed. But I can't stay and argue with you, Father. I simply must go and get my things off. (*To Connie.*) You'll have to receive, dear. I'll be right back. (*Julius Rutland enters. Margaret advances to meet him, shaking his hand.*) You must forgive me for deserting for a moment.

RUTLAND: (*greeting the others*). A family council, I see.

MARGARET: (*on way to exit at rear*). No, a discussion on dreams and dreamers. I leave you to bear my part.

RUTLAND: (*bowing*). With pleasure. The dreamers are the true architects. But—a—what is the dream, and who is the dreamer?

MARGARET: (*pausing in the doorway*). The dream of social justice, of fair play and a square deal to everybody. The dreamer—Mr. Knox.

Rutland is so patently irritated that Margaret lingers in the doorway to enjoy.

RUTLAND: That man! He has insulted and reviled the Church —my calling. He—

CONNIE: (*interrupting*). He said the churchmen stole from God. I remember he once said there had been only one true Christian and that He died on the cross.

MARGARET: He quoted that from Nietzsche.

STARKWEATHER: (*to Rutland, in quiet glee*). He had you there.

RUTLAND: (*in composed fury*). Nietzsche is a blasphemer, sir. Any man who reads Nietzsche or quotes Nietzsche is a

blasphemer. It augurs ill for the future of America when
such pernicious literature has the vogue it has.

MARGARET: (*interrupting, laughing*). I leave the quarrel in
your hands, sir knight. Remember—the dreamer and the
dream.

Margaret makes exit.

RUTLAND: (*shaking his head*). I cannot understand what is
coming over the present generation. Take your daughter,
for instance. Ten years ago she was an earnest, sincere
lieutenant of mine in all our little charities.

STARKWEATHER: Has she given charity up?

CONNIE: It's settlement work now, and kindergartens.

RUTLAND: (*ominously*). It's writers like Nietzsche, and men
who read him, like Knox, who are responsible.

Senator Dowsell and Mrs. Dowsett enter from rear.
Connie advances to greet them. Rutland knows Mrs. Dowsett,
and Connie introduces him to Senator Dowsett.
In the meantime, not bothering to greet anybody, evincing
his own will and way, Starkweather goes across to right
front, selects one of several chairs, seats himself, pulls a thin
notebook from inside coat pocket, and proceeds to immerse
himself in contents of same.
Dowsett and Rutland pair and stroll to left rear and seat
themselves, while Connie and Mrs. Dowsett seat themselves
at tea table to left front. Connie rings the bell for Servant.

MRS. DOWSETT: (*glancing significantly at Starkweather and*
speaking in a low voice). That's your father, isn't it? I have
so wanted to meet him.

CONNIE: (*softly*). You know he's peculiar. He is liable to ignore
everybody here this afternoon and get up and go away
abruptly without saying good-bye.

MRS. DOWSETT: (*sympathetically*). Yes, I know, a man of such
large affairs. He must have so much on his mind. He is a
wonderful man—my husband says the greatest in contem-

porary history—more powerful than a dozen presidents, the King of England, and the Kaiser all rolled into one.

Servant enters with tea urn and accessories, and Connie proceeds to serve tea, all accompanied by appropriate patter—"Two lumps?" "One, please." "Lemon," etc.

Rutland and Dowsett come forward to table for their tea, where they remain.

Connie, glancing apprehensively across at her father and debating a moment, prepares a cup for him and a small plate with crackers, and hands them to Dowsett, who likewise betrays apprehensiveness.

CONNIE: Take it to Father, please, Senator.

Throughout the rest of this act, Starkweather is like a being apart, a king sitting on his throne. He divides the tea function with Margaret. Men come up to him and speak with him. He sends for men. They come and go at his bidding. The whole attitude, perhaps unconsciously on his part, is that wherever he may be, he is master. This attitude is accepted by all the others; forsooth, he is indeed a great man and master. The only one who is not really afraid of him is Margaret, yet she gives in to him insofar as she lets him do as he pleases at her afternoon tea.

Dowsett carries the cup of tea and small plate across stage to Starkweather. Starkweather does not notice him at first.

CONNIE: (*who has been watching*). Tea, Father, won't you have a cup of tea?

Through the following scene between Starkweather and Dowsett, the latter holds cup of tea and crackers, helplessly, at a disadvantage. At the same time Rutland is served with tea and remains at the table, talking with the two women.

STARKWEATHER: (*looking first at Connie, then peering into cup of tea. He grunts refusal and for the first time looks up into the other man's face. He immediately closes notebook down on finger to keep the place.*) Oh, it's you.

DOWSETT: (*painfully endeavoring to be at ease*). A pleasure, Mr. Starkweather, an entirely unexpected pleasure to meet you here. I was not aware you frequented frivolous gatherings of this nature.

STARKWEATHER: (*abruptly and peremptorily*). Why didn't you come when you were sent for this morning?

DOWSETT: I was sick—I was in bed.

STARKWEATHER: That is no excuse, sir. When you are sent for, you are to come. Understand? That bill was reported back. Why was it reported back? You told Dobleman you would attend to it.

DOWSETT: It was a slipup. Such things will happen.

STARKWEATHER: What was the matter with that committee? Have you no influence with the Senate crowd? If not, say so, and I'll get someone who has.

DOWSETT: (*angrily*). I refuse to be treated in this manner, Mr. Starkweather. I have some self-respect— (*Starkweather grunts incredulously.*) Some decency— (*Starkweather grunts.*) A position of prominence in my state. You forget, sir, that in our state organization I occupy no mean place.

STARKWEATHER: (*cutting him off so sharply that Dowsett drops cup and saucer*). Don't you show your teeth to me. I can make you or break you. That state organization of yours belongs to me. (*Dowsett starts—he is learning something new. To hide his feelings, he stoops to pick up cup and saucer.*) Let it alone! I am talking to you. (*Dowsett straightens up to attention with alacrity. Connie, who has witnessed, rings for Servant.*) I bought that state organization and paid for it. You are one of the chattels that came along with the machine. You were made senator to obey my orders. Understand? Do you understand?

DOWSETT: (*beaten*). I—I understand.

STARKWEATHER: That bill is to be killed.

DOWSETT: Yes, sir.

STARKWEATHER: Quietly, no headlines about it. (*Dowsett nods.*)
Now you can go.

*Dowsett proceeds rather limply across to join group at tea
table.*

*Chalmers and Hubbard enter from right, laughing about
something. At sight of Starkweather they immediately
become sober.*

*No hands are shaken. Starkweather barely acknowledges
Hubbard's greeting.*

STARKWEATHER: Tom, I want to see you.

*Hubbard takes his cue and proceeds across to tea table.
Enter Servant. Connie directs him to remove broken cup
and saucer. While this is being done, Starkweather remains
silent. He consults notebook, and Chalmers stands, not quite
at ease, waiting the other's will. At the same time, patter at
tea table. Hubbard, greeting others and accepting or declining
cup of tea.*

Servant makes exit.

STARKWEATHER: (*closing finger on book and looking sharply at
Chalmers*). Tom, this affair of yours in New York must
come to an end. Understand?

CHALMERS: (*starting*). Hubbard has been talking.

STARKWEATHER: No, it is not Hubbard. I have the reports from
other sources.

CHALMERS: It is a harmless affair.

STARKWEATHER: I happen to know better. I have the whole
record. If you wish, I can give you every detail, every
meeting. I know. There is no discussion whatever. I want
no more of it.

CHALMERS: I never dreamed for a moment that I was—er—
indiscreet.

STARKWEATHER: Never forget that every indiscretion of a man
in your position is indiscreet. We have a duty, a great and
solemn duty to perform. Upon our shoulders rest the

destinies of ninety million people. If we fail in our duty,
they go down to destruction. Ignorant demagogues are
working on the beast passions of the people. If they have
their way, they are lost, the country is lost, civilization is
lost. We want no more Dark Ages.

CHALMERS: Really, I never thought it was as serious as all
that.

STARKWEATHER: (*shrugging shoulders and lifting eyebrows*).
After all, why should you? You are only a cog in the
machine. I, and the several men grouped with me, am
the machine. You are a useful cog—too useful to lose—

CHALMERS: Lose?—me?

STARKWEATHER: I have but to raise my hand, anytime—do
you understand?—anytime, and you are lost. You control
your state. Very well. But never forget that tomorrow, if I
wished, I could buy your whole machine out from under
you. I know you cannot change yourself, but for the sake
of the big issues at stake, you must be careful, exceedingly
careful. We are compelled to work with weak tools. You
are a good liver, a fleshpot man. You drink too much.
Your heart is weak. —Oh, I have the report of your doctor.
Nevertheless, don't make a fool of yourself, nor of us.
Besides, do not forget that your wife is my daughter. She
is a strong woman, a credit to both of us. Be careful that
you are not a discredit to her.

CHALMERS: All right, I'll be careful. But while we are—er—on
this subject, there's something I'd like to speak to you
about. (*A pause, in which Starkweather waits noncommit-
tally.*) It's this man Knox and Madge. He comes to the
house. They are as thick as thieves.

STARKWEATHER: Yes?

CHALMERS: (*hastily*). Oh, not a breath of suspicion or anything
of that sort, I assure you. But it doesn't strike me as
exactly appropriate that your daughter and my wife

should be friendly with this fire-eating anarchist who is always attacking us and all that we represent.

STARKWEATHER: I started to speak with her on that subject, but was interrupted. (*Puckers brow and thinks.*) You are her husband. Why don't you take her in hand yourself? *Enters Mrs. Starkweather from rear, looking about, bowing, then locating Starkweather and proceeding toward him.*

CHALMERS: What can I do? She has a will of her own—the same sort of a will that you have. Besides, I think she knows about my—about some of my—indiscretions.

STARKWEATHER: (*slyly*). *Harmless* indiscretions? *Chalmers is about to reply, but observes Mrs. Starkweather approaching.*

MRS. STARKWEATHER: (*speaks in a peevish, complaining voice, and during her harangue Starkweather immerses himself in notebook*). Oh, there you are, Anthony. Talking politics, I suppose. Well, as soon as I get a cup of tea, we must go. Tommy is not looking as well as I could wish. Margaret loves him, but she does not take the right care of him. I don't know what the world is coming to when mothers do not know how to rear their offspring. There is Margaret with her slum kindergartens, taking care of everybody else's children but her own. If she only performed her church duties as eagerly! Mr. Rutland is displeased with her. I shall give her a talking-to—only you'd better do it, Anthony. Somehow, I have never counted much with Margaret. She is as set in doing what she pleases as you are. In my time children paid respect to their parents. This is what comes of speed. There is no time for anything. And now I must get my tea and run. Connie has to dress for that dinner. *Mrs. Starkweather crosses to table, greets others characteristically, and is served with tea by Connie.* *Chalmers waits respectfully on Starkweather.*

STARKWEATHER: (*looking up from notebook*). That will do, Tom. *Chalmers is just starting across to join others when voices are heard outside rear entrance and Margaret enters with Dolores Ortega, wife of the Peruvian Minister, and Matsu Sakari, Secretary of the Japanese Legation—both of whom she has met as they were entering the house.*

Chalmers changes his course and meets the above advancing group. He knows Dolores Ortega, whom he greets, and is introduced to Sakari.

Margaret passes on among guests, greeting them, etc. Then she displaces Connie at tea table and proceeds to dispense tea to the newcomers.

Groups slowly form and seat themselves about stage as follows: Chalmers and Dolores Ortega; Rutland, Dowsett, Mrs. Starkweather; Connie, Mrs. Dowsett, and Hubbard. Chalmers carries tea to Dolores Ortega.

Sakari has been lingering by table, waiting for tea and pattering with Margaret, Chalmers, etc.

MARGARET: (*handing cup to Sakari*). I am very timid in offering you this, for I am sure you must be appalled by our barbarous methods of making tea.

SAKARI: (*bowing*). It is true, your American tea and the tea of the English are quite radically different from the tea in my country. But one learns, you know. I served my apprenticeship to American tea long years ago, when I was at Yale. It was perplexing, I assure you—at first, only at first. I really believe that I am beginning to have a— how shall I call it?—a tolerance for tea in your fashion.

MARGARET: You are very kind in overlooking our shortcomings.

SAKARI: (*bowing*). On the contrary, I am unaware, always unaware, of any shortcomings of this marvelous country of yours.

MARGARET: (*laughing*). You are incorrigibly gracious, Mr. Sakari.

Knox appears at threshold of rear entrance and pauses irresolutely for a moment.

SAKARI: (*noticing Knox and looking about him to select which group he will join*). If I may be allowed, I shall now retire and consume this—tea.

Joins group composed of Connie, Mrs. Dowsett, and Hubbard. Knox comes forward to Margaret, betraying a certain awkwardness due to lack of experience in such social functions. He greets Margaret and those in the group nearest her.

KNOX: (*to Margaret*). I don't know why I come here. I do not belong. All the ways are strange.

MARGARET: (*lightly, at the same time preparing his tea*). The same Ali Baba—once again in the den of the forty thieves. But your watch and pocketbook are safe here, really they are. (*Knox makes a gesture of dissent at her facetiousness.*) Now, don't be serious. You should relax sometimes. You live too tensely. (*Looking at Starkweather.*) There's the arch-anarch over there, the dragon you are trying to slay. (*Knox looks at Starkweather and is plainly perplexed.*) The man who handles all the life insurance funds, who controls more strings of banks and trust companies than all the Rothschilds a hundred times over—the merger of iron and steel and coal and shipping and all the other things—the man who blocks your child labor bill and all the rest of the remedial legislation you advocate. In short, my father.

KNOX: (*looking intently at Starkweather*). I should have recognized him from his photographs. But why do you say such things?

MARGARET: Because they are true. (*He remains silent.*) Now, aren't they? (*She laughs.*) Oh, you don't need to answer. You know the truth, the whole bitter truth. This *is* a den of thieves. There is Mr. Hubbard over there, for instance, the trusty journalist lieutenant of the corporations.

KNOX: (*with an expression of disgust*). I know him. It was he who wrote the Standard Oil side of the story after having abused Standard Oil for years in the pseudo-muckraking magazines. He made them come up to his price, that was all. He's the star writer on *Cartwright's* now, since that magazine changed its policy and became subsidizedly reactionary. I know him—a thoroughly dishonest man. Truly am I Ali Baba, and truly I wonder why I am here.

MARGARET: You are here, sir, because I like you to come.

KNOX: We do have much in common, you and I.

MARGARET: The future.

KNOX: (*gravely, looking at her with shining eyes*). I sometimes fear for more immediate reasons than that. (*Margaret looks at him in alarm and at the same time betrays pleasure in what he has said.*) For you.

MARGARET: (*hastily*). Don't look at me that way. Your eyes are flashing. Someone might see and misunderstand.

KNOX: (*in confusion, awkwardly*). I was unaware that I—that I was looking at you . . . in any way that . . .

MARGARET: I'll tell you why you are here. Because I sent for you.

KNOX: (*with signs of ardor*). I would come whenever you sent for me, and go wherever you might send me.

MARGARET: (*reprovingly*). Please, please . . . It was about that speech. I have been hearing about it from everybody—rumblings and mutterings and dire prophecies. I know how busy you are, and I ought not to have asked you to come. But there was no other way, and I was so anxious.

KNOX: (*pleased*). It seems so strange that you, being what you are, affiliated as you are, should be interested in the welfare of the common people.

MARGARET: (*judicially*). I do seem like a traitor in my own camp. But as Father said a while ago, I, too, have dreamed my dream. I did it as a girl—Plato's *Republic*, Moore's

Utopia—I was steeped in all the dreams of the social dreamers. (*During all that follows of her speech, Knox is keenly interested; his eyes glisten and he hangs on her words.*) And I dreamed that I, too, might do something to bring on the era of universal justice and fair play. In my heart I dedicated myself to the cause of humanity. I made Lincoln my hero—he still is. But I was only a girl, and where was I to find this cause?—how to work for it? I was shut in by a thousand restrictions, hedged in by a thousand conventions. Everybody laughed at me when I expressed the thoughts that burned in me. What could I do? I was only a woman. I had neither vote nor right of utterance. I must remain silent. I must do nothing. Men, in their lordly wisdom, did all. They voted, orated, governed. The place for women was in the home, taking care of some lordly man who did all these lordly things.

KNOX: You understand, then, why I am for equal suffrage.

MARGARET: But I learned—or thought I learned. Power I discovered early. My father had power. He was a "magnate" —I believe that is the correct term. Power was what I needed. But how? I was a woman. Again I dreamed my dream—a modified dream. Only by marriage could I win to power. And there you have the clue to me and what I am and have become. I met the man who was to become my husband. He was clean and strong and an athlete, an outdoor man, a wealthy man and a rising politician. Father told me that if I married him, he would make him the power of his state, make him governor, send him to the United States Senate. And there you have it all.

KNOX: Yes? . . . Yes?

MARGARET: I married. I found that there were greater forces at work than I had ever dreamed of. They took my husband away from me and molded him into the political lieutenant of my father. And I was without power. I could do nothing for the cause. I was beaten. Then it was that I got a new vision. The future belonged to the children. There I could play my woman's part. I was a mother. Very well. I could do no better than to bring into the world a healthy son and bring him up to manhood healthy and wholesome, clean, noble, and alive. Did I do my part well, through him the results would be achieved. Through him would the work of the world be done in making the world healthier and happier for all the human creatures in it. I played the mother's part. That is why I left the pitiful little charities of the church and devoted myself to settlement work and tenement-house reform, established my kindergartens, and worked for the little men and women who come so blindly and to whom the future belongs to make or mar.

KNOX: You are magnificent. I know now why I come when you bid me come.

MARGARET: And then you came. You were magnificent. You were my knight of the windmills, tilting against all power and privilege, striving to wrest the future from the future and realize it here in the present, now. I was sure you would be destroyed. Yet you are still here and fighting valiantly. And that speech of yours tomorrow—

CHALMERS: (*who has approached, bearing Dolores Ortega's cup*). Yes, that speech. How do you do, Mr. Knox. (*They shake hands.*) A cup of tea, Madge. For Mrs. Ortega. Two lumps, please. (*Margaret prepares the cup of tea.*) Everybody is excited over that speech. You are going to give us particular fits tomorrow, I understand.

KNOX: (*smiling*). Really, no more than is deserved.

CHALMERS: The truth, the whole truth, and nothing but the truth?

KNOX: Precisely.

Receiving back cup of tea from Margaret.

CHALMERS: Believe me, we are not so black as we're painted.

There are two sides to this question. Like you, we do our best to do what is right. And we hope, we still hope, to win you over to our side.

Knox shakes his head with a quiet smile.

MARGARET: Oh, Tom, be truthful. You don't hope anything of the sort. You know you are hoping to destroy him.

CHALMERS: (*smiling grimly*). That is what usually happens to those who are not won over. (*Preparing to depart with cup of tea; speaking to Knox.*) You might accomplish much good, were you with us. Against us you accomplish nothing, absolutely nothing.

Returns to Dolores Ortega.

MARGARET: (*hurriedly*). You see. That is why I was anxious— why I sent for you. Even Tom admits that they who are not won over are destroyed. This speech is a crucial event. You know how rigidly they rule the House and gag men like you. It is they, and they alone, who have given you opportunity for this speech. Why?—why?

KNOX: (*smiling confidently*). I know their little scheme. They have heard my charges. They think I am going to make a firebrand speech, and they are ready to catch me without the proofs. They are ready in every way for me. They are going to laugh me down. The Associated Press, the Washington correspondents—all are ready to manufacture, in every newspaper in the land, the great laugh that will destroy me. But I am fully prepared, I have—

MARGARET: The proofs?

KNOX: Yes.

MARGARET: Now?

KNOX: They will be delivered to me tonight—original documents, photographs of documents, affidavits—

MARGARET: Tell me nothing. But, oh, do be careful! Be careful!

MRS. DOWSETT: (*appealing to Margaret*). Do give me some

assistance, Mrs. Chalmers. (*Indicating Sakari.*) Mr. Sakari is trying to make me ridiculous.

MARGARET: Impossible.

MRS. DOWSETT: But he is. He has had the effrontery—

CHALMERS: (*mimicking Mrs. Dowsett*). Effrontery!—O Sakari!

SAKARI: The dear lady is pleased to be facetious.

MRS. DOWSETT: He has had the effrontery to ask me to explain the cause of high prices. Mr. Dowsett says the reason is that the people are living so high.

SAKARI: Such a marvelous country. They are poor because they have so much to spend.

CHALMERS: Are not high prices due to the increased output of gold?

MRS. DOWSETT: Mr. Sakari suggested that himself, and when I agreed with him, he proceeded to demolish it. He has treated me dreadfully.

RUTLAND: (*clearing his throat and expressing himself with ponderous unction*). You will find the solution in the drink traffic. It is liquor, alcohol, that is undermining our industry, our institutions, our faith in God—everything. Yearly the working people drink greater quantities of alcohol. Naturally, through resulting inefficiency the cost of production is higher, and therefore prices are higher.

DOWSETT: Partly so, partly so. And in line with it, and in addition to it, prices are high because the working class is no longer thrifty. If our working class saved as the French peasant does, we would sell more in the world market and have better times.

SAKARI: (*bowing*). As I understand it, then, the more thrifty you are the more you save, and the more you save the more you have to sell, the more you sell, the better the times?

DOWSETT: Exactly so. Exactly.

SAKARI: The less you sell, the harder are the times?

DOWSETT: Just so.

SAKARI: Then, if the people are thrifty and buy less, times will be harder?

DOWSETT: (*perplexed*). Er—it would seem so.

SAKARI: Then it would seem that the present bad times are due to the fact that the people are thrifty, rather than not thrifty?

Dowsett is nonplussed, and Mrs. Dowsett throws up her hands in despair.

MRS. DOWSETT: (*turning to Knox*). Perhaps you can explain to us, Mr. Knox, the reason for this terrible condition of affairs.

Starkweather closes notebook on finger and listens.

Knox smiles, but does not speak.

DOLORES ORTEGA: Please do, Mr. Knox. I am so dreadfully anxious to know why living is so high now. Only this morning, I understand, meat went up again.

Knox hesitates and looks questioningly at Margaret.

HUBBARD: I am sure Mr. Knox can shed new light on this perplexing problem.

CHALMERS: Surely you, the whirlwind of oratorical swords in the House, are not timid here—among friends.

KNOX: (*sparring*). I had no idea that questions of such nature were topics of conversation at affairs like this.

STARKWEATHER: (*abruptly and imperatively*). What causes the high prices?

KNOX: (*equally abrupt and just as positive as the other was imperative*). Theft.

It is a sort of a bombshell he has exploded, but they receive it politely and smilingly, even though it has shaken them up.

DOLORES ORTEGA: What a romantic explanation. I suppose everybody who has anything has stolen it.

KNOX: Not quite, but almost. Take motorcars, for example. This year five hundred million dollars has been spent for motorcars. It required men toiling in the mines and foundries, women sewing their eyes out in sweatshops, shop girls slaving for four and five dollars a week, little children working in the factories and cotton mills—all these it required to produce those five hundred millions spent this year on motorcars. And all this has been stolen from those who did the work.

MRS. STARKWEATHER: I always knew those motorcars were to blame for terrible things.

DOLORES ORTEGA: But, Mr. Knox, I have a motorcar.

KNOX: Somebody's labor made that car. Was it yours?

DOLORES ORTEGA: Mercy, no! I bought it and . . . paid for it.

KNOX: Then did you labor at producing something else and exchange the fruits of that labor for the motorcar? (*A pause.*) You do not answer. Then I am to understand that you have a motorcar which was made by somebody else's labor and for which you gave no labor of your own. This I call theft. You call it property. Yet it is theft.

STARKWEATHER: (*interrupting Dolores Ortega, who was just about to speak*). But surely you have intelligence to see the question in larger ways than stolen motorcars. I am a man of affairs. I don't steal motorcars.

KNOX: (*smiling*). Not concrete little motorcars, no. You do things on a large scale.

STARKWEATHER: Steal?

KNOX: (*shrugging his shoulders*). If you will have it so.

STARKWEATHER: I am like a certain gentleman from Missouri. You've got to show me.

KNOX: And I'm like the man from Texas. It's got to be put in my hand.

STARKWEATHER: I shift my residence at once to Texas. Put it in my hand that I steal on a large scale.

KNOX: Very well. You are the great financier, merger, and magnate. Do you mind a few statistics?

STARKWEATHER: Go ahead.

KNOX: You exercise a controlling interest in nine billion dollars' worth of railways; in two billion dollars' worth of industrial concerns; in one billion dollars' worth of life insurance groups; in one billion dollars' worth of banking groups; in two billion dollars' worth of trust companies. Mind you, I do not say you own all this, but that you exercise a controlling interest. That is all that is necessary. In short, you exercise a controlling interest in such a proportion of the total investments of the United States as to set the pace for all the rest. Now to my point. In the last few years seventy billions of dollars have been artificially added to the capitalization of the nation's industries. By that I mean water—pure, unadulterated water. You, the merger, know what water means. I say seventy billion. It doesn't matter if we call it forty billion or eighty billion; the amount, whatever it is, is a huge one. And what does seventy billions of water mean? It means, at five percent, that three billion and a half must be paid for things this year, and every year, more than things are really worth. The people who labor have to pay this. There is theft for you. There is high prices for you. Who put in the water? Who gets the theft of the water? Have I put it in your hand?

STARKWEATHER: Are there no wages for stewardship?

KNOX: Call it any name you please.

STARKWEATHER: Do I not make two dollars where one was before? Do I not make for more happiness than was before I came?

KNOX: Is that any more than the duty any man owes to his fellowman?

STARKWEATHER: Oh, you unpractical dreamer.

Returns to his notebook.

RUTLAND: (*throwing himself into the breach*). Where do I steal,

Mr. Knox?—I who get a mere salary for preaching the Lord's word.

KNOX: Your salary comes out of that water I mentioned. Do you want to know who pays your salary? Not your parishioners. But the little children toiling in the mills, and all the rest—all the slaves on the wheel of labor pay you your salary.

RUTLAND: I earn it.

KNOX: They pay it.

MRS. DOWSETT: Why, I declare, Mr. Knox, you are worse than Mr. Sakari. You are an anarchist.

She simulates shivering with fear.

CHALMERS: (*to Knox*). I suppose that's part of your speech tomorrow.

DOLORES ORTEGA: (*clapping her hands*). A rehearsal! He's trying it out on us!

SAKARI: How would you remedy this—er—this theft?

Starkweather again closes notebook on finger and listens as Knox begins to speak.

KNOX: Very simply. By changing the governmental machinery by which this household of ninety million people conducts its affairs.

SAKARI: I thought—I was taught so at Yale—that your governmental machinery was excellent, most excellent.

KNOX: It is antiquated. It is ready for the scrap heap. Instead of being our servant, it has mastered us. We are its slaves. All the political brood of grafters and hypocrites have run away with it, and with us as well. In short, from the municipalities up, we are dominated by the grafters. It is a reign of theft.

HUBBARD: But any government is representative of its people. No people is worthy of a better government than it possesses. Were it worthier, it would possess a better government.

Starkweather nods his head approvingly.

KNOX: That is a lie. And I say to you now that the average morality and desire for right conduct of the people of the United States is far higher than that of the government which misrepresents it. The people are essentially worthy of a better government than that which is at present in the hands of the politicians, for the benefit of the politicians and of the interests the politicians represent. I wonder, Mr. Sakari, if you have ever heard the story of the four aces.

SAKARI: I cannot say that I have.

KNOX: Do you understand the game of poker?

SAKARI: (*considering*). Yes, a marvelous game. I have learned it—at Yale. It was very expensive.

KNOX: Well, that story reminds me of our grafting politicians. They have no moral compunctions. They look upon theft as right—eminently right. They see nothing wrong in the arrangement that the man who deals the cards should give himself the best in the deck. Never mind what he deals himself, they'll have the deal next and make up for it.

DOLORES ORTEGA: But the story, Mr. Knox. I, too, understand poker.

KNOX: It occurred out in Nevada, in a mining camp. A tenderfoot was watching a game of poker. He stood behind the dealer, and he saw the dealer deal himself four aces from the bottom of the deck. (*From now on, he tells the story in the slow, slightly drawling western fashion.*) The tenderfoot went around to the player on the opposite side of the table. "Say," he says, "I just seen the dealer give himself four aces off the bottom." The player looked at him a moment and said, "What of it?" "Oh, nothing," said the tenderfoot, "only I thought you might want to know. I tell you I seen the dealer give himself four aces off the bottom." "Look here, mister," said the player, "you'd better get out of this. You don't understand the game. It's *his* deal, ain't it?"

MARGARET: (*arising while they are laughing*). We've talked politics long enough. Dolores, I want you to tell me about your new car.

KNOX: (*as if suddenly recollecting himself*). And I must be going. (*In a low voice to Margaret.*) Do I have to shake hands with all these people?

MARGARET: (*shaking her head, speaking low*). Dear delightful Ali Baba.

KNOX: (*glumly*). I suppose I've made a fool of myself.

MARGARET: (*earnestly*). On the contrary, you were delightful. I am proud of you.

As Knox shakes hands with Margaret, Sakari arises and comes forward.

SAKARI: I, too, must go. I have had a charming half hour, Mrs. Chalmers. But I shall not attempt to thank you.

He shakes hands with Margaret.

Knox and Sakari proceed to make exit to rear.

Just as they go out, Servant enters, carrying card tray, and advances toward Starkweather.

Margaret joins Dolores Ortega and Chalmers, seats herself with them, and proceeds to talk motorcars.

Servant has reached Starkweather, who has taken a telegram from tray, opened it, and is reading it.

STARKWEATHER: Damnation!

SERVANT: I beg your pardon, sir.

STARKWEATHER: Send Senator Chalmers to me, and Mr. Hubbard.

SERVANT: Yes, sir.

Servant crosses to Chalmers and Hubbard, both of whom immediately arise and cross to Starkweather.

While this is being done, Margaret reassembles the three broken groups into one, seating herself so that she can watch

Starkweather and his group across the stage.
Servant lingers to receive a command from Margaret.
Chalmers and Hubbard wait a moment, standing, while
Starkweather rereads telegram.

STARKWEATHER: (*standing up*). Dobleman has just forwarded this telegram. It's from New York—from Martinaw. There's been rottenness. My papers and letter files have been ransacked. It's the confidential stenographer who has been tampered with—you remember that middle-aged, youngish-oldish woman, Tom? That's the one. —Where's that servant? (*Servant is just making exit.*) Here! Come here! (*Servant comes over to Starkweather.*) Go to the telephone and call up Dobleman. Tell him to come here.

SERVANT: (*perplexed*). I beg pardon, sir.

STARKWEATHER: (*irritably*). My secretary. At my house. Dobleman. Tell him to come at once.

Servant makes exit.

CHALMERS: But who can be the principal behind this theft?

Starkweather shrugs his shoulders.

HUBBARD: A blackmailing device, most probably. They will attempt to bleed you—

CHALMERS: Unless—

STARKWEATHER: (*impatiently*). Yes?

CHALMERS: Unless they are to be used tomorrow in that speech of Knox.

Comprehension dawns on the faces of the other two men.

MRS. STARKWEATHER: (*who has arisen*). Anthony, we must go now. Are you ready? Connie has to dress.

STARKWEATHER: I am not going now. You and Connie take the car.

MRS. STARKWEATHER: You mustn't forget you are going to that dinner.

STARKWEATHER: (*wearily*). Do I ever forget?

Servant enters and proceeds toward Starkweather, where

he stands waiting while Mrs. Starkweather finishes the next speech. Starkweather listens to her with a patient, stony face.

MRS. STARKWEATHER: Oh, these everlasting politics! That is what it has been all afternoon—high prices, graft, and theft; theft, graft, and high prices. It is terrible. When I was a girl, we did not talk of such things. Well, come on, Connie.

MRS. DOWSETT: (*rising and glancing at Dowsett*). And we must be going, too.

During the following scene, which takes place around Starkweather, Margaret is saying good-bye to her departing guests.

Mrs. Starkweather and Connie make exit.

Dowsett and Mrs. Dowsett make exit.

The instant Mrs. Dowsett's remark puts a complete end to Mrs. Starkweather's speech, Starkweather, without answer or noticing his wife, turns and interrogates Servant with a glance.

SERVANT: Mr. Dobleman has already left some time to come here, sir.

STARKWEATHER: Show him in as soon as he comes.

SERVANT: Yes, sir.

Servant makes exit.

Margaret, Dolores Ortega, and Rutland are left in a group together, this time around tea table, where Margaret serves Rutland another cup of tea. From time to time Margaret glances curiously at the serious group of men across the stage. Starkweather is thinking hard, with knitted brows. Hubbard is likewise pondering.

CHALMERS: If I were certain Knox had those papers, I would take him by the throat and shake them out of him.

STARKWEATHER: No foolish talk like that, Tom. This is a serious matter.

HUBBARD: But Knox has no money. A Starkweather stenographer comes high.

STARKWEATHER: There is more than Knox behind this.

Enter Dobleman, walking quickly and in a state of controlled excitement.

DOBLEMAN: (*to Starkweather*). You received that telegram, sir? (*Starkweather nods.*) I got the New York office—Martinaw—right along afterward, by long distance. I thought it best to follow and tell you.

STARKWEATHER: What did Martinaw say?

DOBLEMAN: The files seem in perfect order.

STARKWEATHER: Thank God!

During the following speech of Dobleman, Rutland says good-bye to Margaret and Dolores Ortega and makes exit. Margaret and Dolores Ortega rise a minute afterward and go toward exit, throwing curious glances at the men but not disturbing them.

Dolores Ortega makes exit.

Margaret pauses in doorway a moment, giving a final anxious glance at the men, and makes exit.

DOBLEMAN: But they are not. The stenographer, Miss Standish, has confessed. For a long time she has followed the practice of taking two or three letters and documents at a time away from the office. Many have been photographed and returned. But the more important ones were retained and clever copies returned. Martinaw says that Miss Standish herself does not know and cannot tell which of the ones she returned are genuine and which are copies.

HUBBARD: Knox never did this.

STARKWEATHER: Did Martinaw say whom Miss Standish was acting for?

DOBLEMAN: Gherst.

The alarm on the three men's faces is patent.

STARKWEATHER: Gherst!

Pauses to think.

HUBBARD: Then it is not so grave after all. A yellow journal
sensation is the best Gherst can make of it. And, documents
or not, the very medium by which it is made public
discredits it.

STARKWEATHER: Trust Gherst for more ability than that. He
will certainly exploit them in his newspapers, but not until
after Knox has used them in his speech. Oh, the cunning
dog! Never could he have chosen a better mode and
moment to strike at me, at the Administration, at everything. That is Gherst all over. Playing to the gallery.
Inducing Knox to make this spectacular exposure on the
floor of the House just at the critical time when so many
important bills are pending. (*To Dobleman.*) Did Martinaw
give you any idea of the nature of the stolen documents?

DOBLEMAN: (*referring to notes he has brought*). Of course
I don't know anything about it, but he spoke of the
Goodyear letters—(*Starkweather betrays by his face the
gravity of the information*)—the Caledonian letters, all
the Black Rider correspondence. He mentioned, too—
(*referring to notes*)—the Astonbury and Glutz letters. And
there were others, many others, not designated.

STARKWEATHER: This is terrible! (*Recollecting himself.*) Thank
you, Dobleman. Will you please return to the house at
once. Get New York again, and fullest details. I'll follow
you shortly. Have you a machine?

DOBLEMAN: A taxi, sir.

STARKWEATHER: All right, and be careful.

Dobleman makes exit.

CHALMERS: I don't know the import of all these letters, but I
can guess, and it does seem serious.

STARKWEATHER: (*furiously*). Serious! Let me tell you that there
has been no exposure like this in the history of the country.
It means hundreds of millions of dollars. It means more—

the loss of power. And still more, it means the mob, the great mass of the child-minded people rising up and destroying all that I have labored to do for them. Oh, the fools! The fools!

HUBBARD: (*shaking his head ominously*). There is no telling what may happen if Knox makes that speech and delivers the proofs.

CHALMERS: It is unfortunate. The people are restless and excited as it is. They are being constantly prodded on by the mouthings of the radical press, of the muckraking magazines, and of the demagogues. The people are like powder awaiting the spark.

STARKWEATHER: This man Knox is no fool, if he *is* a dreamer. He is a shrewd knave. He is a fighter. He comes from the West—the old pioneer stock. His father drove an ox team across the plains to Oregon. He knows how to play his cards, and never could circumstances have placed more advantageous cards in his hands.

CHALMERS: And nothing like this has ever touched you before.

STARKWEATHER: I have always stood above the muck and ruck—clear and clean and unassailable. But this—this is too much! It is the spark. There is no forecasting what it may develop into.

CHALMERS: A political turnover.

STARKWEATHER: (*nodding savagely*). A new party, a party of demagogues, in power. Government ownership of the railways and telegraphs. A graduated income tax that will mean no less than the confiscation of private capital.

CHALMERS: And all that mass of radical legislation—the Child Labor Bill, the new Employers' Liability Act, the government control of the Alaskan coal fields, that interference with Mexico. And that big power corporation you have worked so hard to form.

STARKWEATHER: It must not be. It is an unthinkable calamity. It means that the very process of capitalistic development is hindered, stopped. It means a setback of ten years in the process. It means work, endless work, to overcome the setback. It means not alone the passage of all this radical legislation with the consequent disadvantages, but it means the fingers of the mob clutching at our grip of control. It means anarchy. It means ruin and misery for all the blind fools and led cattle of the mass who will strike at the very sources of their own existence and comfort.

Tommy enters from left, evidently playing a game, in the course of which he is running away. By his actions he shows that he is pursued. He intends to cross stage, but is stopped by sight of the men. Unobserved by them, he retraces his steps and crawls under the tea table.

CHALMERS: Without doubt, Knox is in possession of the letters right now.

STARKWEATHER: There is but one thing to do, and that is—get them back.

He looks questioningly at the two men.

Margaret enters from left, in flushed and happy pursuit of Tommy—for it is a game she is playing with him. She startles at sight of the three men, whom she first sees as she gains the side of the tea table, where she pauses abruptly, resting one hand on the table.

HUBBARD: I'll undertake it.

STARKWEATHER: There is little time to waste. In twenty hours from now he will be on the floor making his speech. Try mild measures first. Offer him inducements—any inducement. I empower you to act for me. You will find he has a price.

HUBBARD: And if not?

STARKWEATHER: Then you must get them at any cost.

HUBBARD: (*tentatively*). You mean—?

STARKWEATHER: I mean just that. But no matter what happens, I must never be brought in. Do you understand?

HUBBARD: Thoroughly.

MARGARET: (*acting her part and speaking with assumed gaiety*). What are you three conspiring about?
All three men are startled.

CHALMERS: We are arranging to boost prices a little higher.

HUBBARD: And so be able to accumulate more motorcars.

STARKWEATHER: (*taking no notice of Margaret and starting toward exit to rear*). I must be going. Hubbard, you have your work cut out for you. Tom, I want you to come with me.

CHALMERS: (*as the three men move toward exit*). Home?

STARKWEATHER: Yes, we have much to do.

CHALMERS: Then I'll dress first and follow you. (*Turning to Margaret.*) Pick me up on the way to that dinner.
Margaret nods. Starkweather makes exit without speaking. Hubbard says good-bye to Margaret and makes exit, followed by Chalmers.
Margaret remains standing, one hand resting on table, the other hand to her breast. She is thinking, establishing in her mind the connection between Knox and what she has overheard, and in process of reaching the conclusion that Knox is in danger.
Tommy, having vainly waited to be discovered, crawls out dispiritedly and takes Margaret by the hand. She scarcely notices him.

TOMMY: (*dolefully*). Don't you want to play anymore? (*Margaret does not reply*). I was a good Indian.

MARGARET: (*suddenly becoming aware of herself and breaking down. She stoops and clasps Tommy in her arms, crying out in anxiety and fear and from love of her boy.*) Oh, Tommy! Tommy!

CURTAIN

ACT II

*Sitting room of Howard Knox—dimly lighted. Time, eight
o'clock in the evening.*

*Entrance from hallway at side to right. At right rear is
locked door leading to a room which does not belong to
Knox's suite. At rear center is fireplace. At left rear, door
leading to Knox's bedroom. At left are windows facing on
street. Near these windows is a large library table littered
with books, magazines, government reports, etc. To the right
of center, midway forward, is a flattop desk. On it is a desk
telephone. Behind it, so that one sitting in it faces audience,
is revolving desk chair. Also on desk are letters in their
envelopes, etc. Against clear wall spaces are bookcases and
filing cabinets. Of special note is bookcase, containing large
books, and not more than five feet high, which is against
wall between fireplace and door to bedroom. Curtain
discloses empty stage.*

*After a slight interval, door at right rear is shaken and
agitated. After slight further interval, door is opened inward
upon stage. A man's head appears, cautiously looking
around.*

Man enters, turns up lights, is followed by Second Man. Both

209

*are clad decently, in knockabout business suits and starched
collars, cuffs, etc. They are trim, deft, determined men.
Following upon them, enters Hubbard. He looks about room,
crosses to desk, picks up a letter, and reads address.*

HUBBARD: This is Knox's room, all right.

FIRST MAN: Trust us for that.

SECOND MAN: We were lucky the guy with the whiskers
moved out of that other room only this afternoon.

FIRST MAN: His key hadn't come down yet when I engaged it.

HUBBARD: Well, get to work. That must be his bedroom.
(*He goes to door of bedroom, opens, and peers in, turns on
electric lights of bedroom, turns them out, then turns back
to men.*) You know what it is—a bunch of documents and
letters. If we find it, there is a clean five hundred each for
you, in addition to your regular pay.
*While the conversation goes on, all three engage in a careful
search of desk, drawers, filing cabinets, bookcases, etc.*

SECOND MAN: Old Starkweather must want them bad.

HUBBARD: Sh-h. Don't even breathe his name.

SECOND MAN: His nibs is damned exclusive, ain't he?

FIRST MAN: I've never got a direct instruction from him, and
I've worked for him longer than you.

SECOND MAN: Yes, and you worked for him for over two years
before you knew who was hiring you.

HUBBARD: (*to First Man*). You'd better go out in the hall and
keep a watch for Knox. He may come in anytime.
*First Man produces skeleton keys and goes to door at right.
The first key opens it. Leaving door slightly ajar, he makes
exit.*
Desk telephone rings and startles Hubbard.

SECOND MAN: (*grinning at Hubbard's alarm*). It's only the
phone.

HUBBARD: (*proceeding with search*). I suppose you've done lots
of work for Stark—

SECOND MAN: (*mimicking him*). Sh-h. Don't breathe his name.
Telephone rings again and again, insistently, urgently.

HUBBARD: (*disguising his voice*). Hello—yes. (*Shows surprise,
seems to recognize the voice, and smiles knowingly.*) No, this
is not Knox. Some mistake. Wrong number— (*Hanging up
receiver and speaking to Second Man in natural voice.*) She
did hang up quick.

SECOND MAN: You seemed to recognize her.

HUBBARD: No, I only thought I did.

A pause while they search.

SECOND MAN: I've never spoken a word to his nibs in my life.
And I've drawn his pay for years, too.

HUBBARD: What of it?

SECOND MAN: (*complainingly*). He don't know I exist.

HUBBARD: (*pulling open a desk drawer and examining contents*).
The pay's all right, isn't it?

SECOND MAN: It sure is, but I guess I earn every cent of it.
*First Man enters through door at right. He moves hurriedly but
cautiously. Shuts door behind him, but neglects to relock it.*

FIRST MAN: Somebody just left the elevator and is coming
down the hall.

*Hubbard, First Man, and Second Man all start for door at
right rear.*

*First Man pauses and looks around to see if room is in order.
Sees desk drawer which Hubbard has neglected to close; goes
back and closes it.*

Hubbard and Second Man make exit.

First Man turns lights low and makes exit.

Sound of locking door is heard.

A pause.

*A knocking at door to right. A pause. Then door opens and
Gifford enters. He turns up lights, strolls about room, looks
at watch, and sits down in chair near right of fireplace.
Sound of key in lock of door to right.*

Door opens and Knox enters, key in hand. Sees Gifford.

KNOX: (*advancing to meet him at fireplace and shaking hands*).
How did you get in?

GIFFORD: I let myself in. The door was unlocked.

KNOX: I must have forgotten it.

GIFFORD: (*drawing bundle of documents from inside breast
pocket and handing them to Knox*). Well, there they are.

KNOX: (*fingering them curiously*). You are sure they are
originals? (*Gifford nods.*) I can't take any chances, you
know. If Gherst changed his mind after I gave my speech,
and refused to show the originals—such things have
happened.

GIFFORD: That's what I told him. He was firm on giving
duplicates, and for a while it looked as if my trip to New
York was wasted. But I stuck to my guns. It was originals
or nothing with you, I said, and he finally gave in.

KNOX: (*holding up documents*). I can't tell you what they mean
to me, nor how grateful—

GIFFORD: (*interrupting*). That's all right. Don't mention it.
Gherst is wild for the chance. It will do organized labor a
heap of good. And you are able to say your own say at the
same time. How's that compensation act coming on?

KNOX: (*wearily*). The same old story. It will never come
before the House. It is dying in committee. What can you
expect of the Committee of Judiciary?—composed as it is
of ex–railroad judges and ex–railroad lawyers.

GIFFORD: The railroad brotherhoods are keen on getting that
bill through.

KNOX: Well, they won't, and they never will until they learn
to vote right. When will your labor leaders quit the strike
and boycott and lead your men to political action?

GIFFORD: (*holding out hand*). Well, so long. I've got to trot,
and I haven't time to tell you why I think political action
would destroy the trade union movement. (*Knox tosses*

*documents on top of low bookcase between fireplace and
bedroom door and starts to shake hands.*) You're damn
careless with those papers. You wouldn't be if you knew
how much Gherst paid for them.

KNOX: They're safe here.

GIFFORD: You don't appreciate that other crowd. It stops at
nothing.

KNOX: I won't take my eyes off of them. And I'll take them
to bed with me tonight for safety. Besides, there is no
danger. Nobody but you knows I have them.

GIFFORD: (*proceeding toward door to right*). I'd hate to be in
Starkweather's office when he discovers what's happened.
There'll be some bad half hours for somebody. (*Pausing at
door.*) Give them hell tomorrow, good and plenty. I'm
going to be in a gallery. So long.

Makes exit.

*Knox crosses to windows, which he opens, returns to desk,
seats himself in revolving chair, and begins opening his
correspondence.*

A knock at door to right.

KNOX: Come in.

*Hubbard enters, advances to desk, but does not shake hands.
They greet each other, and Hubbard sits down in chair to
left of desk.*

*Knox, still holding an open letter, revolves chair so as to face
his visitor. He waits for Hubbard to speak.*

HUBBARD: There is no use beating about the bush with a man
like you. I know that. You are direct, and so am I. You
know my position well enough to be assured that I am
empowered to treat with you.

KNOX: Oh, yes, I know.

HUBBARD: What we want is to have you friendly.

KNOX: That is easy enough. When the Interests become
upright and honest—

HUBBARD: Save that for your speech. We are talking privately. We can make it well worth your while—

KNOX: (*angrily*). If you think you can bribe me—

HUBBARD: (*suavely*). Not at all. Not the slightest suspicion of it. The point is this. You are a congressman. A congressman's career depends on his membership in good committees. At the present you are buried in the dead Committee on Coinage, Weights, and Measures. If you say the word you can be appointed to the livest committee—

KNOX: (*interrupting*). You have these appointments to give?

HUBBARD: Surely. Else why should I be here? It can be managed.

KNOX: (*meditatively*). I thought our government was rotten enough, but I never dreamed that House appointments were hawked around by the Interests in this fashion.

HUBBARD: You have not given your answer.

KNOX: You should have known my answer in advance.

HUBBARD: There is an alternative. You are interested in social problems. You are a student of sociology. Those whom I represent are genuinely interested in you. We are prepared, so that you may pursue your researches more deeply—we are prepared to send you to Europe. There, in that vast sociological laboratory, far from the jangling strife of politics, you will have every opportunity to study. We are prepared to send you for a period of ten years. You will receive ten thousand dollars a year, and in addition, the day your steamer leaves New York, you will receive a lump sum of one hundred thousand dollars.

KNOX: And this is the way men are bought.

HUBBARD: It is purely an educational matter.

KNOX: Now it is you who are beating about the bush.

HUBBARD: (*decisively*). Very well, then. What price do you set on yourself?

KNOX: You want me to quit—to leave politics, everything? You want to buy my soul?

HUBBARD: More than that. We want to buy those documents and letters.

KNOX: (*showing a slight start*). What documents and letters?

HUBBARD: You are beating around the bush in turn. There is no need for an honest man to lie even—

KNOX: (*interrupting*). To you.

HUBBARD: (*smiling*). Even to me. I watched you closely when I mentioned the letters. You gave yourself away. You knew I meant the letters stolen by Gherst from Starkweather's private files—the letters you intended using tomorrow.

KNOX: Intend using tomorrow.

HUBBARD: Precisely. It is the same thing. What is the price? Set it.

KNOX: I have nothing to sell. I am not on the market.

HUBBARD: One moment. Don't make up your mind hastily. You don't know with whom you have to deal. Those letters will not appear in your speech tomorrow. Take that from me. It would be far wiser to sell for a fortune than to get nothing for them and at the same time not use them.

A knock at door to right startles Hubbard.

KNOX: (*intending to say "Come in"*). Come—

HUBBARD: (*interrupting*). Hush. Don't. I cannot be seen here.

KNOX: (*laughing*). You fear the contamination of my company.

The knock is repeated.

HUBBARD: (*in alarm, rising as Knox purses his lips to bid them enter*). Don't let anybody in. I don't want to be seen here—with you. Besides, my presence will not put you in a good light.

KNOX: (*also rising, starting toward door*). What I do is always open to the world. I see no one whom I should not permit the world to know I saw.

Knox starts toward door to open it.

Hubbard, looking about him in alarm, flees across stage and into bedroom, closing the door. During all the following scene, Hubbard, from time to time, opens door and peers out at what is going on.

KNOX: (*opening door and recoiling*). Margaret! Mrs. Chalmers!
Margaret enters, followed by Tommy and Linda. Margaret is in evening dress covered by evening cloak.

MARGARET: (*shaking hands with Knox*). Forgive me, but I had to see you. I could not get you on the telephone. I called and called, and the best I could do was to get the wrong number.

KNOX: (*recovering from his astonishment*). Yes. I am glad. (*Seeing Tommy.*) Hello, Tommy.
Knox holds out his hand, and Tommy shakes it gravely. Linda stays in background. Her face is troubled.

TOMMY: How do you do?

MARGARET: There was no other way, and it was so necessary for me to warn you. I brought Tommy and Linda along to chaperon me. (*She looks curiously around room, specially indicating filing cabinets and the stacks of government reports on table.*) Your laboratory.

KNOX: Ah, if I were only as great a sociological wizard as Edison is a wizard in physical sciences.

MARGARET: But you are. You labor more mightily than you admit—or dare to think. Oh, I know you—better than you do yourself.

TOMMY: Do you read all those books?

KNOX: Yes, I am still going to school and studying hard. What are you going to study to be when you grow up? (*Tommy meditates, but does not answer.*) President of these great United States?

TOMMY: (*shaking his head*). Father says the President doesn't amount to much.

KNOX: Not a Lincoln?
Tommy is in doubt.

MARGARET: But don't you remember what a great good man Lincoln was? You remember I told you?

TOMMY: (*shaking his head slowly*). But I don't want to be killed. —I'll tell you what!

KNOX: What?

TOMMY: I want to be a senator like Father. He makes them dance.

Margaret is shocked, and Knox's eyes twinkle.

KNOX: Makes whom dance?

TOMMY: (*puzzled*). I don't know. (*With added confidence.*) But he makes them dance just the same.

Margaret makes a signal to Linda to take Tommy across the room.

LINDA: (*starting to cross stage to left*). Come, Tommy. Let us look out of the window.

TOMMY: I'd rather talk with Mr. Knox.

MARGARET: Please do, Tommy. Mama wants to talk to Mr. Knox.

Tommy yields and crosses to right, where he joins Linda in looking out of the window.

MARGARET: You might ask me to take a seat.

KNOX: Oh! I beg pardon.

He draws up a comfortable chair for her and seats himself in desk chair, facing her.

MARGARET: I have only a few minutes. Tom is at Father's, and I am to pick him up there and go on to that dinner after I've taken Tommy home.

KNOX: But your maid?

MARGARET: Linda? Wild horses could not drag from her anything that she thought would harm me. So intense is her fidelity that it almost shames me. I do not deserve it. But this is not what I came to you about. (*She speaks the following hurriedly.*) After you left this afternoon, something happened. Father received a telegram. It seemed most important. His secretary followed upon the heels of the telegram. Father called Tom and Mr. Hubbard to him, and they held a conference. I think they have

discovered the loss of the documents and that they believe
you have them. I did not hear them mention your name,
yet I am absolutely certain that they were talking about
you. Also, I could tell from Father's face that something
was terribly wrong. Oh, be careful! Do be careful!

KNOX: There is no danger, I assure you.

MARGARET: But you do not know them. I tell you, you do not
know them. They will stop at nothing—at nothing. Father
believes he is right in all that he does.

KNOX: I know. That is what makes him so formidable. He has
an ethical sanction.

MARGARET: (*nodding*). It is his religion.

KNOX: And like any religion with a narrow-minded man, it
runs to mania.

MARGARET: He believes that civilization rests on him and that
it is his sacred duty to preserve civilization.

KNOX: I know. I know.

MARGARET: But you? But you? You are in danger.

KNOX: No, I shall remain in tonight. Tomorrow, in the broad
light of midday, I shall proceed to the House and give my
speech.

MARGARET: (*wildly*). Oh, if anything should happen to you!

KNOX: (*looking at her searchingly*). You do care? (*Margaret
nods, with eyes suddenly downcast.*) For Howard Knox, the
reformer? Or for me, the man?

MARGARET: (*impulsively*). Oh, why must a woman forever
remain quiet? Why should I not tell you what you already
know?—what you must already know? I do care for you—
for man and reformer, both—for— (*She is aflame, but
abruptly ceases and glances across at Tommy by the window,
warned instinctively that she must not give way to love in
her child's presence.*) Linda! Will you take Tommy down to
the machine—

KNOX: (*alarmed, interrupting, in low voice*). What are you
doing?

MARGARET: (*hushing Knox with a gesture*). I'll follow you right down.

Linda and Tommy proceed across stage toward right exit.

TOMMY: (*pausing before Knox and gravely extending his hand*). Good evening, Mr. Knox.

KNOX: (*awkwardly*). Good evening, Tommy. You take my word for it and look up this Lincoln question.

TOMMY: I shall. I'll ask Father about it.

MARGARET: (*significantly*). You attend to that, Linda. Nobody must know—this.

Linda nods.

Linda and Tommy make exit to right.

Margaret, seated, slips back her cloak, revealing herself in evening gown, and looks at Knox sumptuously, lovingly, and willingly.

KNOX: (*inflamed by the sight of her*). Don't! Don't! I can't stand it. Such sight of you fills me with madness. (*Margaret laughs low and triumphantly.*) I don't want to think of you as a woman. I must not. Allow me.

He rises and attempts to draw cloak about her shoulders, but she resists him. Yet does he succeed in partly cloaking her.

MARGARET: I want you to see me as a woman. I want you to think of me as a woman. I want you mad for me. (*She holds out her arms, the cloak slipping from them.*) I want— don't you see what I want? (*Knox sinks back in chair, attempting to shield his eyes with his hand. Slipping cloak fully back from her again.*) Look at me.

KNOX: (*looking, coming to his feet, and approaching her, with extended arms, murmuring softly*). Margaret. Margaret.

Margaret rises to meet him, and they are clasped in each other's arms.

Hubbard, peering forth through door, looks at them with an expression of cynical amusement. His gaze wanders, and he sees the documents, within arm's reach, on top of bookcase. He picks up documents, holds them to the light of stage to glance at them, and, with triumphant expression on face, disappears and closes door.

KNOX: (*holding Margaret from him and looking at her*). I love you. I do love you. But I had resolved never to speak it, never to let you know.

MARGARET: Silly man. I have known long that you loved me. You have told me so often and in so many ways. You could not look at me without telling me.

KNOX: You saw?

MARGARET: How could I help seeing? I was a woman. Only, with your voice you never spoke a word. Sit down there where I may look at you, and let me tell you. I shall do the speaking now. (*She urges him back into the desk chair and reseats herself. She makes as if to pull the cloak around her.*) Shall I?

KNOX: (*vehemently*). No, no! As you are. Let me feast my eyes upon you who are mine. I must be dreaming.

MARGARET: (*with a low, satisfied laugh of triumph*). Oh, you men! As of old, and as forever, you must be wooed through your senses. Did I display the wisdom of a Hypatia, the science of a Madame Curie, yet would you keep your iron control, throttling the voice of your heart with silence. But let me for a moment be Lilith, for a moment lay aside this garment constructed for the purpose of keeping out the chill of night, and on the instant you are fire and aflame, all voluble with love's desire.

KNOX: (*protestingly*). Margaret! It is not fair!

MARGARET: I love you—and—you?

KNOX: (*fervently and reverently*). I love you.

MARGARET: Then listen. I have told you of my girlhood and my dreams. I wanted to do what you are so nobly doing. And I did nothing. I could do nothing. I was not permitted. Always was I compelled to hold myself in check. It was to do what you are doing that I married. And that, too, failed me. My husband became a henchman of the Interests, my own father's tool for the perpetuation of the evils against which I desired to fight. (*She pauses.*) It has been a long fight, and I have been very tired, for always did I confront failure. My husband—I did not love him. I never loved him. I sold myself for the cause, and the cause profited nothing. (*Pause.*) Often I have lost faith— faith in everything, in God and man, in the hope of any righteousness ever prevailing. But again and again, by what you are doing, have you awakened me. I came tonight with no thought of self. I came to warn you, to help the good work on. I remained—thank God!—I remained to love you—and to be loved by you. I suddenly found myself, looking at you, very weary. I wanted you— you, more than anything in the world. (*She holds out her arms.*) Come to me. I want you—now.

Knox, in an ecstasy, comes to her. He seats himself on the broad arm of the chair and is drawn into her arms.

KNOX: But I have been tired at times. I was very tired tonight—and you came. And now I am glad, only glad.

MARGARET: I have been wanton tonight. I confess it. I am proud of it. But it was not—professional. It was the first time in my life. Almost do I regret—almost do I regret that I did not do it sooner—it has been crowned with such success. You have held me in your arms—your arms. Oh, you will never know what that first embrace meant to me. I am not a clod. I am not iron nor stone. I am a woman— a warm, breathing woman— (*She rises, and draws him to his feet.*) Kiss me, my dear lord and lover. Kiss me.

They embrace.

KNOX: (*passionately, looking about him wildly as if in search of something*). What shall we do? (*Suddenly releasing her and sinking back in his own chair almost in collapse.*) No. It cannot be. It is impossible. Oh, why could we not have met long ago? We would have worked together. What a comradeship it would have been.

MARGARET: But it is not too late.

KNOX: I have no right to you.

MARGARET: (*misunderstanding*). My husband? He has not been my husband for years. He has no rights. Who but you whom I love has any rights?

KNOX: No, it is not that. (*Snapping his fingers.*) That for him. (*Breaking down.*) Oh, if I were only the man and not the reformer! If I had no work to do!

MARGARET: (*coming to the back of his chair and caressing his hair*). We can work together.

KNOX: (*shaking his head under her fingers*). Don't! Don't! (*She persists and lays her cheek against his.*) You make it so hard. You tempt me so. (*He rises suddenly, takes her two hands in his, leads her gently to her chair, seats her, and reseats himself in desk chair.*) Listen. It is not your husband. But I have no right to you. Nor have you a right to me.

MARGARET: (*interrupting, jealously*). And who but I has any right to you?

KNOX: (*smiling sadly*). No, it is not that. There is no other woman. You are the one woman for me. But there are many others who have greater rights in me than you. I have been chosen by two hundred thousand citizens to represent them in the Congress of the United States. And there are many more— (*He breaks off suddenly and looks at her, at her arms and shoulders.*) Yes, please. Cover them up. Help me not to forget. (*Margaret does not obey.*) There are many more who have rights in me—the people, all the people, whose cause I have made mine. The children— there are two million child laborers in these United States. I cannot betray them. I cannot steal my happiness from them. This afternoon I talked of theft. But would not this, too, be theft?

MARGARET: (*sharply*). Howard! Wake up! Has our happiness turned your head?

KNOX: (*sadly*). Almost—and for a few wild moments, quite. There are all the children. Did I ever tell you of the tenement child who, when asked how he knew when spring came, answered: When he saw the saloons put up their swing doors.

MARGARET: (*irritated*). But what has all that to do with one man and one woman loving?

KNOX: Suppose we loved—you and I; suppose we loosed all the reins of our love. What would happen? You remember Gorki, the Russian patriot, when he came to New York, aflame with passion for the Russian Revolution. His purpose in visiting the land of liberty was to raise funds for that revolution. And because his marriage to the woman he loved was not of the essentially legal sort worshiped by the shopkeepers, and because the newspapers made a sensation of it, his whole mission was brought to failure. He was laughed and derided out of the esteem of the American people. That is what would happen to me. I should be slandered and laughed at. My power would be gone.

MARGARET: And even if so—what of it? Be slandered and laughed at. We will have each other. Other men will rise up to lead the people, and leading the people is a thankless task. Life is so short. We must clutch for the morsel of happiness that may be ours.

KNOX: Ah, if you knew, as I look into your eyes, how easy it would be to throw everything to the winds. But it would be theft.

MARGARET: (*rebelliously*). Let it be theft. Life is so short, dear. We are the biggest facts in the world—to each other.

KNOX: It is not myself alone, nor all my people. A moment ago you said no one but I had any right to you. You were wrong. Your child—

MARGARET: (*in sudden pain, pleadingly*). Don't!

KNOX: I must. I must save myself—and you. Tommy has rights in you. Theft again. What other name for it if you steal your happiness from him?

MARGARET: (*bending her head forward on her hand and weeping*). I have been so lonely—and then you—you came, and the world grew bright and warm—a few short minutes ago you held me—in your arms—a few short minutes ago and it seemed my dream of happiness had come true—and now you dash it from me—

KNOX: (*struggling to control himself now that she is no longer looking at him*). No, I ask you to dash it from yourself. I am not too strong. You must help me. You must call your child to your aid in helping me. I could go mad for you now— (*Rising impulsively and coming to her with arms outstretched to clasp her.*) Right now—

MARGARET: (*abruptly raising her head, and with one outstretched arm preventing the embrace*). Wait. (*She bows her head on her hand for a moment, to think and to win control of herself. Lifting her head and looking at him.*) Sit down— please. (*Knox reseats himself. A pause, during which she looks at him and loves him.*) Dear, I do so love you— (*Knox loses control and starts to rise.*) No! Sit there. I was weak. Yet I am not sorry. You are right. We must forgo each other. We cannot be thieves, even for love's sake. Yet I am glad that this has happened—that I have lain in your arms and had your lips on mine. The memory of it will be sweet always. (*She draws her cloak around her and rises. Knox rises.*) You are right. The future belongs to the children. There lies duty—yours, and mine in my small way. I am going now. We must not see each other ever again. We must work—and forget. But remember, my heart goes with you into the fight. My prayers will accompany every stroke. (*She hesitates, pauses, draws her cloak thoroughly around her in evidence of departure.*) Dear—will you kiss me—once—one last time? (*There is no passion in this kiss, which is the kiss of renunciation. Margaret herself terminates the embrace. Knox accompanies her silently to the door and places hand on knob.*)

KNOX: I wish I had something of you to have with me always —a photograph, that little one, you remember, which I liked so. (*She nods.*) Don't run the risk of sending it by messenger. Just mail it ordinarily.

MARGARET: I shall mail it tomorrow. I'll drop it in the box myself.

KNOX: (*kissing her hand*). Good-bye.

MARGARET: (*lingeringly*). But oh, my dear, I am glad and proud for what has happened. I would not erase a single line of it. (*She indicates for Knox to open door, which he does, but which he immediately closes as she continues speaking.*) There must be immortality. There must be a future life where you and I shall meet again. Good-bye. *They press each other's hands.*

Exit Margaret.

Knox stands a moment, staring at closed door, turns and looks about him indecisively, sees chair in which Margaret sat, goes over to it, kneels down, and buries his face.

Door to bedroom opens slowly and Hubbard peers out cautiously. He cannot see Knox.

HUBBARD: (*advancing, surprised*). What the deuce? Everybody gone?

KNOX: (*startled to his feet*). Where the devil did you come from?

HUBBARD: (*indicating bedroom*). In there. I was in there all the time.

KNOX: (*endeavoring to pass it off*). Oh, I had forgotten about you. Well, my callers are gone.

HUBBARD: (*walking over close to him and laughing at him with affected amusement*). Honest men are such dubs when they do go wrong.

KNOX: The door was closed all the time. You would not have dared to spy upon me.

HUBBARD: There was something familiar about the lady's voice.

KNOX: You heard! —What did you hear?

HUBBARD: Oh, nothing, nothing—a murmur of voices—and the woman's—I could swear I have heard her voice before. (*Knox shows his relief.*) Well, so long. (*Starts to move toward exit to right.*) You won't reconsider your decision?

KNOX: (*shaking his head*). No.

HUBBARD: (*pausing, open door in hand, and laughing cynically*). And yet it was but a moment ago that it seemed I heard you say there was no one whom you would not permit the world to know you saw.

KNOX: (*starting*). What do you mean?

HUBBARD: Good-bye.

Hubbard makes exit and closes door.

Knox wanders aimlessly to his desk, glances at the letter the reading of which had been interrupted by Hubbard's entry of first act, suddenly recollects the package of documents, and walks to low bookcase and looks on top.

KNOX: (*stunned*). The thief!

He looks about him wildly, then rushes like a madman in pursuit of Hubbard, making exit to right and leaving the door flying open.

Empty stage for a moment.

CURTAIN

ACT III

The library, used as a sort of semi-office by Starkweather at such times when he is in Washington. Door to right; also, door to right rear. At left rear is an alcove, without hangings, which is dark. To left are windows. To left, near windows, a flattop desk, with desk chair and desk telephone. Also, on desk, conspicuously, is a heavy dispatch box. At the center rear is a large screen. Extending across center back of room are heavy, old-fashioned bookcases, with swinging glass doors. The bookcases narrow about four feet from the floor, thus forming a ledge. Between left end of bookcases and alcove at left rear, high up on wall, hangs a large painting or steel engraving of Abraham Lincoln. In design and furnishings it is a simple, chaste room, coldly rigid and slightly old-fashioned.

It is 9:30 in the morning of the day succeeding previous act. Curtain discloses Starkweather seated at desk and Dobleman, to right of desk, standing.

STARKWEATHER: All right, though it is an unimportant publication. I'll subscribe.

DOBLEMAN: (*making note on pad*). Very well, sir. Two thousand. (*He consults his notes.*) Then there is *Vanderwater's Magazine.* Your subscription is due.

227

STARKWEATHER: How much?

DOBLEMAN: You have been paying fifteen thousand.

STARKWEATHER: It is too much. What is the regular subscription?

DOBLEMAN: A dollar a year.

STARKWEATHER: (*shaking his head emphatically*). It is too much.

DOBLEMAN: Professor Vanderwater also does good work with his lecturing. He is regularly on the Chautauqua Courses, and at that big meeting of the National Civic Federation his speech was exceptionally telling.

STARKWEATHER: (*doubtfully, about to give in*). All right— (*He pauses, as if recollecting something. Dobleman has begun to write down the note.*) No. I remember there was something in the papers about this Professor Vanderwater—a divorce, wasn't it? He has impaired his authority and his usefulness to me.

DOBLEMAN: It was his wife's fault.

STARKWEATHER: It is immaterial. His usefulness is impaired. Cut him down to ten thousand. It will teach him a lesson.

DOBLEMAN: Very good, sir.

STARKWEATHER: And the customary twenty thousand to *Cartwright's.*

DOBLEMAN: (*hesitatingly*). They have asked for more. They have enlarged the magazine, reorganized the stock, staff, everything.

STARKWEATHER: Hubbard's writing for it, isn't he?

DOBLEMAN: Yes, sir. And though I don't know, it is whispered that he is one of the heavy stockholders.

STARKWEATHER: A very capable man. He has served me well. How much do they want?

DOBLEMAN: They say that Nettman series of articles cost them twelve thousand alone and that they believe, in view of the exceptional service they are prepared to render, and are rendering, fifty thousand—

STARKWEATHER: (*shortly*). All right. How much have I given to University of Hanover this year?

DOBLEMAN: Seven—nine million, including that new library.

STARKWEATHER: (*sighing*). Education does cost. Anything more this morning?

DOBLEMAN: (*consulting notes*). Just one other—Mr. Rutland. His church, you know, sir, and that theological college. He told me he had been talking it over with you. He is anxious to know.

STARKWEATHER: He's very keen, I must say. Fifty thousand for the church and a hundred thousand for the college—I ask you candidly, is he worth it?

DOBLEMAN: The church is a very powerful molder of public opinion, and Mr. Rutland is very impressive. (*Running over the notes and producing a clipping.*) This is what he said in his sermon two weeks ago: "God has given to Mr. Starkweather the talent for making money as truly as God has given to other men the genius which manifests itself in literature and the arts and sciences."

STARKWEATHER: (*pleased*). He says it well.

DOBLEMAN: (*producing another clipping*). And this he said about you in last Sunday's sermon: "We are today rejoicing in the great light of the consecration of a great wealth to the advancement of the race. This vast wealth has been so consecrated by a man who all through life has walked in accord with the word, 'The love of Christ constraineth me.'"

STARKWEATHER: (*meditatively*). Dobleman, I have meant well. I mean well. I shall always mean well. I believe I am one of those few men to whom God, in his infinite wisdom, has given the stewardship of the people's wealth. It is a high trust, and despite the abuse and vilification heaped upon me, I shall remain faithful to it. (*Changing his tone abruptly to businesslike briskness.*) Very well. See that Mr. Rutland gets what he has asked for.

DOBLEMAN: Very good, sir. I shall telephone him. I know he is anxious to hear. (*Starting to leave the room.*) Shall I make the checks out in the usual way?

STARKWEATHER: Yes, except the Rutland one. I'll sign that myself. Let the others go through the regular channels. We take the 2:10 train for New York. Are you ready?

DOBLEMAN: (*indicating dispatch box*). All except the dispatch box.

STARKWEATHER: I'll take care of that myself. (*Dobleman starts to make exit to left, and Starkweather, taking notebook from pocket, glances into it and looks up.*) Dobleman.

DOBLEMAN: (*pausing*). Yes, sir.

STARKWEATHER: Mrs. Chalmers is here, isn't she?

DOBLEMAN: Yes, sir. She came a few minutes ago with her little boy. They are with Mrs. Starkweather.

STARKWEATHER: Please tell Mrs. Chalmers I wish to see her.

DOBLEMAN: Yes, sir.

Dobleman makes exit.

Maidservant enters from right rear, with card tray.

STARKWEATHER: (*examining card*). Show him in.

Maidservant makes exit right rear.

Pause, during which Starkweather consults notebook.

Maidservant reenters, showing in Hubbard.

Hubbard advances to desk.

Starkweather is so glad to see him that he half rises from his chair to shake hands.

STARKWEATHER: (*heartily*). I can only tell you that what you did was wonderful. Your telephone call last night was a great relief. Where are they?

HUBBARD: (*drawing package of documents from inside breast pocket and handing them over*). There they are—the complete set. I was fortunate.

STARKWEATHER: (*opening package and glancing at a number of the documents while he talks*). You are modest, Mr. Hubbard.

It required more—than fortune. It required ability—of no
mean order. The time was short. You had to think—and
act—with too great immediacy to be merely fortunate.
(*Hubbard bows, while Starkweather rearranges package.*)
There is no need for me to tell you how I appreciate your
service. I have increased my subscription to *Cartwright's*
to fifty thousand, and I shall speak to Dobleman, who
will remit to you a more substantial acknowledgment
than my mere thanks for the inestimable service you have
rendered. (*Hubbard bows.*) You—ah—you have read the
documents?

HUBBARD: I glanced through them. They were indeed serious.
But we have spiked Knox's guns. Without them, that
speech of his this afternoon becomes a farce—a howling
farce. Be sure you take good care of them. (*Indicating
documents, which Starkweather still holds.*) Gherst has a
long arm.

STARKWEATHER: He cannot reach me here. Besides, I go to
New York today, and I shall carry them with me. Mr.
Hubbard, you will forgive me— (*Starting to pack dispatch
box with papers and letters lying on desk.*) I am very busy.

HUBBARD: (*taking the hint*). Yes, I understand. I shall be going
now. I have to be at the club in five minutes.

STARKWEATHER: (*in course of packing dispatch box, he sets
certain packets of papers and several medium-sized account
books to one side in an orderly pile. He talks while he packs,
and Hubbard waits.*) I should like to talk with you some
more—in New York. Next time you are in town, be sure to
see me. I am thinking of buying the *Parthenon Magazine,*
and of changing its policy. I should like to have you
negotiate this, and there are other important things as
well. Good day, Mr. Hubbard. I shall see you in New
York—soon.

Hubbard and Starkweather shake hands.

Hubbard starts to make exit to right rear.
Margaret enters from right rear.
Starkweather goes on packing dispatch box through fol-
lowing scene.

HUBBARD: Mrs. Chalmers. (*Holding out hand, which Margaret*
takes very coldly, scarcely inclining her head, and starting to
pass on. Speaking suddenly and savagely.) You needn't be
so high and lofty, Mrs. Chalmers.

MARGARET: (*pausing and looking at him curiously, as if to*
ascertain whether he has been drinking). I do not understand.

HUBBARD: You always treated me this way, but the time for it
is past. I won't stand for your superior goodness anymore.
You really impressed me with it for a long time, and you
made me walk small. But I know better now. A pretty
game you've been playing—you, who are like any other
woman. Well, you know where you were last night. So
do I.

MARGARET: You are impudent.

HUBBARD: (*doggedly*). I said I knew where you were last
night. Mr. Knox also knows where you were. But I'll
wager your husband doesn't.

MARGARET: You spy! (*Indicating her father.*) I suppose you
have told—him.

HUBBARD: Why should I?

MARGARET: You are his creature.

HUBBARD: If it will ease your suspense, let me tell you that I
have not told him. But I do protest to you that you must
treat me with more—more kindness.

Margaret makes no sign but passes on utterly oblivious of him.
Hubbard stares angrily at her and makes exit.
Starkweather, who is finishing packing, puts the documents
last inside box, and closes and locks it. To one side is the
orderly stack of the several account books and packets of
papers.

STARKWEATHER: Good morning, Margaret. I sent for you because we did not finish that talk last night. Sit down. (*She gets a chair for herself and sits down.*) You always were hard to manage, Margaret. You have had too much will for a woman. Yet I did my best for you. Your marriage with Tom was especially auspicious—a rising man, of good family and a gentleman, eminently suitable—

MARGARET: (*interrupting bitterly*). I don't think you were considering your daughter at all in the matter. I know your views on woman and woman's place. I have never counted for anything with you. Neither has Mother, nor Connie, when business was uppermost, and business always is uppermost with you. I sometimes wonder if you think a woman has a soul. As for my marriage—you saw that Tom could be useful to you. He had the various distinctive points you have mentioned. Better than that, he was pliable, capable of being molded to perform your work, to manipulate machine politics and procure for you the legislation you desired. You did not consider what kind of a husband he would make for your daughter whom you did not know. But you gave your daughter to him—sold her to him—because you needed him— (*Laughs hysterically.*) In your business.

STARKWEATHER: (*angrily*). Margaret! You must not speak that way. (*Relaxing.*) Ah, you do not change. You were always that way, always bent on having your will—

MARGARET: Would to God I had been more successful in having it.

STARKWEATHER: (*testily*). This is all beside the question. I sent for you to tell you that this must stop—this association with a man of the type and character of Knox—a dreamer, a charlatan, a scoundrel—

MARGARET: It is not necessary to abuse him.

STARKWEATHER: It must stop—that is all. Do you understand? It must stop.

MARGARET: (*quietly*). It has stopped. I doubt that I shall ever see him again. He will never come to my house again, at any rate. Are you satisfied?

STARKWEATHER: Perfectly. Of course you know I have never doubted you—that—that way.

MARGARET: (*quietly*). How little you know women. In your comprehension we are automatons, puppets, with no hearts nor heats of desire of our own, with no springs of conduct save those of the immaculate and puritanical sort that New England crystallized a century or so ago.

STARKWEATHER: (*suspiciously*). You mean that you and this man—?

MARGARET: I mean nothing has passed between us. I mean that I am Tom's wife and Tommy's mother. What I did mean you have no more understood than you understand me—or any woman.

STARKWEATHER: (*relieved*). It is well.

MARGARET: (*continuing*). And it is so easy. The concept is simple. A woman is human. That is all. Yet I do believe it is news to you.

Enters Dobleman from right carrying a check in his hand. Starkweather, about to speak, pauses.

Dobleman hesitates, and Starkweather nods for him to advance.

DOBLEMAN: (*greeting Margaret, and addressing Starkweather*). This check. You said you would sign it yourself.

STARKWEATHER: Yes, that is Rutland's. (*Looks for pen. Dobleman offers his fountain pen.*) No, my own pen.

Unlocks dispatch box, gets pen, and signs check. Leaves dispatch box open.

Dobleman takes check and makes exit to right.

STARKWEATHER: (*picking up documents from top of pile in*

open box). This man Knox. I studied him yesterday. A man of great energy and ideals. Unfortunately, he is a sentimentalist. He means right—I grant him that. But he does not understand practical conditions. He is more dangerous to the welfare of the United States than ten thousand anarchists. And he is not practical. (*Holding up documents.*) Behold, stolen from my private files by a yellow journal sneak thief and turned over to him. He thought to buttress his speech with them this afternoon. And yet, so hopelessly unpractical is he that, you see, they are already back in the rightful owner's hands.

MARGARET: Then his speech is ruined?

STARKWEATHER: Absolutely. The wheels are all ready to turn. The good people of the United States will dismiss him with roars of laughter—a good phrase, that. Hubbard's, I believe. (*Dropping documents on the open cover of dispatch box, picking up the pile of several account books and packets of papers, and rising.*) One moment. I must put these away. *Starkweather goes to alcove at left rear. He presses a button, and alcove is lighted by electricity, discovering the face of a large safe. During the following scene he does not look around, being occupied with working the combination, opening the safe, putting away account books and packets of papers, and with examining other packets which are in safe.*

Margaret looks at documents lying on open cover of dispatch box and, glancing quickly about room, takes a sudden resolution. She seizes documents, makes as if to run wildly from the room, stops abruptly to reconsider, and changes her mind. She looks about room for a hiding place, and her eyes rest on portrait of Lincoln. Moving swiftly, picking up a light chair on the way, she goes to corner of bookcase nearest to portrait, steps on chair, and from chair to ledge of bookcase, where, clinging, she reaches out and up and drops documents

*behind portrait. Stepping quickly down, with handkerchief
she wipes ledge on which she has stood, also the seat of the
chair. She carries chair back to where she found it, and
reseats herself in chair by desk.*

*Starkweather locks safe, emerges from alcove, turns off
alcove lights, advances to desk chair, and sits down. He is
about to close and lock dispatch box when he discovers
documents are missing. He is very quiet about it and
examines contents of box carefully.*

STARKWEATHER: (*quietly*). Has anybody been in the room?

MARGARET: No.

STARKWEATHER: (*looking at her searchingly*). A most unprecedented thing has occurred. When I went to the safe a
moment ago, I left these documents on the cover of the
dispatch box. Nobody has been in the room but you. The
documents are gone. Give them to me.

MARGARET: I have not been out of the room.

STARKWEATHER: I know that. Give them to me. (*A pause.*) You
have them. Give them to me.

MARGARET: I haven't them.

STARKWEATHER: That is a lie. Give them to me.

MARGARET: (*rising*). I tell you I haven't them—

STARKWEATHER: (*also rising*). That is a lie.

MARGARET: (*turning and starting to cross room*). Very well, if
you do not believe me—

STARKWEATHER: (*interrupting*). Where are you going?

MARGARET: Home.

STARKWEATHER: (*imperatively*). No, you are not. Come back
here. (*Margaret comes back and stands by chair.*) You shall
not leave this room. Sit down.

MARGARET: I prefer to stand.

STARKWEATHER: Sit down. (*She still stands, and he grips her
by arm, forcing her down into chair.*) Sit down. Before
you leave this room, you shall return those documents.
This is more important than you realize. It transcends all

ordinary things of life as you have known it, and you will compel me to do things far harsher than you can possibly imagine. I can forget that you are a daughter of mine. I can forget that you are even a woman. If I have to tear them from you, I shall get them. Give them to me. (*A pause.*) What are you going to do? (*Margaret shrugs her shoulders.*) What have you to say? (*Margaret again shrugs her shoulders.*) What have you to say?

MARGARET: Nothing.

STARKWEATHER: (*puzzled, changing tactics, sitting down, and talking calmly*). Let us talk this over quietly. You have no shred of right of any sort to those documents. They are mine. They were stolen by a sneak thief from my private files. Only this morning—a few minutes ago—did I get them back. They are mine, I tell you. They belong to me. Give them back.

MARGARET: I tell you I haven't them.

STARKWEATHER: You have got them about you somewhere, concealed in your breast there. It will not save you. I tell you, I shall have them. I warn you. I don't want to proceed to extreme measures. Give them to me. (*He starts to press desk button, pauses, and looks at her.*) Well? (*Margaret shrugs her shoulders. He presses button twice.*) I have sent for Dobleman. You have one chance before he comes. Give them to me.

MARGARET: Father, will you believe me just this once? Let me go. I tell you I haven't the documents. I tell you that if you let me leave this room, I shall not carry them away with me. I tell you this on my honor. Do you believe me? Tell me that you do believe me.

STARKWEATHER: I do believe you. You say they are not on you. I believe you. Now tell me where they are—you have them hidden somewhere—(*glancing about room*)—and you can go at once.

Dobleman enters from right and advances to desk.

Starkweather and Margaret remain silent.

DOBLEMAN: You rang for me.

STARKWEATHER: (*with one last questioning glance at Margaret, who remains impassive*). Yes, I did. Have you been in that other room all the time?

DOBLEMAN: Yes, sir.

STARKWEATHER: Did anybody pass through and enter this room?

DOBLEMAN: No, sir.

STARKWEATHER: Very well. We'll see what the maid has to say. (*He presses button once.*) Margaret, I give you one last chance.

MARGARET: I have told you that if I leave this room, I shall not take them with me.

Maid enters from right rear and advances.

STARKWEATHER: Has anybody come into this room from the hall in the last few minutes?

MAID: No, sir, not since Mrs. Chalmers came in.

STARKWEATHER: How do you know?

MAID: I was in the hall, sir, dusting all the time.

STARKWEATHER: That will do. (*Maid makes exit to right rear.*) Dobleman, a very unusual thing has occurred. Mrs. Chalmers and I have been alone in this room. Those letters stolen by Gherst had been returned to me by Hubbard but the moment before. They were on my desk. I turned my back for a moment to go to the safe. When I came back, they were gone.

DOBLEMAN: (*embarrassed*). Yes, sir.

STARKWEATHER: Mrs. Chalmers took them. She has them now.

DOBLEMAN: (*attempts to speak, stammers*). Er—er—yes, sir.

STARKWEATHER: I want them back. What is to be done? (*Dobleman remains in hopeless confusion.*) Well!

DOBLEMAN: (*speaking hurriedly and hopefully*). S-send for Mr. Hubbard. He got them for you before.

STARKWEATHER: A good suggestion. Telephone for him. You should find him at the Press Club. (*Dobleman starts to make exit to right.*) Don't leave the room. Use this telephone. (*Indicating desk telephone. Dobleman moves around to left of desk and uses telephone standing up.*) From now on no one leaves the room. If my daughter can be guilty of such a theft, it is plain I can trust no one—no one.

DOBLEMAN: (*speaking in transmitter*). Red 6-2-4. Yes, please. *Waits.*

STARKWEATHER: (*rising*). Call Senator Chalmers as well. Tell him to come immediately.

DOBLEMAN: Yes, sir—immediately.

STARKWEATHER: (*starting to cross stage to center and speaking to Margaret*). Come over here. (*Margaret follows. She is obedient, frightened, very subdued—but resolved.*) Why have you done this? Were you truthful when you said there was nothing between you and this man Knox?

MARGARET: Father, don't discuss this before the—(*indicating Dobleman*)—the servants.

STARKWEATHER: You should have considered that before you stole the documents.

Dobleman, in the meantime, is telephoning in a low voice.

MARGARET: There are certain dignities—

STARKWEATHER: (*interrupting*). Not for a thief. (*Speaking intensely and in a low voice.*) Margaret, it is not too late. Give them back, and no one shall know.

A pause, in which Margaret is silent, in the throes of indecision.

DOBLEMAN: Mr. Hubbard says he will be here in three minutes. Fortunately, Senator Chalmers is with him.

Starkweather nods and looks at Margaret.

Door at left rear opens, and enter Mrs. Starkweather and Connie. They are dressed for the street and evidently just going out.

MRS. STARKWEATHER: (*speaking in a rush*). We are just going out, Anthony. You were certainly wrong in making us attempt to take that 2:10 train. I simply can't make it. I know I can't. It would have been much wiser— (*Suddenly apprehending the strain of the situation between Starkweather and Margaret.*) Why, what is the matter?

STARKWEATHER: (*patently disturbed by their entrance, speaking to Dobleman, who has finished with the telephone*). Lock the doors.

Dobleman proceeds to obey.

MRS. STARKWEATHER: Mercy me! Anthony! What has happened? (*A pause.*) Madge! What has happened?

STARKWEATHER: You will have to wait here a few minutes, that is all.

MRS. STARKWEATHER: But I must keep my engagements. And I haven't a minute to spare. (*Looking at Dobleman locking doors.*) I do not understand.

STARKWEATHER: (*grimly*). You will shortly. I can trust no one anymore. When my daughter sees fit to steal—

MRS. STARKWEATHER: Steal!—Margaret! What have you been doing now?

MARGARET: Where is Tommy?

Mrs. Starkweather is too confounded to answer and can only stare from face to face.

Margaret looks her anxiety to Connie.

CONNIE: He is already down in the machine waiting for us. You are coming, aren't you?

STARKWEATHER: Let him wait in the machine. Margaret will come when I get done with her.

A knock is heard at right rear.

Starkweather looks at Dobleman and signifies that he is to open door.

Dobleman unlocks door, and Hubbard and Chalmers enter. Beyond the shortest of nods and recognitions with eyes, greetings are cut short by the strain that is on all. Dobleman relocks door.

STARKWEATHER: (*plunging into it*). Look here, Tom. You know those letters Gherst stole. Mr. Hubbard recovered them from Knox and returned them to me this morning. Within five minutes Margaret stole them from me—here, right in this room. She has not left the room. They are on her now. I want them.

CHALMERS: (*who is obviously incapable of coping with his wife, and who is panting for breath, his hand pressed to his side*). Madge, is this true?

MARGARET: I haven't them. I tell you I haven't them.

STARKWEATHER: Where are they, then? (*She does not answer.*) If they are in the room, we can find them. Search the room. Tom, Mr. Hubbard, Dobleman. They must be recovered at any cost.

While a thorough search of the room is being made, Mrs. Starkweather, overcome, has Connie assist her to seat at left. Margaret also seats herself, in same chair at desk.

CHALMERS: (*pausing from search, while others continue*). There is no place to look for them. They are not in the room. Are you sure you didn't mislay them?

STARKWEATHER: Nonsense. Margaret took them. They are a bulky package and not easily hidden. If they aren't in the room, then she has them on her.

CHALMERS: Madge, give them up.

MARGARET: I haven't them.

Chalmers, stepping suddenly up to her, starts feeling for the papers, running his hands over her dress.

MARGARET: (*springing to her feet and striking him in the face with her open palm*). How dare you!

Chalmers recoils; Mrs. Starkweather is threatened with hysteria and is calmed by the frightened Connie, while Starkweather looks on grimly.

HUBBARD: (*giving up search of room*). Possibly it would be better to let me retire, Mr. Starkweather.

STARKWEATHER: No, those papers are here in this room. If nobody leaves, there will be no possible chance for the papers to get out of the room. What would you recommend doing, Hubbard?

HUBBARD: (*hesitatingly*). Under the circumstances I don't like to suggest—

STARKWEATHER: Go on.

HUBBARD: First, I would make sure that she—er—Mrs. Chalmers has taken them.

STARKWEATHER: I have made that certain.

CHALMERS: But what motive could she have for such an act? *Hubbard looks wise.*

STARKWEATHER: (*to Hubbard*). You know more about this than would appear. What is it?

HUBBARD: I'd rather not. It is too—(*looks significantly at Mrs. Starkweather and Connie*)—er—delicate.

STARKWEATHER: This affair has gone beyond all delicacy. What is it?

MARGARET: No! No!
Chalmers and Starkweather look at her with sudden suspicion.

STARKWEATHER: Go on, Mr. Hubbard.

HUBBARD: I'd—I'd rather not.

STARKWEATHER: (*savagely*). I say go on.

HUBBARD: (*with simulated reluctance*). Last night—I saw—I was in Knox's rooms—

MARGARET: (*interrupting*). One moment, please. Let him speak, but first send Connie away.

STARKWEATHER: No one shall leave this room till the documents are produced. Margaret, give me the letters, and Connie can leave quietly, and even will Hubbard's lips remain sealed. They will never breathe a word of whatever shameful thing his eyes saw. This I promise you. (*A pause,*

wherein he waits vainly for Margaret to make a decision.)
Go on, Hubbard.

MARGARET: (*who is terror-stricken and has been wavering*). No!
Don't! I'll tell. I'll give you back the documents. (*All are
expectant. She wavers again and steels herself to resolution.*)
No, I haven't them. Say all you have to say.

STARKWEATHER: You see. She has them. She said she would
give them back. (*To Hubbard.*) Go on.

HUBBARD: Last night—

CONNIE: (*springing up*). I won't stay! (*She rushes to left rear
and finds door locked.*) Let me out! Let me out!

MRS. STARKWEATHER: (*moaning and lying back in chair, legs
stretched out and giving preliminary twitches and jerks of
hysteria*). I shall die! I shall die! I know I shall die!

STARKWEATHER: (*sternly, to Connie*). Go back to your mother.

CONNIE: (*returning reluctantly to side of Mrs. Starkweather,
sitting down beside her, and putting fingers in her own
ears*). I won't listen! I won't listen!

STARKWEATHER: (*sternly*). Take your fingers down.

HUBBARD: Hang it all, Chalmers, I wish I were out of this. I
don't want to testify.

STARKWEATHER: Take your fingers down. (*Connie reluctantly
removes her fingers.*) Now, Hubbard.

HUBBARD: I protest. I am being dragged into this.

CHALMERS: You can't help yourself now. You have cast black
suspicions on my wife.

HUBBARD: All right. She—Mrs. Chalmers visited Knox in his
rooms last night.

MRS. STARKWEATHER: (*bursting out*). Oh! Oh! My Madge! It is
a lie! A lie!

Kicks violently with her legs.

Connie soothes her.

CHALMERS: You've got to prove that, Hubbard. If you have
made any mistake, it will go hard with you.

HUBBARD: (*indicating Margaret*). Look at her. Ask her.

Chalmers looks at Margaret with growing suspicion.

MARGARET: Linda was with me. And Tommy. I had to see Mr. Knox on a very important matter. I went there in the machine. I took Linda and Tommy right into Mr. Knox's room.

CHALMERS: (*relieved*). Ah, that puts a different complexion on it.

HUBBARD: That is not all. Mrs. Chalmers sent the maid and the boy down to the machine and remained.

MARGARET: (*quickly*). But only for a moment.

HUBBARD: Much longer—much, much longer. I know how long I was kicking my heels and waiting.

MARGARET: (*desperately*). I say it was but for a moment—a short moment.

STARKWEATHER: (*abruptly, to Hubbard*). Where were you?

HUBBARD: In Knox's bedroom. The fool had forgotten all about me. He was too delighted with his—er—new visitor.

STARKWEATHER: You said you saw.

HUBBARD: The bedroom door was ajar. I opened it.

STARKWEATHER: What did you see?

MARGARET: (*appealing to Hubbard*). Have you no mercy? I say it was only a moment.

Hubbard shrugs his shoulders.

STARKWEATHER: We'll settle the length of that moment. Tommy is here, and so is the maid. Connie, Margaret's maid is here, isn't she? (*Connie does not answer.*) Answer me!

CONNIE: Yes.

STARKWEATHER: Dobleman. Ring for a maid and tell her to fetch Tommy and Mrs. Chalmers's maid.

Dobleman goes to desk and pushes button once.

MARGARET: No! Not Tommy!

STARKWEATHER: (*looking shrewdly at Margaret, to Dobleman*). Mrs. Chalmers's maid will do.

A knock is heard at left rear. Dobleman opens door and talks to maid. Closes door.

STARKWEATHER: Lock it.

Dobleman locks door.

CHALMERS: (*coming over to Margaret*). So you, the immaculate one, have been playing fast and loose.

MARGARET: You have no right to talk to me that way, Tom—

CHALMERS: I am your husband.

MARGARET: You have long since ceased being that.

CHALMERS: What do you mean?

MARGARET: I mean just what you have in mind about yourself right now.

CHALMERS: Madge, you are merely conjecturing. You know nothing against me.

MARGARET: I know everything—and without evidence, if you please. I am a woman. It is your atmosphere. Faugh! You have exhaled it for years. I doubt not that proofs, as you would call them, could have been easily obtained. But I was not interested. I had my boy. When he came, I gave you up, Tom. You did not seem to need me anymore.

CHALMERS: And so, in retaliation, you took up with this fellow Knox.

MARGARET: No, no. It is not true, Tom. I tell you it is not true.

CHALMERS: You were there last night, in his rooms alone— how long, we shall soon find out— (*Knock is heard at left rear. Dobleman proceeds to unlock door.*) And now you have stolen your father's private papers for your lover.

MARGARET: He is not my lover.

CHALMERS: But you have acknowledged that you have the papers. For whom, save Knox, could you have stolen them?

Linda enters. She is white and strained and looks at Margaret for some cue as to what she is to do.

STARKWEATHER: That is the woman. (*To Linda.*) Come here.

(*Linda advances reluctantly.*) Where were you last night?
You know what I mean. (*She does not speak.*) Answer me.

LINDA: I don't know what you mean, sir—unless—

STARKWEATHER: Yes, that's it. Go on.

LINDA: But I don't think you have any right to ask me such
questions. What if I—if I did go out with my young man—

STARKWEATHER: (*to Margaret*). A very faithful young woman
you've got. (*Briskly, to the others.*) There's nothing to be
got out of her. Send for Tommy. Dobleman, ring the bell.
Dobleman starts to obey.

MARGARET: (*stopping Dobleman*). No, no, not Tommy. Tell
them, Linda. (*Linda looks appealingly at her. Kindly.*) Don't
mind me. Tell them the truth.

CHALMERS: (*breaking in*). The whole truth.

MARGARET: Yes, Linda, the whole truth.
Linda, looking very woeful, nerves herself for the ordeal.

STARKWEATHER: Never mind, Dobleman. (*To Linda.*) Very
well. You were at Mr. Knox's rooms last night, with your
mistress and Tommy.

LINDA: Yes, sir.

STARKWEATHER: Your mistress sent you and Tommy out of
the room.

LINDA: Yes, sir.

STARKWEATHER: You waited in the machine.

LINDA: Yes, sir.

STARKWEATHER: (*abruptly springing the point he has been
working up to*). How long?
*Linda perceives the gist of the questioning just as she is
opening her mouth to reply, and she does not speak.*

MARGARET: (*with deliberate calmness of despair*). Half an
hour—an hour—any length of time your shameful minds
dictate. That will do, Linda. You can go.

STARKWEATHER: No, you don't. Stand over there to one side.
(*To the others.*) The papers are in this room, and I shall
keep my mind certain on that point.

HUBBARD: I think I have shown the motive.

CONNIE: You are a beast!

CHALMERS: You haven't told what you saw.

HUBBARD: I saw them in each other's arms—several times. Then I found the stolen documents where Knox had thrown them down. So I pocketed them and closed the door.

CHALMERS: How long after that did they remain together?

HUBBARD: Quite a time, quite a long time.

CHALMERS: And when you last saw them?

HUBBARD: They were in each other's arms—quite enthusiastically, I may say, in each other's arms.
Chalmers is crushed.

MARGARET: (*to Hubbard*). You coward. (*Hubbard smiles. To Starkweather.*) When are you going to call off this hound of yours?

STARKWEATHER: When I get the papers. You see what you've been made to pay for them already. Now listen to me closely. Tom, you listen, too. You know the value of these letters. If they are not recovered, they will precipitate a turnover that means not merely money but control and power. I doubt that even you would be reelected. So what we have heard in this room must be forgotten—absolutely forgotten. Do you understand?

CHALMERS: But it is adultery.

STARKWEATHER: It is not necessary for that word to be mentioned. The point is that everything must be as it was formerly.

CHALMERS: Yes, I understand.

STARKWEATHER: (*to Margaret*). You hear. Tom will make no trouble. Now give me the papers. They are mine, you know.

MARGARET: It seems to me the people, who have been lied to, and cajoled, and stolen from, are the rightful owners, not you.

STARKWEATHER: Are you doing this out of love for this—this man, this demagogue?

MARGARET: For the people, the children, the future.

STARKWEATHER: Faugh! Answer me.

MARGARET: (*slowly*). Almost I do not know. Almost I do not know.

A knock is heard at left rear. Dobleman answers.

DOBLEMAN: (*looking at card Maid has given him, to Starkweather*). Mr. Rutland.

STARKWEATHER: (*making an impatient gesture, then abruptly changing his mind, speaking grimly*). Very well. Bring him in. I've paid a lot for the Church; now we'll see what the Church can do for me.

CONNIE: (*impulsively crossing stage to Margaret, putting arms around her, and weeping*). Please, please, Madge, give up the papers, and everything will be hushed up. You heard what Father said. Think what it means to me if this scandal comes out. Father will hush it up. Not a soul will dare to breathe a word of it. Give him the papers.

MARGARET: (*kissing her, shaking head, and setting her aside*). No, I can't. But Connie, dearest— (*Connie pauses.*) It is not true, Connie. He—he is not my lover. Tell me that you believe me.

CONNIE: (*caressing her*). I do believe you. But won't you return the papers—for my sake?

A knock at door.

MARGARET: I can't.

Enter Rutland.

Connie returns to take care of Mrs. Starkweather.

RUTLAND: (*advances beamingly upon Starkweather*). My, what a family gathering. I hastened on at once, my dear Mr. Starkweather, to thank you in person, ere you fled away to New York, for your generously splendid—yes, generously splendid—contribution—

Here the strained situation dawns upon him, and he remains helplessly with mouth open, looking from one to another.

STARKWEATHER: A theft has been committed, Mr. Rutland. My daughter has stolen something very valuable from me—a package of private papers so important—well, if she succeeds in making them public, I shall be injured to such an extent financially that there won't be any more generously splendid donations for you or anybody else. I have done my best to persuade her to return what she has stolen. Now you try. Bring her to a realization of the madness of what she is doing.

RUTLAND: (*quite at sea, hemming and hawing*). As your spiritual adviser, Mrs. Chalmers—if this be true—I recommend—I suggest—I—ahem—I entreat—

MARGARET: Please, Mr. Rutland, don't be ridiculous. Father is only making a stalking horse out of you. Whatever I may have done, or not done, I believe I am doing right. The whole thing is infamous. The people have been lied to and robbed, and you are merely lending yourself to the infamy of perpetuating the lying and the robbing. If you persist in obeying my father's orders—yes, orders—you will lead me to believe that you are actuated by desire for more of those generously splendid donations.

Starkweather sneers.

RUTLAND: (*embarrassed, hopelessly at sea*). This is, I fear—ahem—too delicate a matter, Mr. Starkweather, for me to interfere. I would suggest that it be advisable for me to withdraw—ahem—

STARKWEATHER: (*musingly*). So the Church fails me, too. (*To Rutland.*) No, you shall stay right here.

MARGARET: Father, Tommy is down in the machine alone. Won't you let me go?

STARKWEATHER: Give me the papers.

Mrs. Starkweather rises and totters across to Margaret, moaning and whimpering.

MRS. STARKWEATHER: Madge, Madge, it can't be true. I don't believe it. I know you have not done this awful thing. No daughter of mine could be guilty of such wickedness. I refuse to believe my ears—

Mrs. Starkweather sinks suddenly on her knees before Margaret, with clasped hands, weeping hysterically.

STARKWEATHER: (*stepping to her side*). Get up. (*Hesitates and thinks.*) No, go on. She might listen to you.

MARGARET: (*attempting to raise her mother*). Don't, Mother, don't. Please get up. (*Mrs. Starkweather resists her hysterically.*) You don't understand, Mother. Please, please, get up.

MRS. STARKWEATHER: Madge, I, your mother, implore you on my bended knees. Give up the papers to your father, and I shall forget all I have heard. Think of the family name. I don't believe it, not a word of it; but think of the shame and disgrace. Think of me. Think of Connie, your sister. Think of Tommy. You'll have your father in a terrible state. And you'll kill me. (*Moaning and rolling her head.*) I'm going to be sick. I know I am going to be sick.

MARGARET: (*bending over mother and raising her, while Connie comes across stage to help support mother*). Mother, you do not understand. More is at stake than the good name of the family or—(*looking at Rutland*)—God. You speak of Connie and Tommy. There are two millions of Connies and Tommys working as child laborers in the United States today. Think of them. And besides, Mother, these are all lies you have heard. There is nothing between Mr. Knox and me. He is not my lover. I am not the—the shameful thing—these men have said I am.

CONNIE: (*appealingly*). Madge.

MARGARET: (*appealingly*). Connie. Trust me. I am right. I know I am right.

Mrs. Starkweather, supported by Connie, moaning incoherently, is led back across stage to chair.

STARKWEATHER: Margaret, a few minutes ago, when you told me there was nothing between you and this man, you lied to me—lied to me as only a wicked woman can lie.

MARGARET: It is clear that you believe the worst.

STARKWEATHER: There is nothing less than the worst to be believed. Besides, more heinous than your relations with this man is what you have done here in this room, stolen from me, and practically before my very eyes. Well, you have crossed your will with mine, and in affairs beyond your province. This is a man's game in which you are attempting to play, and you shall take the consequences. Tom will apply for a divorce.

MARGARET: That threat, at least, is without power.

STARKWEATHER: And by that means we can break Knox as effectually as by any other. That is one thing the good stupid people will not tolerate in a chosen representative. We will make such a scandal of it—

MRS. STARKWEATHER: (*shocked*). Anthony!

STARKWEATHER: (*glancing irritably at his wife and continuing*). Another thing. Being proven an adulterous woman, morally unfit for companionship with your child, your child will be taken away from you.

MARGARET: No, no. That cannot be. I have done nothing wrong. No court, no fair-minded judge, would so decree on the evidence of a creature like that.
Indicating Hubbard.

HUBBARD: My evidence is supported. In an adjoining room were two men. I happen to know, because I placed them there. They were your father's men, at that. There is such a thing as seeing through a locked door. They saw.

MARGARET: And they would swear to—to anything.

HUBBARD: I doubt not they will know to what to swear.

STARKWEATHER: Margaret, I have told you some, merely some, of the things I shall do. It is not too late. Return the papers, and everything will be forgotten.

MARGARET: You would condone this—this adultery. You, who have just said that I was morally unfit to have my own boy, will permit me to retain him. I had never dreamed, Father, that your own immorality would descend to such vile depths. Believing this shameful thing of me, you will forgive and forget it all for the sake of a few scraps of paper that stand for money, that stand for a license to rob and steal from the people. Is this your morality—money?

STARKWEATHER: I have my morality. It is not money. I am only a steward, but so highly do I conceive the duties of my stewardship—

MARGARET: (*interrupting, bitterly*). The thefts and lies and all common little sins like adulteries are not to stand in the way of your high duties—that the end hallows the means.

STARKWEATHER: (*shortly*). Precisely.

MARGARET: (*to Rutland*). There is Jesuitism, Mr. Rutland. I would suggest that you, as my father's spiritual adviser—

STARKWEATHER: Enough of this foolery. Give me the papers.

MARGARET: I haven't them.

STARKWEATHER: What's to be done, Hubbard?

HUBBARD: She has them. She has as much as acknowledged that they are not elsewhere in the room. She has not been out of the room. There is nothing to do but search her.

STARKWEATHER: Nothing else remains to be done. Dobleman and you, Hubbard, take her behind the screen. Strip her. Recover the papers.

Dobleman is in a proper funk, but Hubbard betrays no unwillingness.

CHALMERS: No, that I shall not permit. Hubbard shall have nothing to do with this.

MARGARET: It is too late, Tom. You have stood by and allowed me to be stripped of everything else. A few clothes do not matter now. If I am to be stripped and searched by men, Mr. Hubbard will serve as well as any other man. Perhaps Mr. Rutland would like to lend his assistance.

CONNIE: Oh, Madge! Give them up. (*Margaret shakes her head. To Starkweather.*) Then let me search her, Father.

STARKWEATHER: You are too willing. I don't want volunteers. I doubt that I can trust you any more than your sister.

CONNIE: Let Mother, then.

STARKWEATHER: (*sneering*). Margaret could smuggle a steamer trunk of documents past her.

CONNIE: But not the men, Father! Not the men!

STARKWEATHER: Why not? She has shown herself dead to all shame. (*Imperatively.*) Dobleman!

DOBLEMAN: (*thinking his time has come, and almost dying*). Y-y-yes, sir.

STARKWEATHER: Call in the servants.

MRS. STARKWEATHER: (*crying out in protest*). Anthony!

STARKWEATHER: Would you prefer her to be searched by the men?

MRS. STARKWEATHER: (*subsiding*). I shall die, I shall die. I know I shall die.

STARKWEATHER: Dobleman. Ring for the servants. (*Dobleman, who has been hesitant, crosses to desk and pushes button, then returns toward door.*) Send in the maids and the housekeeper. (*Linda, blindly desiring to be of some assistance, starts impulsively toward Margaret.*) Stand over there—in the corner.

Indicating right front.

Linda pauses irresolutely, and Margaret nods to her to obey and smiles encouragement. Linda, protesting in every fiber of her, goes to right front.

A knock at right rear, and Dobleman unlocks door, confers with Maid, and closes and locks door.

STARKWEATHER: (*to Margaret*). This is no time for trifling, nor for mawkish sentimentality. Return the papers or take the consequences.

Margaret makes no answer.

CHALMERS: You have taken a hand in a man's game, and you've got to play it out or quit. Give up the papers.

Margaret remains resolved and impassive.

HUBBARD: (*suavely*). Allow me to point out, my dear Mrs. Chalmers, that you are not merely stealing from your father. You are playing the traitor to your class.

STARKWEATHER: And causing irreparable damage.

MARGARET: (*firing up suddenly and pointing to Lincoln's portrait*). I doubt not he caused irreparable damage when he freed the slaves and preserved the Union. Yet he recognized no classes. I'd rather be a traitor to my class than to him.

STARKWEATHER: Demagoguery. Demagoguery.

A knock at right rear. Dobleman opens door. Enter Mrs. Middleton, who is the Housekeeper, followed by two House-maids. They pause at rear. Housekeeper to the fore and looking expectantly at Starkweather. The Maids appear timid and frightened.

HOUSEKEEPER: Yes, sir.

STARKWEATHER: Mrs. Middleton, you have the two maids to assist you. Take Mrs. Chalmers behind that screen there and search her. Strip all her clothes from her and make a careful search.

Maids show perturbation.

HOUSEKEEPER: (*self-possessed*). Yes, sir. What am I to search for?

STARKWEATHER: Papers, documents, anything unusual. Turn them over to me when you find them.

MARGARET: (*in a sudden panic*). This is monstrous! This is monstrous!

STARKWEATHER: So is your theft of the documents monstrous.

MARGARET: (*appealing to the other men, ignoring Rutland and not considering Dobleman at all*). You cowards! Will you stand by and permit this thing to be done? Tom, have you one atom of manhood in you?

CHALMERS: (*doggedly*). Return the papers, then.

MARGARET: Mr. Rutland—

RUTLAND: (*very awkwardly and oilily*). My dear Mrs. Chalmers. I assure you the whole circumstance is unfortunate. But you are so palpably in the wrong that I cannot interfere— (*Margaret turns from him in withering scorn*)—that I cannot interfere.

DOBLEMAN: (*breaking down unexpectedly*). I cannot stand it. I leave your employ, sir. It is outrageous. I resign now, at once. I cannot be a party to this. (*Striving to unlock door.*) I am going at once. You brutes! You brutes!
Breaks into convulsive sobbings.

CHALMERS: Ah, another lover, I see.
Dobleman manages to unlock door and starts to open it.

STARKWEATHER: You fool! Shut that door! (*Dobleman hesitates.*) Shut it! (*Dobleman obeys.*) Lock it!
Dobleman obeys.

MARGARET: (*smiling wistfully, benignantly*). Thank you, Mr. Dobleman. (*To Starkweather.*) Father, you surely will not perpetrate this outrage when I tell you, I swear to you—

STARKWEATHER: (*interrupting*). Return the documents, then.

MARGARET: I swear to you that I haven't them. You will not find them on me.

STARKWEATHER: You have lied to me about Knox, and I have no reason to believe you will not lie to me about this matter.

MARGARET: (*steadily*). If you do this thing, you shall cease to be my father forever. You shall cease to exist so far as I am concerned.

STARKWEATHER: You have too much of my own will in you for you ever to forget whence it came. Mrs. Middleton, go ahead.

Housekeeper, summoning Maids with her eyes, begins to advance on Margaret.

CONNIE: (*in a passion*). Father, if you do this, I shall never speak to you again.

Breaks down weeping.

Mrs. Starkweather, during following scene, has mild but continuous shuddering and weeping hysteria.

STARKWEATHER: (*briskly, looking at watch*). I've wasted enough time on this. Mrs. Middleton, proceed.

MARGARET: (*wildly, backing away from Housekeeper*). I will not tamely submit. I will resist, I promise you.

STARKWEATHER: Use force, if necessary.

The Maids are reluctant, but Housekeeper commands them with her eyes to close in on Margaret, and they obey.

Margaret backs away until she brings up against desk.

HOUSEKEEPER: Come, Mrs. Chalmers.

Margaret stands trembling, but refuses to notice Housekeeper. Housekeeper places hand on Margaret's arm.

MARGARET: (*violently flinging the hand off, crying imperiously*). Stand back! (*Housekeeper instinctively shrinks back, as do Maids. But it is only for the moment. They close in upon Margaret to seize her. Crying frantically for help.*) Linda! Linda!

Linda springs forward to help her mistress, but is caught and held struggling by Chalmers, who twists her arm and finally compels her to become quiet.

Margaret, struggling and resisting, is hustled across stage and behind screen, the Maids warming up to their work. One of them emerges from behind screen for the purpose of getting a chair, upon which Margaret is evidently forced to sit. The screen is of such height that occasionally, when standing up and struggling, Margaret's bare arms are visible above the top of it. Muttered exclamations are heard, and the voice of Housekeeper trying to persuade Margaret to submit.

MARGARET: (*abruptly, piteously*). No! No!

The struggle becomes more violent, and the screen is overturned, disclosing Margaret seated on chair, partly undressed, and clutching an envelope in her hand, which they are trying to force her to relinquish.

MRS. STARKWEATHER: (*crying wildly*). Anthony! They are taking her clothes off!

Renewed struggle of Linda with Chalmers at the sight. Starkweather, calling Rutland to his assistance, stands screen up again, then, as an afterthought, pulls screen a little further away from Margaret.

MARGARET: No! No!

Housekeeper appears triumphantly with envelope in her hand and hands it to Hubbard.

HUBBARD: (*immediately*). That's not it. (*Glances at address and starts.*) It's addressed to Knox.

STARKWEATHER: Tear it open. Read it.

Hubbard tears envelope open.

While this is going on, struggle behind screen is suspended.

HUBBARD: (*withdrawing contents of envelope*). It is only a photograph—of Mrs. Chalmers. (*Reading.*) "For the future —Margaret."

CHALMERS: (*thrusting Linda back to right front and striding up to Hubbard*). Give it to me.

Hubbard passes it to him, and he looks at it, crumples it in his hand, and grinds it underfoot.

STARKWEATHER: That is not what we wanted, Mrs. Middleton. Go on with the search.

The search goes on behind the screen without any further struggling.

A pause, during which screen is occasionally agitated by the searchers, removing Margaret's garments.

HOUSEKEEPER: (*appearing around corner of screen*). I find nothing else, sir.

STARKWEATHER: Is she stripped?

HOUSEKEEPER: Yes, sir.

STARKWEATHER: Every stitch?

HOUSEKEEPER: (*disappearing behind screen instead of answering for a pause, during which it is patent that the ultimate stitch is being removed, then reappearing*). Yes, sir.

STARKWEATHER: Nothing?

HOUSEKEEPER: Nothing.

STARKWEATHER: Throw out her clothes—everything.

A confused mass of feminine apparel is tossed out, falling near Dobleman's feet, who, in consequence, is hugely mortified and embarrassed.

Chalmers examines garments, then steps behind screen a moment, and reappears.

CHALMERS: Nothing.

Chalmers, Starkweather, and Hubbard gaze at each other dumbfoundedly.

The two Maids come out from behind screen and stand near door to right rear.

Starkweather is loath to believe and steps to Margaret's garments and overhauls them.

STARKWEATHER: (*to Chalmers, looking inquiringly toward screen*). Are you sure?

CHALMERS: Yes, I made certain. She hasn't them.

STARKWEATHER: (*to Housekeeper*). Mrs. Middleton, examine those girls.

HOUSEKEEPER: (*passing hands over dresses of Maids*). No, sir.

MARGARET: (*from behind screen, in a subdued, spiritless voice*). May I dress—now? (*Nobody answers.*) It—it is quite chilly. (*Nobody answers.*) Will you let Linda come to me, please?

Starkweather nods savagely to Linda to obey.

Linda crosses to garments, gathers them up, and disappears behind screen.

STARKWEATHER: (*to Housekeeper*). You may go.

Exit Housekeeper and the two Maids.

DOBLEMAN: (*hesitating, after closing door*). Shall I lock it?

Starkweather does not answer, and Dobleman leaves door unlocked.

CONNIE: (*rising*). May I take Mother away?

Starkweather, who is in a brown study, nods.

Connie assists Mrs. Starkweather to her feet.

MRS. STARKWEATHER: (*staggering weakly and sinking back into chair*). Let me rest a moment, Connie. I'll be better. (*To Starkweather, who takes no notice.*) Anthony, I am going to bed. This has been too much for me. I shall be sick. I shall never catch that train today.

Shudders and sighs, leans head back, closes eyes, and Connie fans her or administers smelling salts.

CHALMERS: (*to Hubbard*). What's to be done?

HUBBARD: (*shrugging shoulders*). I'm all at sea. I had just left the letters with him when Mrs. Chalmers entered the room. What's become of them? She hasn't them, that's certain.

CHALMERS. But why? Why should she have taken them?

HUBBARD: (*dryly, pointing to crumpled photograph on floor*). It seems very clear to me.

CHALMERS: You think so? You think so?

HUBBARD: I told you what I saw last night at his rooms. There is no other explanation.

CHALMERS: (*angrily*). And that's the sort he is—vaunting his moral superiority—mouthing phrases about theft—our theft—and himself the greatest thief of all, stealing the dearest and sacredest things—

Margaret appears from behind screen, pinning on her hat.

She is dressed, but somewhat in disarray, and Linda follows, pulling and touching and arranging. Margaret pauses near to Rutland, but does not seem to see him.

RUTLAND: (*lamely*). It is a sad happening—ahem—a sad happening. I am grieved, deeply grieved. I cannot tell you, Mrs. Chalmers, how grieved I am to have been compelled to be present at this—ahem—this unfortunate—

Margaret withers him with a look, and he awkwardly ceases.

MARGARET: After this, Father, there is one thing I shall do—

CHALMERS: (*interrupting*). Go to your lover, I suppose.

MARGARET: (*coldly*). Have it that way if you choose.

CHALMERS: And take him what you have stolen—

STARKWEATHER: (*arousing suddenly from brown study*). But she hasn't them on her. She hasn't been out of the room. They are not in the room. Then where are they?

During the following, Margaret goes to the door, which Dobleman opens. She forces Linda to go out and herself pauses in open door to listen.

HUBBARD: (*uttering an exclamation of enlightenment, going rapidly across to window at left and raising it*). It is not locked. It moves noiselessly. There's the explanation. (*To Starkweather.*) While you were at the safe with your back turned, she lifted the window, tossed the papers out to somebody waiting— (*He sticks head and shoulders out of window, peers down, then brings head and shoulders back.*) —No, they are not there. Somebody was waiting for them.

STARKWEATHER: But how should she know I had them? You had only just recovered them.

HUBBARD: Didn't Knox know right away last night that I had taken them? I took the up elevator instead of the down when I heard him running along the hall. Trust him to let her know what had happened. She was the only one who could recover them for him. Else why did she come here so immediately this morning? To steal the package, of course. And she had someone waiting outside. She tossed them out and closed the window—(*he closes window*)—you notice it makes no sound—and sat down again—all while your back was turned.

STARKWEATHER: Margaret, is this true?

MARGARET: (*excitedly*). Yes, the window. Why didn't you think of it before? Of course, the window. He—somebody was waiting. They are gone now—miles and miles away. You will never get them. They are in his hands now. He will use them in his speech this afternoon. (*Laughs wildly. Suddenly changing her tone to mock meekness, subtle with defiance.*) May I go—now?

Nobody answers, and she makes exit.

A moment's pause, during which Starkweather, Chalmers, and Hubbard look at each other in stupefaction.

CURTAIN

ACT IV

Same as Act I. It is half past one of same day.

Curtain discloses Knox seated at right front and waiting. He is dejected in attitude.

Margaret enters from right rear and advances to him. He rises awkwardly and shakes hands. She is very calm and self-possessed.

MARGARET: I knew you would come. Strange that I had to send for you so soon after last night— (*With alarm and sudden change of manner.*) What is the matter? You are sick. Your hand is cold.

She warms it in both of her hands.

KNOX: It is flame or freeze with me. (*Smiling.*) And I'd rather flame.

MARGARET: (*becoming aware that she is warming his hand*). Sit down and tell me what is the matter.

Leading him by the hand, she seats him, at the same time seating herself.

KNOX: (*abruptly*). After you left last night, Hubbard stole those documents back again.

MARGARET: (*very matter-of-fact*). Yes, he was in your bedroom while I was there.

KNOX: (*startled*). How do you know that? Anyway, he did not know who you were.

MARGARET: Oh, yes, he did.

KNOX: (*angrily*). And he has dared—?

MARGARET: Yes, not two hours ago. He announced the fact before my father, my mother, Connie, the servants, everybody.

KNOX: (*rising to his feet and beginning to pace perturbedly up and down*). The cur!

MARGARET: (*quietly*). I believe, among other things, I told him he was that myself. (*She laughs cynically.*) Oh, it was a pretty family party, I assure you. Mother said she didn't believe it—but that was only hysteria. Of course she believes it—the worst. So does Connie—everybody.

KNOX: (*stopping abruptly and looking at her horror-stricken*). You don't mean they charged—?

MARGARET: No, I don't mean that. I mean more. They didn't charge. They accepted it as a proven fact that I was guilty. That you were my—lover.

KNOX: On that man's testimony?

MARGARET: He had two witnesses in an adjoining room.

KNOX: (*relieved*). All the better. They can testify to nothing more than the truth, and the truth is not serious. In our case it is good, for we renounced each other.

MARGARET: You don't know these men. It is easy to guess that they have been well trained. They would swear to anything. (*She laughs bitterly.*) They are my father's men, you know, his paid sleuthhounds.

KNOX: (*collapsing in chair, holding head in hands, and groaning*). How you must have suffered. What a terrible time, what a terrible time! I can see it all—before everybody —your nearest and dearest. Ah, I could not understand, after our parting last night, why you should have sent for me today. But now I know.

MARGARET: No, you don't at all.

KNOX: (*ignoring her and again beginning to pace back and forth, thinking on his feet*). What's the difference? I am ruined politically. Their scheme has worked out only too well. Gifford warned me, you warned me, everybody warned me. But I was a fool, blind—with a fool's folly. There is nothing left but you now. (*He pauses, and the light of a new thought irradiates his face.*) Do you know, Margaret, I thank God it has happened as it has. What if my usefulness is destroyed? There will be other men—other leaders. I but make way for another. The cause of the people can never be lost. And though I am driven from the fight, I am driven to you. We are driven together. It is fate. Again I thank God for it.

He approaches her and tries to clasp her in his arms, but she steps back.

MARGARET: (*smiling sadly*). Ah, now you flame. The tables are reversed. Last night it was I. We are fortunate that we choose diverse times for our moods—else there would be naught but one sweet melting mad disaster.

KNOX: But it is not as if we had done this thing deliberately and selfishly. We have renounced. We have struggled against it until we were beaten. And now we are driven together, not by our doing but fate's. After this affair this morning, there is nothing for you but to come to me. And as for me, despite my best I am finished. I have failed. As I told you, the papers are stolen. There will be no speech this afternoon.

MARGARET: (*quietly*). Yes, there will.

KNOX: Impossible. I would make a triple fool of myself. I would be unable to substantiate my charges.

MARGARET: You will substantiate them. What a chain of theft it is. My father steals from the people. The documents that prove his stealing are stolen by Gherst. Hubbard steals

them from you and returns them to my father. And I steal
them from my father and pass them back to you.

KNOX: (*astounded*). You? You?

MARGARET: Yes, this very morning. That was the cause of all
the trouble. If I hadn't stolen them, nothing would have
happened. Hubbard had just returned them to my father.

KNOX: (*profoundly touched*). And you did this for me—?

MARGARET: Dear man, I didn't do it for you. I wasn't brave
enough. I should have given in. I don't mind confessing
that I started to do it for you, but it soon grew so terrible
that I was afraid. It grew so terrible that, had it been for
you alone, I should have surrendered. But out of the
terror of it all, I caught a wider vision, and all that you
said last night rose before me. And I knew that you were
right. I thought of all the people, and of the little children.
I did it for them, after all. You speak for them. I stole the
papers so that you could use them in speaking for the
people. Don't you see, dear man? (*Changing to angry
recollection.*) Do you know what they cost me? Do you
know what was done to me today, this morning, in my
father's house? I was shamed, humiliated, as I would
never have dreamed it possible. Do you know what they
did to me? The servants were called in, and by them I was
stripped before everybody—my family, Hubbard, the
Reverend Mr. Rutland, the secretary, everybody.

KNOX: (*stunned*). Stripped—you?

MARGARET: Every stitch. My father commanded it.

KNOX: (*suddenly visioning the scene*). My God!

MARGARET: (*recovering herself and speaking cynically, with a
laugh at his shocked face*). No, it was not so bad as that.
There was a screen. (*Knox appears somewhat relieved.*) But
it fell down in the midst of the struggle.

KNOX: But in heaven's name, why was this done to you?

MARGARET: Searching for the lost letters. They knew I had

taken them. (*Speaking gravely.*) So, you see, I have earned those papers. And I have earned the right to say what shall be done with them. I shall give them to you, and you will use them in your speech this afternoon.

KNOX: I don't want them.

MARGARET: (*going to bell and ringing*). Oh, yes, you do. They are more valuable right now than anything else in the world.

KNOX: (*shaking his head*). I wish it hadn't happened.

MARGARET: (*returning to him, pausing by his chair, and caressing his hair*). What?

KNOX: This morning—your recovering the letters. I had adjusted myself to their loss, and the loss of the fight, and the finding of—you. (*He reaches up, draws down her hand, and presses it to his lips.*) So—give them back to your father.

Margaret draws quickly away from him.

Enter Manservant at right rear.

MARGARET: Send Linda to me.

Exit Manservant.

KNOX: What are you doing?

MARGARET: (*sitting down*). I am going to send Linda for them. They are still in my father's house, hidden, of all places, behind Lincoln's portrait. He will guard them safely, I know.

KNOX: (*with fervor*). Margaret! Margaret! Don't send for them. Let them go. I don't want them. (*Rising and going toward her impulsively. Margaret rises and retreats, holding him off.*) I want you—you—you.

He catches her hand and kisses it. She tears it away from him, but tenderly.

MARGARET: (*still retreating, roguishly and tenderly*). Dear, dear man, I love to see you so. But it cannot be. (*Looking anxiously toward right rear.*) No, no, please, please sit down.

Enter Linda from right rear. She is dressed for the street.

MARGARET: (*surprised*). Where are you going?

LINDA: Tommy and the nurse and I were going downtown. There is some shopping she wants to do.

MARGARET: Very good. But go first to my father's house. Listen closely. In the library, behind the portrait of Lincoln —you know it? (*Linda nods.*) You will find a packet of papers. It took me five seconds to put it there. It will take you no longer to get it. Let no one see you. Let it appear as though you had brought Tommy to see his grandmother and cheer her up. You know she is not feeling very well just now. After you get the papers, leave Tommy there and bring them immediately back to me. Step on a chair to the ledge of the bookcase, and reach behind the portrait. You should be back inside fifteen minutes. Take the car.

LINDA: Tommy and the nurse are already in it, waiting for me.

MARGARET: Be careful. Be quick.

Linda nods to each instruction and makes exit.

KNOX: (*bursting out passionately*). This is madness. You are sacrificing yourself, and me. I don't want them. I want you. I am tired. What does anything matter except love? I have pursued ideals long enough. Now I want you.

MARGARET: (*gravely*). Ah, there you have expressed the pith of it. You will now forsake ideals for me— (*He attempts to interrupt.*) No, no; not that I am less than an ideal. I have no silly vanity that way. But I want you to remain ideal, and you can only by going on—not by being turned back. Anybody can play the coward and assert they are fatigued. I could not love a coward. It was your strength that saved us last night. I could not have loved you as I do now, had you been weak last night. You can only keep my love—

KNOX: (*interrupting, bitterly*). By forgoing it—for an ideal. Margaret, what is the biggest thing in the world? Love. There is the greatest ideal of all.

MARGARET: (*playfully*). Love of man and woman?

KNOX: What else?

MARGARET: (*gravely*). There is one thing greater—love of man for his fellowman.

KNOX: Oh, how you turn my preachments back on me. It is a lesson. Nevermore shall I preach. Henceforth—

MARGARET: Yes.

Chalmers enters unobserved at left, pauses, and looks on.

KNOX: Henceforth I love. Listen.

MARGARET: You are overwrought. It will pass, and you will see your path straight before you and know that I am right. You cannot run away from the fight.

KNOX: I can—and will. I want you, and you want me—the man's and woman's need for each other. Come, go with me—now. Let us snatch at happiness while we may. (*He arises, approaches her, and gets her hand in his. She becomes more complaisant and, instead of repulsing him, is willing to listen and receive.*) As I have said, the fight will go on just the same. Scores of men, better men, stronger men than I, will rise to take my place. Why do I talk this way? Because I love you, love you, love you. Nothing else exists in all the world but love of you.

MARGARET: (*melting and wavering*). Ah, you flame, you flame.

Chalmers utters an inarticulate cry of rage and rushes forward at Knox.

Margaret and Knox are startled by the cry and discover Chalmers's presence.

MARGARET: (*confronting Chalmers and thrusting him slightly back from Knox, and continuing to hold him off from Knox*). No, Tom, no dramatics, please. This excitement of yours is only automatic and conventional. You really don't mean it. You don't even feel it. You do it because it is expected of you and because it is your training. Besides, it is bad for your heart. Remember Dr. West's warning—

*Chalmers, making an unusually violent effort to get at Knox,
suddenly staggers weakly back, signs of pain on his face,
holding a hand convulsively clasped over his heart. Margaret
catches him and supports him to a chair, into which he
collapses.*

CHALMERS: (*muttering weakly*). My heart! My heart!

KNOX: (*approaching*). Can I do anything?

MARGARET: (*calmly*). No, it is all right. He will be better
presently.

*She is bending over Chalmers, her hand on his wrist, when
suddenly, as a sign he is recovering, he violently flings her
hand off and straightens up.*

KNOX: (*undecidedly*). I shall go now.

MARGARET: No. You will wait until Linda comes back. Besides,
you can't run away from this and leave me alone to face it.

KNOX: (*hurt, showing that he will stay*). I am not a coward.

CHALMERS: (*in a stifled voice that grows stronger*). Yes, wait. I
have a word for you. (*He pauses a moment, and when he
speaks again, his voice is all right. Witheringly.*) A nice
specimen of a reformer, I must say. You, who babbled
yesterday about theft. The most high, righteous, and noble
Ali Baba, who has come into the den of thieves and who is
also a thief. (*Mimicking Margaret.*) "Ah, you flame, you
flame!" (*In his natural voice.*) I should call you—you thief,
you thief, you wife stealer, you.

MARGARET: (*coolly*). I should scarcely call it theft.

CHALMERS: (*sneeringly*). Yes, I forgot. You mean it is not theft
for him to take what already belongs to him.

MARGARET: Not quite that—but in taking what has been
freely offered to him.

CHALMERS: You mean you have so forgotten your womanhood
as to offer—

MARGARET: Just that. Last night. And Mr. Knox did himself
the honor of refusing me.

KNOX: (*bursting forth*). You see, nothing else remains, Margaret.

CHALMERS: (*twittingly*). Ah, "Margaret."

KNOX: (*ignoring him*). The situation is intolerable.

CHALMERS: (*emphatically*). It is intolerable. Don't you think you had better leave this house? Every moment of your presence dishonors it.

MARGARET: Don't talk of honor, Tom.

CHALMERS: I make no excuses for myself. I fancy I never fooled you very much. But at any rate, I never used my own house for such purposes.

KNOX: (*springing at him*). You cur!

MARGARET: (*interposing*). No, don't. His heart.

CHALMERS: (*mimicking Margaret*). No dramatics, please.

MARGARET: (*plaintively, looking from one man to the other*). Men are so strangely and wonderfully made. What am I to do with the pair of you? Why won't you reason together like rational human beings?

CHALMERS: (*bitterly gay, rising to his feet*). Yes, let us come and reason together. Be rational. Sit down and talk it over like civilized humans. This is not the Stone Age. Be reassured, Mr. Knox. I won't brain you. Margaret—(*indicating chair*)—sit down. Mr. Knox—(*indicating chair*)—sit down. (*All three seat themselves, in a triangle.*) Behold the problem— the ever-ancient and ever-young triangle of the playwright and the short-story writer—two men and a woman.

KNOX: True, and yet not true. The triangle is incomplete. Only one of the two men loves the woman.

CHALMERS: Yes?

KNOX: And I am that man.

CHALMERS: I fancy you're right. (*Nodding his head.*) But how about the woman?

MARGARET: She loves one of the two men.

KNOX: And what are you going to do about it?

CHALMERS: (*judicially*). She has not yet indicated the man.

(*Margaret is about to indicate Knox.*) Be careful, Madge. Remember who is Tommy's father.

MARGARET: Tom, honestly, remembering what the last years have been, can you imagine that I love you?

CHALMERS: I'm afraid I've not—er—not flamed sufficiently.

MARGARET: You have possibly spoken nearer the truth than you dreamed. I married you, Tom, hoping great things of you. I hoped you would be a power for good—

CHALMERS: Politics again. When will women learn they must leave politics alone?

MARGARET: And also I hoped for love. I knew you didn't love me when we married, but I hoped for it to come.

CHALMERS: And—er—may I be permitted to ask if you loved me?

MARGARET: No, but I hoped that, too, would come.

CHALMERS: It was, then, all a mistake.

MARGARET: Yes, yours, and mine, and my father's.

KNOX: We have sat down to reason this out, and we get nowhere. Margaret and I love each other. Your triangle breaks.

CHALMERS: It isn't a triangle after all. You forget Tommy.

KNOX: (*petulantly*). Make it four-sided, then, but let us come to some conclusion.

CHALMERS: (*reflecting*). Ah, it is more than that. There is a fifth side. There are the stolen letters which Madge has just this morning restolen from her father. Whatever settlement takes place, they must enter into it. (*Changing his tone.*) Look here, Madge, I am a fool. Let us talk sensibly, you and Knox and I. Knox, you want my wife. You can have her—on one consideration. Madge, you want Knox. You can have him on one consideration, the same consideration. Give up the letters and we'll forget everything.

MARGARET: Everything?

CHALMERS: Everything. Forgive and forget. You know.

MARGARET: You will forgive my—I—this—this adultery?

CHALMERS: (*doggedly*). I'll forgive anything for the letters. I've played fast and loose with you, Madge, and I fancy your playing fast and loose only evens things up. Return the letters and you can go with Knox quietly. I'll see to that. There won't be a breath of scandal. I'll give you a divorce. Or you can stay on with me if you want to. I don't care. What I want is the letters. Is it agreed?

Margaret seems to hesitate.

KNOX: (*pleadingly*). Margaret.

MARGARET: And Tommy?

CHALMERS: (*testily*). Am I not giving you each other? What more do you want? Tommy stays with me. If you want Tommy, then stay with me, but you must give up the letters.

MARGARET: I shall not go with Mr. Knox. I shall not give up the letters. I shall remain with Tommy.

CHALMERS: So far as I am concerned, Knox doesn't count in this. I want the letters and I want Tommy. If you don't give them up, I'll divorce you on statutory grounds, and no woman, so divorced, can keep her child. In any event, I shall keep Tommy.

MARGARET: (*speaking steadily and positively*). Listen, Tom, and you, too, Howard. I have never for a moment entertained the thought of giving up the letters. I may have led you to think so, but I wanted to see just how low you, Tom, could sink. I saw how low you—all of you—this morning sank. I have learned—much. Where is this fine honor, Tom, which put you on a man-killing rage a moment ago? You'll barter it all for a few scraps of paper and forgive and forget adultery which does not exist—(*Chalmers laughs skeptically*)—though I know when I say it, you will not believe me. At any rate, I shall not give up the letters. Not if you do take Tommy away from me. Not even for

Tommy will I sacrifice all the people. As I told you this morning, there are two million Tommys, child laborers all, who cannot be sacrificed for Tommy's sake or anybody's sake.

Chalmers shrugs his shoulders and smiles in ridicule.

KNOX: Surely, Margaret, there is a way out for us. Give up the letters. What are they?—only scraps of paper. Why match them against happiness—our happiness?

MARGARET: But as you told me yourself, those scraps of paper represent the happiness of millions of lives. It is not our happiness that is matched against some scraps of paper. It is our happiness against millions of lives—like ours. All these millions have hearts, and loves, and desires, just like ours.

KNOX: But it is a great social and cosmic process. It does not depend on one man. Kill off, at this instant, every leader of the people, and the process will go on just the same. The people will come into their own. Theft will be unseated. It is destiny. It is the process. Nothing can stop it.

MARGARET: But it can be retarded.

KNOX: You and I are no more than straws in relation to it. We cannot stop it any more than straws can stop an ocean tide. We mean nothing—except to each other—and to each other we mean all the world.

MARGARET: (*sadly and tenderly*). All the world and immortality thrown in.

CHALMERS: (*breaking in*). Nice situation, sitting here and listening to a strange man woo my wife in terms of sociology and scientific slang.

Both Margaret and Knox ignore him.

KNOX: Dear, I want you so.

MARGARET: (*despairingly*). Oh! It is so hard to do right!

KNOX: (*eagerly*). He wants the letters very badly. Give them up for Tommy. He will give Tommy for them.

CHALMERS: No, emphatically no. If she wants Tommy, she can

stay on, but she must give up the letters. If she wants you, she may go, but she must give up the letters.

KNOX: (*pleading for a decision*). Margaret.

MARGARET: Howard. Don't tempt me and press me. It is hard enough as it is.

CHALMERS: (*standing up*). I've had enough of this. The thing must be settled, and I leave it to you, Knox. Go on with your lovemaking. But I won't be a witness to it. Perhaps I—er—retard the—er—the flame process. You two must make up your minds, and you can do it better without me. I am going to get a drink and settle my nerves. I'll be back in a minute. (*He moves toward exit to right.*) She will yield, Knox. Be warm, be warm. (*Pausing in doorway.*) Ah, you flame! Flame to some purpose.

Exit Chalmers.

Knox rests his head despairingly on his hand, and Margaret, pausing and looking at him sadly for a moment, crosses to him, stands beside him, and caresses his hair.

MARGARET: It is hard, I know, dear. And it is hard for me as well.

KNOX: It is so unnecessary.

MARGARET: No, it is necessary. What you said last night, when I was weak, was wise. We cannot steal from my child—

KNOX: But if he gives you Tommy?

MARGARET: (*shaking her head*). Nor can we steal from any other woman's child—from all the children of all the women. And other things I heard you say, and you were right. We cannot live by ourselves alone. We are social animals. Our good and our ill—all is tied up with all humanity.

KNOX: (*catching her hand and caressing it*). I do not follow you. I hear your voice, but I do not know a word you say. Because I am loving your voice—and you. I am so filled with love that there is no room for anything else. And you, who yesterday were so remote and unattainable, are so near and possible, so immediately possible. All you have to do is to say the word, one little word. Say it —say it.

He carries her hand to his lips and holds it there.

MARGARET: (*wistfully*). I should like to. I should like to. But I can't.

KNOX: You must.

MARGARET: There are other and greater things that say "must" to me. Oh, my dear, have you forgotten them? Things you yourself have spoken to me—the great stinging things of the spirit that are greater than you and I, greater even than our love.

KNOX: I exhaust my arguments—but still I love you.

MARGARET: And I love you for it.

Chalmers enters from right and sees Margaret still caressing Knox's hair.

CHALMERS: (*with mild elation, touched with sarcasm*). Ah, I see you have taken my advice and reached a decision. (*They do not answer. Margaret moves slowly away and seats herself. Knox remains with head bowed on hand.*) No? (*Margaret shakes her head.*) Well, I've thought it over, and I've changed my terms. Madge, go with Knox, take Tommy with you. (*Margaret wavers, but Knox, head bowed on hand, does not see her.*) There will be no scandal. I'll give you a proper divorce. And you can have Tommy.

KNOX: (*suddenly raising his head, joyfully, pleadingly*). Margaret!

Margaret is swayed, but does not speak.

CHALMERS: You and I never hit it off together any too extraordinarily well, Madge, but I'm not altogether a bad sort. I am easygoing. I always have been easygoing. I'll make everything easy for you now. But you see the fix I am in. You love another man, and I simply must regain those letters. It is more important than you realize.

MARGARET: (*incisively*). You make me realize how important those letters are.

KNOX: Give him the letters, Margaret.

CHALMERS: So she hasn't turned them over to you yet?

MARGARET: No, I still have them.

KNOX: Give them to him.

CHALMERS: Selling out for a petticoat. A pretty reformer.

KNOX: (*proudly*). A better lover.

MARGARET: (*to Chalmers*). He is weak today. What of it? He was strong last night. He will win back his strength again. It is human to be weak. And in his very weakness now, I have my pride, for it is the weakness of love. God knows I have been weak, and I am not ashamed of it. It was the weakness of love. It is hard to stifle one's womanhood always with morality. (*Quickly.*) But do not mistake, Tom. This of mine is no conventional morality. I do not care about nasty, gossipy tongues and sensation-mongering sheets; nor do I care what any persons, of all the persons I know, would say if I went away with Mr. Knox this instant. I would go, and go gladly and proudly with him, divorce or no divorce, scandal or scandal triplefold—if—if no one else were hurt by what I did. (*To Knox.*) Howard, I tell you that I would go with you now in all willingness and joy, with Maytime and the songs of all singing birds in my heart—were it not for the others. But there is a higher morality. We must not hurt those others. We dare not steal our happiness from them. The future belongs to them, and we must not, dare not, sacrifice that future nor give it in pledge for our own happiness. Last night I came to you. I was weak—yes. More than that—I was ignorant. I did not know, even as late as last night, the monstrous vileness, the consummate wickedness of present-day

conditions. I learned that today, this morning, and now.
I learned that the morality of the Church was a pretense.
Far deeper than it, and vastly more powerful, was the
morality of the dollar. My father, my family, my husband,
were willing to condone what they believed was my
adultery. And for what? For a few scraps of paper that
to them represented only the privilege to plunder, the
privilege to steal from the people. (*To Chalmers.*) Here are
you, Tom, not only willing and eager to give me into the
arms of the man you believe my lover, but you throw in
your boy—your child and mine—to make it good measure
and acceptable. And for what? Love of some woman?—
any woman? No. Love of humanity? No. Love of God? No.
Then for what? For the privilege of perpetuating your
stealing from the people—money, bread and butter, hats,
shoes, and stockings—for stealing all these things from
the people. (*To Knox.*) Now, and at last, do I realize how
stern and awful is the fight that must be waged—the fight
in which you and I, Howard, must play our parts and play
them bravely and uncomplainingly—you as well as I, but I
even more than you. This is the den of thieves. I am a
child of thieves. All my family is composed of thieves. I
have been fed and reared on the fruits of thievery. I have
been a party to it all my life. Somebody must cease from
this theft, and it is I. And you must help me, Howard.

CHALMERS: (*emitting a low long whistle*). Strange that you
never went into the suffragette business. With such
speech-making ability you would have been a shining
light.

KNOX: (*sadly*). The worst of it is, Margaret, you are right. But
it is hard that we cannot be happy save by stealing from
the happiness of others. Yet it hurts, deep down and
terribly, to forgo you.

Margaret thanks him with her eyes.

CHALMERS: (*sarcastically*). Oh, believe me, I am not too anxious to give up my wife. Look at her. She's a pretty good woman for any man to possess.

MARGARET: Tom, I'll accept a quiet divorce, marry Mr. Knox, and take Tommy with me—on one consideration.

CHALMERS: And what is that?

MARGARET: That I retain the letters. They are to be used in his speech this afternoon.

CHALMERS: No, they're not.

MARGARET: Whatever happens, do whatever worst you can possibly do, that speech will be given this afternoon. Your worst to me will be none too great a price for me to pay.

CHALMERS: No letters, no divorce, no Tommy, nothing.

MARGARET: Then will you compel me to remain here? I have done nothing wrong, and I don't imagine you will make a scandal. (*Enter Linda at right rear, pausing and looking inquiringly.*) There they are now. (*To Linda.*) Yes, give them to me.

Linda, advancing, draws package of documents from her breast. As she is handing them to Margaret, Chalmers attempts to seize them.

KNOX: (*springing forward and thrusting Chalmers back*). That you shall not!

Chalmers is afflicted with heart seizure and staggers.

MARGARET: (*maternally, solicitously*). Tom, don't! Your heart! Be careful! (*Chalmers starts to stagger toward bell.*) Howard! Stop him! Don't let him ring, or the servants will get the letters away from us. (*Knox starts to interpose, but Chalmers, growing weaker, sinks into a chair, head thrown back and legs out straight before him.*) Linda, a glass of water.

Linda gives documents to Margaret and makes running exit to right rear.

Margaret bends anxiously over Chalmers.

A pause.

KNOX: (*touching her hand*). Give them to me.

Margaret gives him the documents, which he holds in his hand; at the same time she thanks him with her eyes.

Enter Linda with glass of water, which she hands to Margaret.

Margaret tries to place the glass to Chalmers's lips.

CHALMERS: (*dashing the glass violently from her hand to the floor and speaking in smothered voice*). Bring me a whiskey and soda.

Linda looks at Margaret interrogatively. Margaret is undecided what to say, shrugs her shoulders in helplessness, and nods her head.

Linda makes hurried exit to right.

MARGARET: (*to Knox*). You will go now and you will give the speech.

KNOX: (*placing documents in inside coat pocket*). I will give the speech.

MARGARET: And all the forces making for the good time coming will be quickened by your words. Let the voices of the millions be in it. (*Chalmers, legs still stretched out, laughs cynically.*) You know where my heart lies. Someday, in all pride and honor, stealing from no one, hurting no one, we shall come together—to be together always.

KNOX: (*drearily*). And in the meantime?

MARGARET: We must wait.

KNOX: (*decidedly*). We will wait.

CHALMERS: (*straightening up*). For me to die, eh?

During the following speech Linda enters from right with whiskey and soda and gives it to Chalmers, who thirstily drinks half of it. Margaret dismisses Linda with her eyes, and Linda makes exit to right rear.

KNOX: I hadn't that in mind, but now that you mention it, it seems to the point. That heart of yours isn't going to carry you much farther. You have played fast and loose with it, as with everything else. You are like the carter who steals hay from his horse that he may gamble. You have stolen from your heart. Someday soon, like the horse, it will quit. We can afford to wait. It won't be long.

CHALMERS: (*after laughing incredulously and sipping his whiskey*). Well, Knox, neither of us wins. You don't get the woman. Neither do I. She remains under my roof, and I fancy that is about all. I won't divorce her. What's the good? But I've got her tied hard and fast by Tommy. You won't get her.

Knox, ignoring him, goes to right rear and pauses in doorway.

MARGARET: Work. Bravely work. You are my knight. Go.

Knox makes exit.

Margaret stands quietly, face averted from audience and turned toward where Knox was last to be seen.

CHALMERS: Madge. (*Margaret neither moves nor answers.*) I say, Madge. (*He stands up and moves toward her, holding whiskey glass in one hand.*) That speech is going to make a devil of a row. But I don't think it will be so bad as your father says. It looks pretty dark, but such things blow over. They always do blow over. And so with you and me. Maybe we can manage to forget all this and patch it up somehow. (*She gives no sign that she is aware of his existence.*) Why don't you speak? (*Pause. He touches her arm.*) Madge.

MARGARET: (*turning upon him in a blaze of wrath and with unutterable loathing*). Don't touch me!

Chalmers recoils.

CURTAIN

THE ACORN PLANTER

A CALIFORNIA FOREST PLAY

PLANNED TO BE SUNG BY EFFICIENT SINGERS
ACCOMPANIED BY A CAPABLE ORCHESTRA

ARGUMENT

In the morning of the world, while his tribe makes its camp for the night in a grove, Red Cloud, the first man of men, and the first man of the Nishinam, save in war, sings of the duty of life, which duty is to make life more abundant. The Shaman, or medicine man, sings of foreboding and prophecy. The War Chief, who commands in war, sings that war is the only way to life. This Red Cloud denies, affirming that the way of life is the way of the acorn planter and that whoso slays one man slays the planter of many acorns. Red Cloud wins the Shaman and the people to his contention.

After the passage of thousands of years, again in the grove appear the Nishinam. In Red Cloud, the War Chief, the Shaman, and the Dew Woman are repeated the eternal figures of the philosopher, the soldier, the priest, and the woman—types ever realizing themselves afresh in the social adventures of man. Red Cloud recognizes the wrecked explorers as planters and life makers and is for treating them with kindness. But the War Chief and the idea of war are dominant. The Shaman joins with the war party and is privy to the massacre of the explorers.

A hundred years pass, when on their seasonal migration the

Nishinam camp for the night in the grove. They still live, and the war formula for life seems vindicated, despite the imminence of the superior life makers, the whites, who are flooding into California from north, south, east, and west—the English, the Americans, the Spaniards, and the Russians. The massacre by the white men follows, and Red Cloud, dying, recognizes the white men as brother acorn planters, the possessors of the superior life formula of which he had always been a protagonist.

In the Epilogue, or Apotheosis, occur the celebration of the death of war and the triumph of the acorn planters.

PROLOGUE

In the morning of the world.
A forest hillside where great trees stand with wide spaces
between. A stream flows from a spring that bursts out of the
hillside. It is a place of lush ferns and brakes, also of thickets
of such shrubs as inhabit a redwood forest floor. At the left,
in the open level space at the foot of the hillside, extending
out of sight among the trees, is visible a portion of a Nishinam
Indian camp. It is a temporary camp for the night. Small
cooking fires smolder. Standing about are withe-woven
baskets for the carrying of supplies and dunnage. Spears
and bows and quivers of arrows lie about. Boys drag in dry
branches for firewood. Young women fill gourds with water
from the stream and proceed about their camp tasks. A
number of older women are pounding acorns in stone
mortars with stone pestles. An old man and a Shaman, or
priest, look expectantly up the hillside. All wear moccasins
and are skin-clad, primitive in their garmenting. Neither
iron nor woven cloth occurs in the weapons and gear.
SHAMAN: (*looking up hillside*). Red Cloud is late.
OLD MAN: (*after inspection of hillside*). He has chased the deer
far. He is patient. In the chase he is patient like an old man.

SHAMAN: His feet are as fleet as the deer's.

OLD MAN: (*nodding*). And he is more patient than the deer.

SHAMAN: (*assertively, as if inculcating a lesson*). He is a mighty chief.

OLD MAN: (*nodding*). His father was a mighty chief. He is like to his father.

SHAMAN: (*more assertively*). He is his father. It is so spoken. He is his father's father. He is the first man, the first Red Cloud, ever born, and born again, to chiefship of his people.

OLD MAN: It is so spoken.

SHAMAN: His father was the Coyote. His mother was the Moon. And he was the first man.

OLD MAN: (*repeating*). His father was the Coyote. His mother was the Moon. And he was the first man.

SHAMAN: He planted the first acorns, and he is very wise.

OLD MAN: (*repeating*). He planted the first acorns, and he is very wise.

Cries from the women and a turning of faces. Red Cloud appears among his hunters descending the hillside. All carry spears, and bows and arrows. Some carry rabbits and other small game. Several carry deer.

PLAINT OF THE NISHINAM

Red Cloud, the meat bringer!
Red Cloud, the acorn planter!
Red Cloud, first man of the Nishinam!
Thy people hunger.
Far have they fared.
Hard has the way been.
Day long they sought,
High in the mountains,
Deep in the pools,
Wide 'mong the grasses,

In the bushes, and treetops,
Under the earth and flat stones.
Few are the acorns,
Past is the time for berries,
Fled are the fishes, the prawns, and the grasshoppers,
Blown far are the grass seeds,
Flown far are the young birds,
Old are the roots and withered.
Built are the fires for the meat.
Laid are the boughs for sleep,
Yet thy people cannot sleep.
Red Cloud, thy people hunger.

RED CLOUD: (*still descending*). Good hunting! Good hunting!
HUNTERS: Good hunting! Good hunting!
*Completing the descent, Red Cloud motions to the meat
bearers. They throw down their burdens before the women,
who greedily inspect the spoils.*

MEAT SONG OF THE NISHINAM

Meat that is good to eat,
Tender for old teeth,
Gristle for young teeth,
Big deer and fat deer,
Lean meat and fat meat,
Haunch meat and knucklebone,
Liver and heart.
Food for the old men,
Life for all men,
For women and babes.
Easement of hunger pangs,
Sorrow destroying,
Laughter provoking,
Joy invoking,

In the smell of its smoking
And its sweet in the mouth.

*The younger women take charge of the meat, and the older
women resume their acorn-pounding. Red Cloud approaches
the acorn pounders and watches them with pleasure. All
group about him, the Shaman to the fore, and hang upon
his every action, his every utterance.*

RED CLOUD: The heart of the acorn is good?

FIRST OLD WOMAN: (*nodding*). It is good food.

RED CLOUD: When you have pounded and winnowed and
washed away the bitter.

SECOND OLD WOMAN: As thou taught'st us, Red Cloud,
when the world was very young and thou wast the
first man.

RED CLOUD: It is a fat food. It makes life, and life is good.

SHAMAN: It was thou, Red Cloud, gathering the acorns and
teaching the storing, who gavest life to the Nishinam in
the lean years aforetime, when the tribes not of the
Nishinam passed like the dew of the morning.

He nods a signal to the Old Man.

OLD MAN

In the famine in the old time,
When the old man was a young man,
When the heavens ceased from raining,
When the grasslands parched and withered,
When the fishes left the river,
And the wild meat died of sickness,
In the tribes that knew not acorns,
All their women went dry-breasted,
All their younglings chewed the deer hides,
All their old men sighed and perished,
And the young men died beside them,
Till they died by tribe and totem,

And o'er all was death upon them.
Yet the Nishinam unvanquished,
Did not perish by the famine.
Oh, the acorns Red Cloud gave them!
Oh, the acorns Red Cloud taught them
How to store in willow baskets
'Gainst the time and need of famine!

SHAMAN: (*who, throughout the Old Man's recital, has nodded approbation, turning to Red Cloud*). Sing to thy people, Red Cloud, the song of life which is the song of the acorn.

RED CLOUD: (*making ready to begin*). And which is the song of woman, O Shaman.

SHAMAN: (*hushing the People to listen, solemnly*). He sings with his father's lips, and with the lips of his father's fathers to the beginning of time and men.

SONG OF THE FIRST MAN

RED CLOUD

I am Red Cloud,
The first man of the Nishinam.
My father was the Coyote.
My mother was the Moon.
The Coyote danced with the stars,
And wedded the Moon on a midsummer night.
The Coyote is very wise,
The Moon is very old,
Mine is his wisdom,
Mine is her age.
I am the first man.
I am the life maker and the father of life.

I am the fire bringer.
The Nishinam were the first men,

And they were without fire,
And knew the bite of the frost of bitter nights.
The panther stole the fire from the East,
The fox stole the fire from the panther,
The ground squirrel stole the fire from the fox,
And I, Red Cloud, stole the fire from the ground squirrel.
I, Red Cloud, stole the fire for the Nishinam,
And hid it in the heart of the wood.
To this day is the fire there in the heart of the wood.

I am the Acorn Planter.
I brought down the acorns from heaven.
I planted the short acorns in the valley.
I planted the long acorns in the valley.
I planted the black oak acorns that sprout, that sprout!
I planted the *sho-kum* and all the roots of the ground.
I planted the oat and the barley, the beaver-tail grass nut,
The tar weed and crowfoot, rock lettuce and ground lettuce,
And I taught the virtue of clover in the season of blossom,
The yellow-flowered clover, ball-rolled in its yellow dust.
I taught the cooking in baskets by hot stones from the fire,
Took the bite from the buckeye and soap root
By ground-roasting and washing in the sweetness of water,
And of the manzanita the berry I made into flour,
Taught the way of its cooking with hot stones in sand pools,
And the way of its eating with the knobbed tail of the deer.

Taught I likewise the gathering and storing,
The parching and pounding
Of the seeds from the grasses and grass roots;
And taught I the planting of seeds in the Nishinam home camps,
In the Nishinam hills and their valleys,
In the due times and seasons,
To sprout in the spring rains and grow ripe in the sun.

SHAMAN: Hail, Red Cloud, the first man!

PEOPLE: Hail, Red Cloud, the first man!

SHAMAN: Who showedst us the way of our feet in the world!

PEOPLE: Who showedst us the way of our feet in the world!

SHAMAN: Who showedst us the way of our food in the world!

PEOPLE: Who showedst us the way of our food in the world!

SHAMAN: Who showedst us the way of our hearts in the world!

PEOPLE: Who showedst us the way of our hearts in the world!

SHAMAN: Who gavest us the law of family!

PEOPLE: Who gavest us the law of family!

SHAMAN: The law of tribe!

PEOPLE: The law of tribe!

SHAMAN: The law of totem!

PEOPLE: The law of totem!

SHAMAN: And madest us strong in the world among men!

PEOPLE: And madest us strong in the world among men!

RED CLOUD: Life is good, O Shaman, and I have sung but half its song. Acorns are good. So is woman good. Strength is good. Beauty is good. So is kindness good. Yet are all these things without power except for woman. And by these things woman makes strong men, and strong men make for life, ever for more life.

WAR CHIEF: (with gesture of interruption that causes remonstrance from the Shaman but which Red Cloud acknowledges). I care not for beauty. I desire strength in battle and wind in the chase, that I may kill my enemy and run down my meat.

RED CLOUD: Well spoken, O War Chief. By voices in council we learn our minds, and that, too, is strength. Also is it kindness. For kindness and strength and beauty are one. The eagle in the high blue of the sky is beautiful. The salmon leaping the white water in the sunlight is beautiful. The young man fastest of foot in the race is beautiful. And because they fly well, and leap well, and run well, are they beautiful. Beauty must beget beauty.

The ringtail cat begets the ringtail cat, the dove the dove. Never does the dove beget the ringtail cat. Hearts must be kind. The little turtle is not kind. That is why it is the little turtle. It lays its eggs in the sun-warm sand and forgets its young forever. And the little turtle is forever the little turtle. But we are not little turtles because we are kind. We do not leave our young to the sun in the sand. Our women keep our young warm under their hearts, and, after, they keep them warm with deerskin and campfire. Because we are kind, we are men and not little turtles, and that is why we eat the little turtle that is not strong because it is not kind.

WAR CHIEF: (*gesturing to be heard*). The Modoc come against us in their strength. Often the Modoc come against us. We cannot be kind to the Modoc.

RED CLOUD: That will come after. Kindness grows. First must we be kind to our own. After, long after, all men will be kind to all men, and all men will be very strong. The strength of the Nishinam is not the strength of its strongest fighter. It is the strength of all the Nishinam added together that makes the Nishinam strong. We talk, you and I, War Chief and First Man, because we are kind one to the other; and thus we add together our wisdom, and all the Nishinam are stronger because we have talked. *A voice is heard singing. Red Cloud holds up his hand for silence.*

MATING SONG

DEW WOMAN

In the morning by the river,
    In the evening at the fire,
In the night when all lay sleeping,
    Torn was I with life's desire.

There were stirrings 'neath my heartbeats
  Of the dreams that came to me;
In my ears were whispers, voices,
  Of the children yet to be.

RED CLOUD

(*As Red Cloud sings, Dew Woman steals from
    behind a tree and approaches him.*)
In the morning by the river
  Saw I first my maid of dew,
Daughter of the dew and dawn light,
  Of the dawn and honeydew.
She was laughter, she was sunlight,
  Woman, maid, and mate, and wife;
She was sparkle, she was gladness,
  She was all the song of life.

DEW WOMAN

In the night I built my fire,
  Fire that maidens foster when
In the ripe of mating season
  Each builds for her man of men.

RED CLOUD

In the night I sought her, proved her,
  Found her ease, content, and rest,
After day of toil and struggle
  Man's reward on woman's breast.

DEW WOMAN

Came to me my mate and lover;
  Kind the hands he laid on me;
Wooed me gently as a man may,
  Father of the race to be.

RED CLOUD

Soft her arms about me bound me,
  First man of the Nishinam,
Arms as soft as dew and dawn light,
  Daughter of the Nishinam.

RED CLOUD

She was life and she was woman!

DEW WOMAN

He was life and he was man!

RED CLOUD and DEW WOMAN
(*Arms about each other.*)
In the dusktime of our love night,
  There beside the marriage fire,
Proved we all the sweets of living,
  In the arms of our desire.

WAR CHIEF: (*angrily*). The councils of men are not the place for women.

RED CLOUD: (*gently*). As men grow kind and wise, there will be women in the councils of men. As men grow, their women must grow with them if they would continue to be the mothers of men.

WAR CHIEF: It is told of old time that there are women in the councils of the Sun. And is it not told that the Sun Man will destroy us?

RED CLOUD: Then is the Sun Man the stronger; it may be because of his kindness and wiseness, and because of his women.

YOUNG BRAVE: Is it told that the women of the Sun are good to the eye, soft to the arm, and a fire in the heart of man?

SHAMAN: (*holding up hand solemnly*). It were well, lest

the young do not forget, to repeat the old word
again.

WAR CHIEF: (*nodding confirmation*). Here, where the tale is
told. (*Pointing to the spring.*) Here, where the water burst
from under the heel of the Sun Man mounting into the sky.
*War Chief leads the way up the hillside to the spring and
signals to the Old Man to begin.*

THE SNARING OF THE SUN

OLD MAN

When the world was in the making,
Here within the mighty forest,
Came the Sun Man every morning.
White and shining was the Sun Man,
Blue his eyes were as the sky-blue,
Bright his hair was as dry grass is,
Warm his eyes were as the sun is,
Fruit and flower were in his glances;
All he looked on grew and sprouted,
As these trees we see about us,
Mightiest trees in all the forest,
For the Sun Man looked upon them.
Where his glance fell grasses seeded,
Where his feet fell sprang upstarting
Buckeye woods and hazel thickets,
Berry bushes, manzanita,
Till his pathway was a garden,
Flowing after like a river,
Laughing into bud and blossom.
There was never frost nor famine
And the Nishinam were happy,
Singing, dancing through the seasons,
Never cold and never hungered,
When the Sun Man lived among us.

But the foxes mean and cunning,
Hating Nishinam and all men,
Laid their snares within this forest,
Caught the Sun Man in the morning,
With their ropes of sinew caught him,
Bound him down to steal his wisdom
And become themselves bright Sun Men,
Warm of glance and fruitful-footed,
Masters of the frost and famine.

Swiftly the Coyote running
Came to aid the fallen Sun Man,
Swiftly killed the cunning foxes,
Swiftly cut the ropes of sinew,
Swiftly the Coyote freed him.

But the Sun Man in his anger,
Lightning flashing, thunder throwing,
Loosed the frost and fanged the famine,
Thorned the bushes, pinched the berries,
Put the bitter in the buckeye,
Rocked the mountains to their summits,
Flung the hills into the valleys,
Sank the lakes and shoaled the rivers,
Poured the fresh sea in the salt sea,
Stamped his foot here in the forest,
Where the water burst from under
Heel that raised him into heaven—
Angry with the world forever
Rose the Sun Man into heaven.

SHAMAN: (*solemnly*). I am the Shaman. I know what has gone
    before and what will come after. I have passed down
    through the gateway of death and talked with the dead.
    My eyes have looked upon the unseen things. My ears

have heard the unspoken words. And now I shall tell you
of the Sun Man in the days to come.

*Shaman stiffens suddenly with hideous facial distortions,
with in-turned eyeballs and loosened jaw. He waves his arms
about, writhes and twists in torment, as if in epilepsy. The
women break into a wailing, inarticulate chant, swaying
their bodies to the accent. The men join them somewhat
reluctantly, all save Red Cloud, who betrays vexation, and
War Chief, who betrays truculence. Shaman, leading the
rising frenzy, with convulsive shiverings and tremblings,
tears off his skin garments so that he is quite naked save for
a girdle of eagle claws about his thighs. His long black hair
flies about his face. With an abruptness that is startling, he
ceases all movement and stands erect, rigid. This is greeted
with a low moaning that slowly dies away.*

CHANT OF PROPHECY

SHAMAN

The Sun never grows cold.
The Sun Man is like the Sun.
His anger never grows cold.
The Sun Man will return.
The Sun Man will come back from the Sun.

PEOPLE

The Sun Man will return.
The Sun Man will come back from the Sun.

SHAMAN

There is a sign.
As the water burst forth when he rose into the sky,
So will the water cease to flow when he returns from the sky.
The Sun Man is mighty.
In his eyes is blue fire.

In his hands he bears the thunder.
The lightnings are in his hair.

PEOPLE

In his hands he bears the thunder.
The lightnings are in his hair.

SHAMAN

There is a sign.
The Sun Man is white.
His skin is white like the sun.
His hair is bright like the sunlight.
His eyes are blue like the sky.

PEOPLE

There is a sign.
The Sun Man is white.

SHAMAN

The Sun Man is mighty.
He is the enemy of the Nishinam.
He will destroy the Nishinam.

PEOPLE

He is the enemy of the Nishinam.
He will destroy the Nishinam.

SHAMAN

There is a sign.
The Sun Man will bear the thunder in his hand.

PEOPLE

There is a sign.
The Sun Man will bear the thunder in his hand.

SHAMAN

In the day the Sun Man comes
The water from the spring will no longer flow.
And in that day he will destroy the Nishinam.
With the thunder will he destroy the Nishinam.
The Nishinam will be like last year's grasses.
The Nishinam will be like the smoke of last year's campfires.
The Nishinam will be less than the dreams that trouble the
sleeper.
The Nishinam will be like the days no man remembers.
I am the Shaman.
I have spoken.

The People set up a sad wailing.
WAR CHIEF: (*striking his chest with his fist*). Hoh! Hoh! Hoh!
*The People cease from their wailing and look to the War
Chief with hopeful expectancy.*
WAR CHIEF: I am the War Chief. In war I command. Nor the
Shaman nor Red Cloud may say me nay when in war I
command. Let the Sun Man come back. I am not afraid. If
the foxes snared him with ropes, then can I slay him with
spear thrust and war club. I am the War Chief. In war I
command.
*The People greet War Chief's pronouncement with warlike
cries of approval.*
RED CLOUD: The foxes are cunning. If they snared the Sun
Man with ropes of sinew, then let us be cunning and snare
him with ropes of kindness. In kindness, O War Chief, is
strength, much strength.
SHAMAN: Red Cloud speaks true. In kindness is strength.
WAR CHIEF: I am the War Chief.
SHAMAN: You cannot slay the Sun Man.
WAR CHIEF: I am the War Chief.
SHAMAN: The Sun Man fights with the thunder in his hand.

WAR CHIEF: I am the War Chief.

RED CLOUD: (*as he speaks, the People are visibly won by his argument*). You speak true, O War Chief. In war you command. You are strong, most strong. You have slain the Modoc. You have slain the Napa. You have slain the Clam Eaters of the big water till the last one is not. Yet you have not slain all the foxes. The foxes cannot fight, yet are they stronger than you because you cannot slay them. The foxes are foxes, but we are men. When the Sun Man comes, we will not be cunning like the foxes. We will be kind. Kindness and love will we give to the Sun Man, so that he will be our friend. Then will he melt the frost, pull the teeth of famine, give us back our rivers of deep water, our lakes of sweet water, take the bitter from the buckeye, and in all ways make the world the good world it was before he left us.

PEOPLE

Hail, Red Cloud, the first man!
Hail, Red Cloud, the Acorn Planter!
Who showed us the way of our feet in the world!
Who showed us the way of our food in the world!
Who showed us the way of our hearts in the world!
Who gave us the law of family,
The law of tribe,
The law of totem,
And made us strong in the world among men!

While the People sing, the hillside slowly grows dark.

ACT I

*Ten thousand years have passed, and it is the time of the
early voyaging from Europe to the waters of the Pacific,
when the deserted hillside is again revealed as the moon
rises. The stream no longer flows from the spring. Since
the grove is used only as a camp for the night when the
Nishinam are on their seasonal migration, there are no signs
of previous camps.*

*Enter from right, at end of day's march, women, old men,
and Shaman, the women bending under their burdens of
camp gear and dunnage.*

*Enter from left youths carrying fish spears and large fish.
Appear, coming down the hillside, Red Cloud and the
Hunters, many carrying meat.*

*The various repeated characters, despite differences of skin
garmenting and decoration, resemble their prototypes of
the prologue.*

RED CLOUD: Good hunting! Good hunting!

HUNTERS: Good hunting! Good hunting!

YOUTHS: Good fishing! Good fishing!

WOMEN: Good berries! Good acorns!

*The women and youths and hunters, as they reach the
campsite, begin throwing down their burdens.*

DEW WOMAN: (*discovering the dry spring*). The water no longer flows!

SHAMAN: (*stilling the excitement that is immediate on the discovery*). The word of old time that has come down to us from all the Shamans who have gone before! The Sun Man has come back from the Sun.

DEW WOMAN: (*looking to Red Cloud*). Let Red Cloud speak. Since the morning of the world has Red Cloud ever been reborn with the ancient wisdom to guide us.

WAR CHIEF: Save in war. In war I command. (*He picks out Hunters by name.*) Deer Foot . . . Elk Man . . . Antelope. Run through the forest, climb the hilltops, seek down the valleys, for aught you may find of this Sun Man.
At a wave of the War Chief's hand the three Hunters depart in different directions.

DEW WOMAN: Let Red Cloud speak his mind.

RED CLOUD: (*quietly*). Last night the earth shook and there was a roaring in the air. Often have I seen, when the earth shakes and there is a roaring, that springs in some places dry up and that in other places where were no springs, springs burst forth.

SHAMAN: There is a sign.
The Shamans told it of old.
The Sun Man will bear the thunder in his hand.

PEOPLE: There is a sign.
The Sun Man will bear the thunder in his hand.

SHAMAN: The roaring in the air was the thunder of the Sun Man's return. Now will he destroy the Nishinam. Such is the word.

WAR CHIEF: Hoh! Hoh!
From right Deer Foot runs in.

DEER FOOT: (*breathless*). They come! He comes!

WAR CHIEF: Who comes?

DEER FOOT: The Sun Men. The Sun Man. He is their chief. He marches before them. And he is white.

PEOPLE: There is a sign.

There is a sign.
    The Sun Man is white.

RED CLOUD: Carries he the thunder in his hand?

DEER FOOT: (*puzzled*). He looks hungry.

WAR CHIEF: Hoh! Hoh! The Sun Man is hungry. It will be easy to kill a hungry Sun Man.

RED CLOUD: It would be easy to be kind to a hungry Sun Man and give him food. We have much. The hunting has been good.

WAR CHIEF: Better to kill the Sun Man.

He turns upon People, indicating most commands in gestures as he prepares the ambush, making women and boys conceal all the camp outfit and game and disposing the armed hunters among the ferns and behind trees till all are hidden.

ELK MAN and ANTELOPE: (*running down hillside*). The Sun Man comes.

War Chief sends them to hiding places.

WAR CHIEF: (*preparing himself to hide*). You have not hidden, O Red Cloud.

RED CLOUD: (*stepping into shadow of big tree, where he remains inconspicuous though dimly visible*). I would see this Sun Man and talk with him.

The sound of singing is heard, and War Chief conceals himself.

Sun Man, with handful of followers, singing to ease the tedium of the march, enters from right. They are patently survivors of a wrecked exploring ship, making their way inland.

SONG OF THE SEA CUNIES

SUN MEN
We sailed three hundred strong
For the far Barbaree;

Our voyage has been most long
  For the far Barbaree;
    So—it's a long pull,
    Give a strong pull,
  For the far Barbaree.

We sailed the oceans wide
  For the coast of Barbaree;
And left our ship a-sinking
  On the coast of Barbaree;
    So—it's a long pull,
    Give a strong pull,
  For the far Barbaree.

Our ship went fast alee
  On the rocks of Barbaree;
That's why we quit the sea
  On the rocks of Barbaree.
    So—it's a long pull,
    Give a strong pull,
  For the far Barbaree.

We quit the bitter seas
  On the coast of Barbaree;
To seek the savag-ees
  Of the far Barbaree.
    So—it's a long pull,
    Give a strong pull,
  For the far Barbaree.

Our feet are lame and sore
  In the far Barbaree;
From treading of the shore
  Of the far Barbaree.

> So—it's a long pull,
> Give a strong pull,
> For the far Barbaree.
>
> A weary brood are we
> In the far Barbaree;
> Sea cunies of the sea
> In the far Barbaree.
> So—it's a long pull,
> Give a strong pull,
> For the far Barbaree.

SUN MAN: (*who alone carries a musket, and who is evidently captain of the wrecked company*). No farther can we go this night. Mayhap tomorrow we may find the savages and food. (*He glances about.*) This far world grows noble trees. We shall sleep as in a temple.

FIRST SEA CUNY: (*espying Red Cloud and pointing*). Look, Captain!

SUN MAN: (*making the universal peace sign, arm raised and out, palm outward*). Who are you? Speak. We come in peace. We kindness seek.

RED CLOUD: (*advancing out of the shadow*). Whence do you come?

SUN MAN: From the great sea.

RED CLOUD: I do not understand. No one journeys on the great sea.

SUN MAN: We have journeyed many moons.

RED CLOUD: Have you come from the sun?

SUN MAN: God wot! We have journeyed across the sun, high and low in the sky, and over the sun and under the sun the round world 'round.

RED CLOUD: (*with conviction*). You come from the Sun. Your hair is like the summer sunburned grasses. Your eyes are blue. Your skin is white. (*With absolute conviction.*) You are the Sun Man.

SUN MAN: (*with a shrug of shoulders*). Have it so. I come from the Sun. I am the Sun Man.

RED CLOUD: Do you carry the thunder in your hand?

SUN MAN: (*nonplussed for the moment, glances at his musket, then smiles*). Yes, I carry the thunder in my hand.
War Chief and the Hunters leap suddenly from ambush. Sun Man warns Sea Cunies not to resist. War Chief captures and holds Sun Man, and Sea Cunies are similarly captured and held. Women and boys appear, and examine prisoners curiously.

WAR CHIEF: Hoh! Hoh! Hoh! I have captured the Sun Man! Like the foxes, I have captured the Sun Man! Deer Foot! Elk Man! The foxes held the Sun Man. I now hold the Sun Man. Then can you hold the Sun Man.
Deer Foot and Elk Man seize the Sun Man.

RED CLOUD: (*to Shaman*). He said he came in kindness.

WAR CHIEF: (*sneering*). In kindness, with the thunder in his hand.

SHAMAN: (*deflected to partisanship of War Chief by War Chief's success*). By his own lips has he said it, with the thunder in his hand.

WAR CHIEF: You are the Sun Man.

SUN MAN: (*shrugging shoulders*). My names are many as the stars. Call me White Man.

RED CLOUD: I am Red Cloud, the first man.

SUN MAN: Then am I Adam, the first man and your brother. (*Glancing about.*) And this is Eden, to look upon it.

RED CLOUD: My father was the Coyote.

SUN MAN: My father was Jehovah.

RED CLOUD: I am the Fire Bringer. I stole the fire from the ground squirrel and hid it in the heart of the wood.

SUN MAN: Then am I Prometheus, your brother. I stole

the fire from heaven and hid it in the heart of the
wood.

RED CLOUD: I am the Acorn Planter. I am the Food Bringer,
the Life Maker. I make food for more life, ever more life.

SUN MAN: Then am I truly your brother. Life Maker am I,
tilling the soil in the sweat of my brow from the beginning
of time, planting all manner of good seeds for the harvest.
(*Looking sharply at Red Cloud's skin garments.*) Also am
I the Weaver and Cloth Maker. (*Holding out arm so that
Red Cloud may examine the cloth of the coat.*) From the
hair of the goat and the wool of the sheep, and from
beaten and spun grasses, do I make the cloth to keep
man warm.

SHAMAN: (*breaking in boastfully*). I am the Shaman. I know
all secret things.

SUN MAN: I know my pathway under the sun over all the
seas, and I know the secrets of the stars that show me my
path where no path is. I know when the Wolf of Darkness
shall eat the moon. (*Pointing toward moon.*) On this night
shall the Wolf of Darkness eat the moon. (*He turns suddenly
to Red Cloud, drawing sheath knife and passing it to him.*)
More, O First Man and Acorn Planter. I am the Iron Maker.
Behold!

*Red Cloud examines knife, understands immediately its
virtue, cuts easily a strip of skin from his skin garment, and
is overcome with the wonder of the knife.*

WAR CHIEF: (*exhibiting a long bow*). I am the War Chief. No
man, save me, has strength to bend this bow. I can slay
farther than any man.

*A huge bear has come out among the bushes far up the
hillside.*

SUN MAN: I, too, am War Chief over men, and I can slay
farther than you.

WAR CHIEF: Hoh! Hoh!

SUN MAN: (*pointing to bear*). Can you slay that with your strong bow?

WAR CHIEF: (*dubiously*). It is a far shot. Too far. No man can slay a great bear so far.

Sun Man, shaking off from his arms the hands of Deer Foot and Elk Man, aims musket and fires. The bear falls, and the Nishinam betray astonishment and awe.

At a quick signal from War Chief, Sun Man is again seized. War Chief takes away musket and examines it.

SHAMAN: There is a sign.

PEOPLE: There is a sign.

He carries the thunder in his hand.

He slays with the thunder in his hand.

He is the enemy of the Nishinam.

He will destroy the Nishinam.

SHAMAN: There is a sign.

PEOPLE: There is a sign.

In the day the Sun Man comes,

The waters from the spring will no longer flow,

And in that day will he destroy the Nishinam.

WAR CHIEF: (*exhibiting musket*). Hoh! Hoh! I have taken the Sun Man's thunder.

SHAMAN: Now shall the Sun Man die, that the Nishinam may live.

RED CLOUD: He is our brother. He, too, is an acorn planter. He has spoken.

SHAMAN: He is the Sun Man, and he is our eternal enemy. He shall die.

WAR CHIEF: In war I command. (*To Hunters.*) Tie their feet with stout thongs that they may not run. And then make ready with bow and arrow to do the deed.

Hunters obey, urging and thrusting the Sea Cunies into a compact group behind the Sun Man.

RED CLOUD: Shaman I am not.

I know not the secret things.
I say the things I know.
When you plant kindness, you harvest kindness.
When you plant blood, you harvest blood.
He who plants one acorn makes way for life.
He who slays one man slays the planter of a thousand
                                                           acorns.

SHAMAN: Shaman I am.
I see the dark future.
I see the Sun Man's death,
The journey he must take
Through thick and endless forest
Where lost souls wander howling
A thousand moons of moons.

PEOPLE: Through thick and endless forest
Where lost souls wander howling
A thousand moons of moons.

*War Chief arranges Hunters with their bows and arrows for
the killing.*

SUN MAN: (*to Red Cloud*). You will slay us?

RED CLOUD: (*indicating War Chief*). In war he commands.

SUN MAN: (*addressing the Nishinam*). Nor am I a Shaman. But
I will tell you true things to be. Our brothers are acorn
planters, cloth weavers, ironworkers. Our brothers are life
makers and masters of life. Many are our brothers and
strong. They will come after us. Your First Man has spoken
true words. When you plant blood, you harvest blood.
Our brothers will come to the harvest with the thunder in
their hands. There is a sign. This night, and soon, will the
Wolf of Darkness eat the moon. And by that sign will our
brothers come on the trail we have broken.

*As final preparation for the killing is completed, and as
Hunters are arranged with their bows and arrows, Sun Man
sings.*

SONG OF THE BROTHERS

SUN MAN

Our brothers will come after,
On our trail to farthest lands;
Our brothers will come after
With the thunder in their hands.

SUN MEN

Loud will be the weeping,
Red will be the reaping,
High will be the heaping
Of the slain their law commands.

SUN MAN

Givers of law, our brothers,
This is the law they say:
Who takes the life of a brother
Ten of the slayers shall pay.

SUN MEN

Our brothers will come after,
On our trail to farthest lands;
Our brothers will come after
With the thunder in their hands.
Loud will be the weeping,
Red will be the reaping,
High will be the heaping
Of the slain their law commands.

SUN MAN

Our brothers will come after
By the courses that we lay;
Many and strong our brothers,
Masters of life are they.

SUN MEN

Our brothers will come after
  On our trail to farthest lands;
Our brothers will come after
    With the thunder in their hands.
      Loud will be the weeping,
      Red will be the reaping,
      High will be the heaping
Of the slain their law commands.

SUN MAN

Plowers of land, our brothers,
  Of the hills and pleasant leas;
Under the sun our brothers
    With their keels will plow the seas.

SUN MEN

Our brothers will come after,
  On our trail to farthest lands;
Our brothers will come after
    With the thunder in their hands.
      Loud will be the weeping,
      Red will be the reaping,
      High will be the heaping
Of the slain their law commands.

SUN MAN

Mighty men are our brothers,
  Quick to forgive and to wrath,
Sailing the seas, our brothers
    Will follow us on our path.

SUN MEN

Our brothers will come after,
  On our trail to farthest lands;

Our brothers will come after
With the thunder in their hands.
Loud will be the weeping,
Red will be the reaping,
High will be the heaping
Of the slain their law commands.

*At signal from War Chief the arrows are discharged, and
repeatedly discharged. The Sun Men fall. The War Chief
himself kills the Sun Man.*

*In what follows, Red Cloud and Dew Woman stand aside,
taking no part. Red Cloud is depressed and at the same time
is overcome with the wonder of the knife which he still
holds.*

WAR CHIEF: (*brandishing musket and drifting stiff-legged, as he
sings, into the beginning of a war dance of victory*).
Hoh! Hoh! Hoh!
I have slain the Sun Man!
Hoh! Hoh! Hoh!
I hold his thunder in my hand!
Hoh! Hoh! Hoh!
Greatest of War Chiefs am I!
Hoh! Hoh! Hoh!
I have slain the Sun Man!
The dance grows wilder.
After a time the hillside begins to darken.

DEW WOMAN: (*pointing to the moon entering eclipse*). Lo! The
Wolf of Darkness eats the Moon!
In consternation the dance is broken off for the moment.

SHAMAN: (*reassuringly*). It is a sign.
The Sun Man is dead.

WAR CHIEF: (*recovering courage and resuming dance*).
Hoh! Hoh! Hoh!
The Sun Man is dead!

PEOPLE: (*resuming dance*). Hoh! Hoh! Hoh!
  The Sun Man is dead!
  As darkness increases, the dance grows into a saturnalia
  until complete darkness settles down and hides the hillside.

ACT II

A hundred years have passed, when the hillside and the Nishinam in their temporary camp are revealed. The spring is flowing, and women are filling gourds with water. Red Cloud and Dew Woman stand apart from their people.

SHAMAN: (*pointing*). There is a sign.

    The spring lives.

    The water flows from the spring

    And all is well with the Nishinam.

PEOPLE: There is a sign.

    The spring lives.

    The water flows from the spring.

WAR CHIEF: (*boastingly*). Hoh! Hoh! Hoh!

    All is well with the Nishinam.

    Hoh! Hoh! Hoh!

    It is I who have made all well with the Nishinam.

    Hoh! Hoh! Hoh!

    I led our young men against the Napa.

    Hoh! Hoh! Hoh!

    We left no man living of the camp.

    Hoh! Hoh! Hoh!

SHAMAN: Great is our War Chief!

Good is war!
No more will the Napa hunt our meat.
No more will the Napa pick our berries.
No more will the Napa catch our fish.

PEOPLE: No more will the Napa hunt our meat.
No more will the Napa pick our berries.
No more will the Napa catch our fish.

WAR CHIEF: Hoh! Hoh! Hoh!
The War Chiefs before me made all well with the Nishinam.
Hoh! Hoh! Hoh!
The War Chief of long ago slew the Sun Man.
Hoh! Hoh! Hoh!
The Sun Man said his brothers would come after.
Hoh! Hoh! Hoh!
The Sun Man lied.

PEOPLE: Hoh! Hoh! Hoh!
The Sun Man lied.
Hoh! Hoh! Hoh!
The Sun Man lied.

SHAMAN: (*derisively*). Red Cloud is sick. He lives in dreams.
Ever he dreams of the wonders of the Sun Man.

RED CLOUD: The Sun Man was strong. The Sun Man was a
life maker. The Sun Man planted acorns, and cut quickly
with a knife not of bone nor stone, and of grasses and
hides made cunning cloth that is better than all grasses
and hides. —Old Man, where is the cunning cloth that is
better than all grasses and hides?

OLD MAN: (*fumbling in his skin pouch for the cloth*).
In the many moons aforetime,
Hundred moons and many hundred,
When the old man was the young man,
When the young man was the youngling,
Dragging branches for the campfire,
Stealing suet from the bear meat,

Cause of trouble to his mother,
Came the Sun Man in the nighttime.
I alone of all the Nishinam
Live today to tell the story;
I alone of all the Nishinam
Saw the Sun Man come among us,
Heard the Sun Man and his Sun Men
Sing their death song here among us
Ere they died beneath our arrows,
War Chief's arrows sharp and feathered—

WAR CHIEF: (*interrupting braggartly*). Hoh! Hoh! Hoh!

OLD MAN: (*producing cloth*). And the Sun Man and his Sun Men
Wore nor hair nor hide nor birdskin.
Cloth they wore from beaten grasses
Woven like our willow baskets,
Willow-woven acorn baskets
Women make in acorn season.

Old Man hands piece of cloth to Red Cloud.

RED CLOUD: (*admiring cloth*). The Sun Man was an acorn
planter, and we killed the Sun Man. We were not kind.
We made a blood debt. Blood debts are not good.

SHAMAN: The Sun Man lied. His brothers did not come after.
There is no blood debt when there is no one to make
us pay.

RED CLOUD: He who plants acorns reaps food, and food is
life. He who sows war reaps war, and war is death.

PEOPLE: (*encouraged by Shaman and War Chief to drown out
Red Cloud's voice*). Hoh! Hoh! Hoh!
The Sun Man is dead!
Hoh! Hoh! Hoh!
The Sun Man and his Sun Men are dead!

RED CLOUD: (*shaking his head*). His brothers of the Sun are
coming after. I have reports.

*Red Cloud beckons one after another of the young hunters to
speak.*

FIRST HUNTER: To the south, not far, I wandered and lived
with the Petaluma. With my eyes I did not see, but it was
told me by those whose eyes had seen, that still to the
south, not far, were many Sun Men—war chiefs who carry
the thunder in their hands; cloth makers and weavers of
cloth like to that in Red Cloud's hand; acorn planters who
plant all manner of strange seeds that ripen to rich harvests
of food that is good. And there had been trouble. The
Petaluma had killed Sun Men, and many Petaluma had
the Sun Men killed.

SECOND HUNTER: To the east, not far, I wandered and lived
with the Solano. With my own eyes I did not see, but it
was told me by those whose eyes had seen, that still to
the east, not far, and just beyond the lands of the Tule
tribes, were many Sun Men—war chiefs and cloth makers
and acorn planters. And there had been trouble. The
Solano had killed Sun Men, and many Solano had the
Sun Men killed.

THIRD HUNTER: To the north, and far, I wandered and lived
with the Klamath. With my own eyes I did not see, but it
was told me by those whose eyes had seen, that still to
the north, and far, were many Sun Men—war chiefs and
cloth makers and acorn planters. And there had been
trouble. The Klamath had killed Sun Men, and many
Klamath had the Sun Men killed.

FOURTH HUNTER: To the west, not far, three days gone I
wandered, where from the mountain I looked down upon
the great sea. With my own eyes I saw. It was like a great
bird that swam upon the water. It had great wings like to
our great trees here. And on its back I saw men, many
men, and they were Sun Men. With my own eyes I saw.

RED CLOUD: We shall be kind to the Sun Men when they
come among us.

WAR CHIEF: (*dancing stiff-legged*). Hoh! Hoh! Hoh!
Let the Sun Men come!

Hoh! Hoh! Hoh!

We will kill the Sun Men when they come!

PEOPLE: (*as they join in the war dance*). Hoh! Hoh! Hoh!

Let the Sun Men come!

Hoh! Hoh! Hoh!

We will kill the Sun Men when they come.

The dance grows wilder, the Shaman and War Chief encouraging it, while Red Cloud and Dew Woman stand sadly at a distance.

Rifle shots ring out from every side. Up the hillside appear Sun Men firing rifles. The Nishinam reel to death from their dancing.

Red Cloud shields Dew Woman with one arm about her and, with the other arm, makes the peace sign.

The massacre is complete, Dew Woman and Red Cloud being the last to fall. Red Cloud, wounded, the sole survivor, rests on his elbow and watches the Sun Men assemble about their leader.

The Sun Men are the type of pioneer Americans who, even before the discovery of gold, were already drifting across the Sierras and down into Oregon and California with their oxen and great wagons. With here and there a Rocky Mountain trapper or a buckskin-clad scout of the Kit Carson type, in the main they are backwoods farmers. All carry the long rifle of the period.

The Sun Man is buckskin-clad, with long blond hair sweeping his shoulders.

SUN MEN

(*Led by Sun Man.*)

We crossed the Western Ocean
    Three hundred years ago,
We cleared New England's forests
    Three hundred years ago.

Blow high, blow low,
Heigh hi, heigh ho,
We cleared New England's forests
Three hundred years ago.

We climbed the Alleghenies
Two hundred years ago,
We reached the Susquehanna
Two hundred years ago.
Blow high, blow low,
Heigh hi, heigh ho,
We reached the Susquehanna
Two hundred years ago.

We crossed the Mississippi
One hundred years ago,
And glimpsed the Rocky Mountains
One hundred years ago.
Blow high, blow low,
Heigh hi, heigh ho,
And glimpsed the Rocky Mountains
One hundred years ago.

We passed the Rocky Mountains
A year or so ago,
And crossed the salty deserts
A year or so ago.
Blow high, blow low,
Heigh hi, heigh ho,
And crossed the salty deserts
A year or so ago.

We topped the high Sierras
But a few days ago,

And saw great California
But a few days ago.
　　Blow high, blow low,
　　Heigh hi, heigh ho,
And saw great California
But a few days ago.

We crossed Sonoma's mountains
　　An hour or so ago,
And found this mighty forest
　　An hour or so ago.
　　Blow high, blow low,
　　Heigh hi, heigh ho,
And found this mighty forest
　　An hour or so ago.

SUN MAN: (*glancing about at the slain and at the giant forest*).
Good the day, good the deed, and good this California
land.

RED CLOUD: Not with these eyes, but with other eyes in my
lives before, have I beheld you. You are the Sun Man.
*The attention of all is drawn to Red Cloud, and they group
about him and the Sun Man.*

SUN MAN: Call me White Man. Though in truth we follow the
sun. All our lives have we followed the sunset sun, as our
fathers followed it before us.

RED CLOUD: And you slay us with the thunder in your hand.
You slay us because we slew your brothers.

SUN MAN: (*nodding to Red Cloud and addressing his own
followers*). You see, it was no mistake. He confesses it.
Other white men have they slain.

RED CLOUD: There will come a day when men will not slay
men and when all men will be brothers. And in that day
all men will plant acorns.

SUN MAN: You speak well, brother.

RED CLOUD: Ever was I for peace, but in war I did not command.
Ever I sought the secrets of the growing things, the times
and seasons for planting. Ever I planted acorns, making
two black oak trees grow where one grew before. And
now all is ended. Oh, my black oak acorns! My black oak
acorns! Who will plant them now?

SUN MAN: Be of good cheer. We, too, are planters. Rich is
your land here. Not from poor soil can such trees sprout
heavenward. We will plant many seeds and grow mighty
harvests.

RED CLOUD: I planted the short acorns in the valley. I planted
the long acorns in the valley. I made food for life.

SUN MAN: You planted well, brother, but not well enough. It
is for that reason that you pass. Your fat valley grows food
but for a handful of men. We shall plant your fat valley
and grow food for ten thousand men.

RED CLOUD: Ever I counseled peace and planting.

SUN MAN: Some day all men will counsel peace. No man will
slay his fellow. All men will plant.

RED CLOUD: But before that day you will slay, as you have
this day slain us?

SUN MAN: You killed our brothers first. Blood debts must
be paid. It is man's way upon the earth. But more, O
brother! We follow the sunset sun, and the way before us
is red with war. The way behind us is white with peace.
Ever before us we make room for life. Ever we slay the
squalling, crawling things of the wild. Ever we clear the
land and destroy the weeds that block the way of life
for the seeds we plant. We are many, and many are our
brothers that come after along the way of peace we blaze.
Where you make two black oaks grow in the place of one,
we make a hundred. And where we make one grow, our
brothers who come after make a hundred hundred.

RED CLOUD: Truly are you the Sun Man. We knew about you of old time. Our old men knew and sang of you:

> White and shining was the Sun Man,
> Blue his eyes were as the sky-blue,
> Bright his hair was as dry grass is,
> Warm his eyes were as the sun is,
> Fruit and flower were in his glances;
> All he looked on grew and sprouted,
> Where his glance fell grasses seeded,
> Where his feet fell sprang upstarting
> Buckeye woods and hazel thickets,
> Berry bushes, manzanita,
> Till his pathway was a garden,
> Flowing after like a river
> Laughing into bud and blossom.

SONG OF THE PIONEERS

SUN MEN

Our brothers follow on the trail we blaze;
Where howled the wolf and ached the naked plain
Spring bounteous harvests at our brothers' hands;
In place of war's alarums, peaceful days;
Above the warrior's grave the golden grain
Turns deserts grim and stark to laughing lands.

SUN MAN

We cleared New England's flinty slopes and plowed
Her rocky fields to fairness in the sun,
But fared we westward always for we sought
A land of golden richness and we knew
The land was waiting on the sunset trail.
Where we found forest we left fertile fields,
We bridled rivers wild to grind our corn,

The deer paths turned to roadways at our heels,
Our axes felled the trees that bridged the streams,
And fenced the meadow pastures for our kine.

SUN MEN

Our brothers follow on the trail we blaze;
    Where howled the wolf and ached the naked plain
        Spring bounteous harvests at our brothers' hands;
In place of war's alarums, peaceful days;
    Above the warrior's grave the golden grain
        Turns deserts grim and stark to laughing lands.

SUN MAN

Beyond the Mississippi still we fared,
And rested weary by the River Platte
Until the young grass velveted the Plains,
Then yoked again our oxen to the trail
That ever led us west to farthest west.
Our women toiled beside us, and our young,
And helped to break the soil and plant the corn,
And fought beside us in the battlefront
To fight of arrow, whine of bullet, when
We chained our circled wagons wheel to wheel.

SUN MEN

Our brothers follow on the trail we blaze;
    Where howled the wolf and ached the naked plain
        Spring bounteous harvests at our brothers' hands;
In place of war's alarums, peaceful days;
    Above the warrior's grave the golden grain
        Turns deserts grim and stark to laughing lands.

SUN MAN

The rivers sank beneath the desert sand,
The tall pines dwarfed to sagebrush, and the grass

Grew sparse and bitter in the alkali,
But fared we always toward the setting sun.
Our oxen famished till the last one died
And our great wagons rested in the snow.
We climbed the high Sierras and looked down
From winter bleak upon the land we sought,
A sunny land, a rich and fruitful land,
The warm and golden California land.

SUN MEN

Our brothers follow on the trail we blaze;
  Where howled the wolf and ached the naked plain
    Spring bounteous harvests at our brothers' hands;
In place of war's alarums, peaceful days;
  Above the warrior's grave the golden grain
    Turns deserts grim and stark to laughing lands.

The hillside begins to darken.

RED CLOUD: (*faintly*). The darkness is upon me. You are acorn
planters. You are my brothers. The darkness is upon me
and I pass.

SUN MEN

(*As total darkness descends.*)
Our brothers follow on the trail we blaze;
  Where howled the wolf and ached the naked plain
    Spring bounteous harvests at our brothers' hands;
In place of war's alarums, peaceful days;
  Above the warrior's grave the golden grain
    Turns deserts grim and stark to laughing lands.

EPILOGUE

RED CLOUD: Good tidings! Good tidings
    To the sons of men!
    Good tidings! Good tidings!
    War is dead!
    Light begins to suffuse the hillside, revealing Red Cloud
    far up the hillside in a commanding position on an out-jut
    of rock.
    Lo, the New Day dawns,
    The day of brotherhood,
    The day when all men
    Shall be kind to all men,
    And all men shall be sowers of life.
VOICES: (*from every side a burst of voices*). Hail to Red Cloud!
    The Acorn Planter!
    The Life Maker!
    Hail! All hail!
    The New Day dawns,
    The day of brotherhood,
    The day of man.
    A band of Warriors appears on hillside.
WARRIORS: Hail, Red Cloud!

Mightier than all fighting men!
The slayer of War!
We are not sad.
Our eyes were blinded.
We did not know one acorn planted
Was mightier than a hundred fighting men.
We are not sad.
Our red work was when
The world was young and wild.
The world has grown wise.
No man slays his brother.
Our work is done.
In the light of the New Day are we glad.
A band of Pioneers and Sea Explorers appears.

PIONEERS and EXPLORERS: Hail, Red Cloud!
The first planter!
The Acorn Planter!
We sang that War would die,
The anarch of our wild and wayward past.
We sang our brothers would come after,
Turning desert into garden,
Sowing friendship, and not hatred,
Planting seeds instead of dead men,
Growing men to manhood in the sun.
A band of Husbandmen appear, bearing fruit and sheaves of grain and corn.

HUSBANDMEN: Hail, Red Cloud!
The first planter!
The Acorn Planter!
The harvests no more are red, but golden.
We are thy children.
We plant for increase,
Increase of wheat and corn,
Of fruit and flower,

Of sheep and kine,
Of love and lovers;
Rich are our harvests
And many are our lovers.

RED CLOUD: Death is a stench in the nostrils,
Life is beauty and joy.
The planters are ever brothers.
Never are the warriors brothers;
Their ways are set apart,
Their hands raised each against each.
The planters' ways are the one way.
Ever they plant for life,
For life more abundant,
For beauty of head and hand,
For the voices of children playing,
And the laughter of maids in the twilight
And the lover's song in the gloom.

ALL VOICES: Hail, Red Cloud!
The first planter!
The Acorn Planter!
The maker of life!
Hail! All hail!
The New Day dawns,
The day of brotherhood,
The day of man!

THE FIRST POET

*A summer plain, the eastern side of which is bounded by
grassy hills of limestone, the other sides by a forest. The
hill nearest to the plain terminates in a cliff, in the face of
which, nearly at the level of the ground, are four caves, with
low, narrow entrances. Before the caves, and distant from
them less than one hundred feet, is a broad, flat rock, on
which are laid several sharp slivers of flint, which, like the
rock, are blood-stained. Between the rock and the cave
entrances, on a low pile of stones, is squatted a man, stout
and hairy. Across his knees is a thick club, and behind
him crouches a woman. At his right and left are two men
somewhat resembling him, and like him, bearing wooden
clubs. These four face the west, and between them and the
bloody rock squat some threescore of cave folk, talking
loudly among themselves. It is late afternoon.
The name of him on the pile of stones is Uk, the name
of his mate, Ala; and of those at his right and left, Ok
and Un.*

UK: Be still! (*Turning to the woman behind him.*) Thou seest
that they become still. None save me can make his kind
be still, except perhaps the chief of the apes when in the

331

night he deems he hears a serpent. . . . At whom dost thou stare so long? At Oan? Oan, come to me!

OAN: I am thy cub.

UK: Oan, thou art a fool!

OK and UN: Ho! Ho! Oan is a fool!

ALL THE TRIBE: Ho! Ho! Oan is a fool!

OAN: Why am I a fool?

UK: Dost thou not chant strange words? Last night I heard thee chant strange words at the mouth of thy cave.

OAN: Ay! They are marvelous words; they were born within me in the dark.

UK: Art thou a woman, that thou shouldst bring forth? Why dost thou not sleep when it is dark?

OAN: I did half sleep; perhaps I dreamed.

UK: And why shouldst thou dream, not having had more than thy portion of flesh? Hast thou slain a deer in the forest and brought it not to the Stone?

ALL THE TRIBE: Wa! Wa! He hath slain in the forest and brought not the meat to the Stone!

UK: Be still, ye! (*To Ala.*) Thou seest that they become still. . . . Oan, hast thou slain and kept to thyself?

OAN: Nay, thou knowest that I am not apt at the chase. Also it irks me to squat on a branch all day above a path, bearing a rock upon my thighs. Those words did but awaken within me when I was peaceless in the night.

UK: And why wast thou peaceless in the night?

OAN: Thy mate wept, for that thou didst beat her.

UK: Ay! She lamented loudly. But thou shalt make thy half-sleep henceforth at the mouth of the cave, so that when Gurr the tiger cometh, thou shalt hear him sniff between the boulders and shalt strike the flints, whose stare he hatest. Gurr cometh nightly to the caves.

ONE OF THE TRIBE: Ay! Gurr smelleth the Stone!

UK: Be still! (*To Ala.*) Had he not become still, Ok and Un would have beaten him with their clubs. . . . But, Oan, tell us those words that were born to thee when Ala did weep.

OAN: (*arising*). They are wonderful words. They are such:

> The bright day is gone—

UK: Now I see thou art liar as well as fool: Behold, the day is not gone!

OAN: But the day was gone in that hour when my song was born to me.

UK: Then shouldst thou have sung it only at that time and not when it is yet day. But beware lest thou awaken me in the night. Make thou many stars, that they fly in the whiskers of Gurr.

OAN: My song is even of stars.

UK: It was Ul thy father's wont, ere I slew him with four great stones, to climb to the tops of the tallest trees and reach forth his hand, to see if he might not pluck a star. But I said, "Perhaps they be as chestnut burs." And all the tribe did laugh. Ul was also a fool. But what dost thou sing of stars?

OAN: I will begin again:

> The bright day is gone.
> The night maketh me sad, sad, sad—

UK: Nay, the night maketh thee sad; not sad, sad, sad. For when I say to Ala, "Gather thou dried leaves," I say not, "Gather thou dried leaves, leaves, leaves." Thou art a fool!

OK and UN: Thou art a fool!

ALL THE TRIBE: Thou art a fool!

UK: Yea, he is a fool. But say on, Oan, and tell us of thy chestnut burs.

OAN: I will begin again:

> The bright day is gone—

UK: Thou dost not say, "gone, gone, gone"!

OAN: I am thy cub. Suffer that I speak: So shall the tribe admire greatly.

UK: Speak on!

OAN: I will begin once more:

> The bright day is gone.
> The night maketh me sad, sad—

UK: Said I not that "sad" should be spoken but once? Shall I set Ok and Un upon thee with their branches?

OAN: But it was so born within me—even "sad, sad—"

UK: If again thou twice or thrice say "sad," thou shalt be dragged to the Stone.

OAN: Ow! Ow! I am thy cub! Yet listen:

> The bright day is gone.
> The night maketh me sad—

Ow! Ow! Thou makest me more sad than the night doth! The song—

UK: Ok! Un! Be prepared!

OAN: (*hastily*). Nay! Have mercy! I will begin afresh:

> The bright day is gone.
> The night maketh me sad.
> The—the—the—

UK: Thou hast forgotten and art a fool! See, Ala, he is a fool!

OK and UN: He is a fool!

ALL THE TRIBE: He is a fool!

OAN: I am not a fool! This is a new thing. In the past, when
ye did chant, O men, ye did leap about the Stone, beating
your breasts and crying, "Hai, hai, hai!" Or, if the moon
was great, "Hai, hai! Hai, hai, hai!" But this song is made
even with such words as ye do speak, and is a great
wonder. One may sit at the cave's mouth and moan it
many times as the light goeth out of the sky.

ONE OF THE TRIBE: Ay! Even thus doth he sit at the mouth
of our cave, making us marvel, and more especially the
women.

UK: Be still! . . . When I would make women marvel, I do
show them a wolf's brains upon my club, or the great
stone that I cast, or perhaps do whirl my arms mightily, or
bring home much meat. How should a man do otherwise?
I will have no songs in this place.

OAN: Yet suffer that I sing my song unto the tribe. Such things
have not been before. It may be that they shall praise
thee, seeing that I who do make this song am thy cub.

UK: Well, let us have the song.

OAN: (facing the tribe).

> The bright day is gone.
> The night maketh me sa—sad.
> But the stars are very white.
> They whisper that the day shall return.
> O stars; little pieces of the day!

UK: This is indeed madness. Hast thou heard a star whisper?
Did Ul, thy father, tell thee that he heard the stars whisper
when he was in the treetop? And of what moment is it
that a star be a piece of the day, seeing that its light is of
no value? Thou art a fool!

OK and UN: Thou art a fool!

ALL THE TRIBE: Thou art a fool!

OAN: But it was so born unto me. And at that birth it was as though I would weep, yet had not been stricken; I was moreover glad, yet none had given me a gift of meat.

UK: It is a madness. How shall the stars profit us? Will they lead us to a bear's den, or where the deer foregather, or break for us great bones, that we come at their marrow? Will they tell us anything at all? Wait thou until the night, and we shall peer forth from between the boulders, and all men shall take note that the stars cannot whisper. . . . Yet it may be that they are pieces of the day. This is a deep matter.

OAN: Ay! They are pieces of the moon!

UK: What further madness is this? How shall they be pieces of two things that are not the same? Also it was not thus in the song.

OAN: I will make me a new song. We do change the shape of wood and stone, but a song is made out of nothing. Ho! Ho! I can fashion things from nothing! Also I say that the stars come down at morning and become the dew.

UK: Let us have no more of these stars. It may be that a song is a good thing, if it be of what a man knoweth. Thus, if thou singest of my club, or of the bear that I slew, of the stain on the Stone, or the cave and the warm leaves in the cave, it might be well.

OAN: I will make thee a song of Ala!

UK: (*furiously*). Thou shalt make me no such song! Thou shalt make me a song of the deer liver that thou hast eaten! Did I not give to thee of the liver of the she-deer, because thou didst bring me crawfish?

OAN: Truly I did eat of the liver of the she-deer, but to sing thereof is another matter.

UK: It was no labor for thee to sing of the stars. See now our clubs and casting stones, with which we slay flesh to eat;

also the caves in which we dwell, and the Stone whereon we make sacrifice; wilt thou sing no song of those?

OAN: It may be that I shall sing thee songs of them. But now, as I strive here to sing of the doe's liver, no words are born unto me: I can but sing, "O liver! O red liver!"

UK: That is a good song: Thou seest that the liver is red. It is red as blood.

OAN: But I love not the liver, save to eat of it.

UK: Yet the song of it is good. When the moon is full, we shall sing it about the Stone. We shall beat upon our breasts and sing, "O liver! O red liver!" And all the women in the caves shall be affrighted.

OAN: I will not have that song of the liver! It shall be Ok's song; the tribe must say, "Ok hath made the song!"

OK: Ay! I shall be a great singer; I shall sing of a wolf's heart and say, "Behold, it is red!"

UK: Thou art a fool, and shalt sing only, "Hai, hai!" as thy father before thee. But Oan shall make me a song of my club, for the women listen to his songs.

OAN: I will make thee no songs, neither of thy club, nor thy cave, nor thy doe's liver. Yea! Though thou give me no more flesh, yet will I live alone in the forest and eat the seed of grasses and likewise rabbits that are easily snared. And I will sleep in a treetop, and I will sing nightly:

> The bright day is gone.
> The night maketh me sad, sad, sad, sad, sad, sad—

UK: Ok and Un, arise and slay!
Ok and Un rush upon Oan, who stoops and picks up two casting stones, with one of which he strikes Ok between the eyes, and with the other mashes the hand of Un, so that he drops his club. Uk arises.

UK: Behold! Gurr cometh! He cometh swiftly from the wood!

*The Tribe, including Oan and Ala, rush for the cave mouths.
As Oan passes Uk, the latter runs behind Oan and crushes
his skull with a blow of his club.*

UK: O men! O men with the heart of hyenas! Behold, Gurr
cometh not! I did but strive to deceive you, that I might
the more easily slay this singer, who is very swift of foot.
. . . Gather ye before me, for I would speak wisdom. . . .
It is not well that there be any song among us other
than what our fathers sang in the past, or, if there be
songs, let them be of such matters as are of common
understanding. If a man sing of a deer, so shall he be
drawn, it may be, to go forth and slay a deer, or even a
moose. And if he sing of his casting stones, it may be that
he become more apt in the use thereof. And if he sing of
his cave, it may be that he shall defend it more stoutly
when Gurr teareth at the boulders. But it is a vain thing
to make songs of the stars that seem scornful even of
me; or of the moon, which is never two nights the same;
or of the day, which goeth about its business and will
not linger, though one pierce a she-babe with a flint.
But as for me, I would have none of these songs. For if
I sing of such in the council, how shall I keep my wits?
And if I think thereof when at the chase, it may be that
I babble it forth and the meat hear and escape. And ere
it be time to eat, I do give my mind solely to the care of
my hunting gear. And if one sing when eating, he may
fall short of his just portion. And when one hath eaten,
doth not he go straightway to sleep? So where shall
men find a space for singing? But do ye as ye will: As
for me, I will have none of these songs and stars. Be it
also known to all the women that if, remembering these
wild words of Oan, they do sing them to themselves or
teach them to the young ones, they shall be beaten with
brambles. Cause swiftly that the wife of Ok cease from

her wailing, and bring hither the horses that were slain yesterday, that I may apportion them. Had Oan wisdom, he might have eaten thereof; and had a mammoth fallen into our pit, he might have feasted many days. But Oan was a fool!

UN: Oan was a fool!

ALL THE TRIBE: Oan was a fool!

CURTAIN

A WICKED WOMAN

Scene: California.

Time: Afternoon of a summer day.

CHARACTERS

LORETTA: A sweet young thing. Frightfully innocent. About nineteen years old. Slender, delicate, a fragile flower. Ingenuous.

NED BASHFORD: A jaded young man of the world, who has philosophized his experiences and who is without faith in the veracity or purity of women.

BILLY MARSH: A boy from a country town who is just about as innocent as Loretta. Awkward. Positive. Raw and callow youth.

ALICE HEMINGWAY: A society woman, good-hearted, and a matchmaker.

JACK HEMINGWAY: Her husband.

MAID.

Curtain rises on a conventional living room of a country house in California. It is the Hemingway house at Santa Clara. The room is remarkable for magnificent stone fireplace at rear center. On either side of fireplace are generous diamond-paned windows. Wide, curtained doorways to right and left. To left, front, table, with vase of flowers and chairs. To right, front, grand piano.

Curtain discovers Loretta seated at piano, not playing, her back to it, facing Ned Bashford, who is standing.

LORETTA: (*petulantly, fanning herself with sheet of music*). No, I won't go fishing. It's too warm. Besides, the fish won't bite so early in the afternoon.

NED: Oh, come on. It's not warm at all. And anyway, we won't really fish. I want to tell you something.

LORETTA: (*still petulantly*). You are always wanting to tell me something.

NED: Yes, but only in fun. This is different. This is serious. Our . . . my happiness depends upon it.

LORETTA: (*speaking eagerly, no longer petulant, looking serious and delighted, divining a proposal*). Then don't wait. Tell me right here.

NED: (*almost threateningly*). Shall I?

LORETTA: (*challenging*). Yes.

> *He looks around apprehensively, as though fearing inter-*
> *ruption; clears his throat, takes resolution, also takes*
> *Loretta's hand.*
> *Loretta is startled, timid, yet willing to hear, naively unable*
> *to conceal her love for him.*

NED: (*speaking softly*). Loretta . . . I . . . ever since I met you,
I have—

> *Jack Hemingway appears in the doorway to the left, just*
> *entering.*
> *Ned suddenly drops Loretta's hand. He shows exasperation.*
> *Loretta shows disappointment at interruption.*

NED: Confound it!

LORETTA: (*shocked*). Ned! Why will you swear so?

NED: (*testily*). That isn't swearing.

LORETTA: What is it, pray?

NED: Displeasuring.

JACK HEMINGWAY: (*who is crossing over to right*). Squabbling
again?

LORETTA: (*indignantly and with dignity*). No, we're not.

NED: (*gruffly*). What do you want now?

JACK HEMINGWAY: (*enthusiastically*). Come on fishing.

NED: (*snappily*). No. It's too warm.

JACK HEMINGWAY: (*resignedly, going out right*). You needn't
take a fellow's head off.

LORETTA: I thought you wanted to go fishing.

NED: Not with Jack.

LORETTA: (*accusingly, fanning herself vigorously*). And you told
me it wasn't warm at all.

NED: (*speaking softly*). That isn't what I wanted to tell you,
Loretta. (*He takes her hand.*) Dear Loretta—

> *Enter abruptly Alice Hemingway from right.*
> *Loretta sharply jerks her hand away and looks put out.*

Ned tries not to look awkward.

ALICE HEMINGWAY: Goodness! I thought you'd both gone fishing!

LORETTA: (*sweetly*). Is there anything you want, Alice?

NED: (*trying to be courteous*). Anything I can do?

ALICE HEMINGWAY: (*speaking quickly and trying to withdraw*). No, no. I only came to see if the mail had arrived.

LORETTA and NED: (*speaking together*). No, it hasn't arrived.

LORETTA: (*suddenly moving toward door to right*). I am going to see.

Ned looks at her reproachfully.

Loretta looks back tantalizingly from doorway and disappears.

Ned flings himself disgustedly into morris chair.

ALICE HEMINGWAY: (*moving over and standing in front of him. Speaks accusingly.*) What have you been saying to her?

NED: (*disgruntled*). Nothing.

ALICE HEMINGWAY: (*threateningly*). Now, listen to me, Ned.

NED: (*earnestly*). On my word, Alice, I've been saying nothing to her.

ALICE HEMINGWAY: (*with sudden change of front*). Then you ought to have been saying something to her.

NED: (*irritably. Getting chair for her, seating her, and seating himself again.*) Look here, Alice, I know your game. You invited me down here to make a fool of me.

ALICE HEMINGWAY: Nothing of the sort, sir. I asked you down to meet a sweet and unsullied girl—the sweetest, most innocent and ingenuous girl in the world.

NED: (*dryly*). That's what you said in your letter.

ALICE HEMINGWAY: And that's why you came. Jack had been trying for a year to get you to come. He did not know what kind of a letter to write.

NED: If you think I came because of a line in a letter about a girl I'd never seen—

ALICE HEMINGWAY: (*mockingly*). The poor, jaded, world-worn

man, who is no longer interested in women . . . and girls!
The poor, tired pessimist who has lost all faith in the
goodness of women—

NED: For which you are responsible.

ALICE HEMINGWAY: (*incredulously*). I?

NED: You are responsible. Why did you throw me over and
marry Jack?

ALICE HEMINGWAY: Do you want to know?

NED: Yes.

ALICE HEMINGWAY: (*judiciously*). First, because I did not love
you. Second, because you did not love me. (*She smiles
at his protesting hand and at the protesting expression
on his face.*) And third, because there were just about
twenty-seven other women at that time that you loved, or
thought you loved. That is why I married Jack. And that is
why you lost faith in the goodness of women. You have
only yourself to blame.

NED: (*admiringly*). You talk so convincingly. I almost believe
you as I listen to you. And yet I know all the time that you
are like all the rest of your sex—faithless, unveracious,
and . . .

He glares at her, but does not proceed.

ALICE HEMINGWAY: Go on. I'm not afraid.

NED: (*with finality*). And immoral.

ALICE HEMINGWAY: Oh! You wretch!

NED: (*gloatingly*). That's right. Get angry. You may break the
furniture if you wish. I don't mind.

ALICE HEMINGWAY: (*with sudden change of front, softly*). And
how about Loretta?

Ned gasps and remains silent.

ALICE HEMINGWAY: The depths of duplicity that must lurk
under that sweet and innocent exterior . . . according to
your philosophy!

NED: (*earnestly*). Loretta is an exception, I confess. She is all

that you said in your letter. She is a little fairy, an angel. I
never dreamed of anything like her. It is remarkable to
find such a woman in this age.

ALICE HEMINGWAY: (*encouragingly*). She is so naive.

NED: (*taking the bait*). Yes, isn't she? Her face and her tongue
betray all her secrets.

ALICE HEMINGWAY: (*nodding her head*). Yes, I have noticed it.

NED: (*delightedly*). Have you?

ALICE HEMINGWAY: She cannot conceal anything. Do you
know that she loves you?

NED: (*falling into the trap, eagerly*). Do you think so?

ALICE HEMINGWAY: (*laughing and rising*). And to think I once
permitted you to make love to me for three weeks!
Ned rises.
*Maid enters from left with letters, which she brings to Alice
Hemingway.*

ALICE HEMINGWAY: (*running over letters*). None for you, Ned.
(*Selecting two letters for herself.*) Tradesmen. (*Handing
remainder of letters to Maid.*) And three for Loretta.
(*Speaking to Maid.*) Put them on the table, Josie.
Maid puts letters on table to left front and makes exit to left.

NED: (*with shade of jealousy*). Loretta seems to have quite a
correspondence.

ALICE HEMINGWAY: (*with a sigh*). Yes, as I used to when I was
a girl.

NED: But hers are family letters.

ALICE HEMINGWAY: Yes, I did not notice any from Billy.

NED: (*faintly*). Billy?

ALICE HEMINGWAY: (*nodding*). Of course she has told you
about him?

NED: (*gasping*). She has had lovers . . . already?

ALICE HEMINGWAY: And why not? She is nineteen.

NED: (*haltingly*). This . . . er . . . this Billy . . . ?

ALICE HEMINGWAY: (*laughing and putting her hand reassuringly on his arm).* Now, don't be alarmed, poor, tired philosopher. She doesn't love Billy at all.

Loretta enters from right.

ALICE HEMINGWAY: (*to Loretta, nodding toward table*). Three letters for you.

LORETTA: (*delightedly*). Oh! Thank you.

Loretta trips swiftly across to table, looks at letters, sits down, opens letters, and begins to read.

NED: (*suspiciously*). But Billy?

ALICE HEMINGWAY: I am afraid he loves her very hard. That is why she is here. They had to send her away. Billy was making life miserable for her. They were little children together—playmates. And Billy has been, well, importunate. And Loretta, poor child, does not know anything about marriage. That is all.

NED: (*reassured*). Oh, I see.

Alice Hemingway starts slowly toward right exit, continuing conversation and accompanied by Ned.

ALICE HEMINGWAY: (*calling to Loretta*). Are you going fishing, Loretta?

Loretta looks up from letter and shakes head.

ALICE HEMINGWAY: (*to Ned*). Then you're not, I suppose.

NED: No, it's too warm.

ALICE HEMINGWAY: Then I know the place for you.

NED: Where?

ALICE HEMINGWAY: Right here. (*Looks significantly in direction of Loretta.*) Now is your opportunity to say what you ought to say.

Alice Hemingway laughs teasingly and goes out to right. Ned hesitates, starts to follow her, looks at Loretta, and stops. He twists his mustache and continues to look at her meditatively.

Loretta is unaware of his presence and goes on reading. Finishes letter, folds it, replaces in envelope, looks up, and discovers Ned.

LORETTA: (*startled*). Oh! I thought you were gone.

NED: (*walking across to her*). I thought I'd stay and finish our conversation.

LORETTA: (*willingly, settling herself to listen*). Yes, you were going to . . .

Drops eyes and ceases talking.

NED: (*taking her hand, tenderly*). I little dreamed when I came down here visiting that I was to meet my destiny in—

Abruptly releases Loretta's hand.

Maid enters from left with tray.

Loretta glances into tray and discovers that it is empty. She looks inquiringly at Maid.

MAID: A gentleman to see you. He hasn't any card. He said for me to tell you that it was Billy.

LORETTA: (*starting, looking with dismay and appeal to Ned*). Oh! . . . Ned!

NED: (*gracefully and courteously, rising to his feet and preparing to go*). If you'll excuse me now, I'll wait till afterward to tell you what I wanted.

LORETTA: (*in dismay*). What shall I do?

NED: (*pausing*). Don't you want to see him? (*Loretta shakes her head.*) Then don't.

LORETTA: (*slowly*). I can't do that. We are old friends. We . . . were children together. (*To the Maid.*) Send him in. (*To Ned, who has started to go out toward right.*) Don't go, Ned.

Maid makes exit to left.

NED: (*hesitating a moment*). I'll come back.

Ned makes exit to right.

Loretta, left alone on stage, shows perturbation and dismay. Billy enters from left. Stands in doorway a moment. His shoes are dusty. He looks overheated. His eyes and face brighten at sight of Loretta. .

BILLY: (*stepping forward, ardently*). Loretta!

LORETTA: (*not exactly enthusiastic in her reception, going slowly to meet him*). You never said you were coming.

Billy shows that he expects to kiss her, but she merely shakes his hand.

BILLY: (*looking down at his very dusty shoes*). I walked from the station.

LORETTA: If you had let me know, the carriage would have been sent for you.

BILLY: (*with expression of shrewdness*). If I had let you know, you wouldn't have let me come.

Billy looks around stage cautiously, then tries to kiss her.

LORETTA: (*refusing to be kissed*). Won't you sit down?

BILLY: (*coaxingly*). Go on, just one. (*Loretta shakes head and holds him off.*) Why not? We're engaged.

LORETTA: (*with decision*). We're not. You know we're not. You know I broke it off the day before I came away. And . . . and . . . you'd better sit down.

Billy sits down on edge of chair. Loretta seats herself by table. Billy, without rising, jerks his chair forward till they are facing each other, his knees touching hers. He yearns toward her. She moves back her chair slightly.

BILLY: (*with supreme confidence*). That's what I came to see you for—to get engaged over again.

Billy nudges chair forward and tries to take her hand. Loretta nudges her chair back.

BILLY: (*drawing out large silver watch and looking at it*). Now, look here, Loretta, I haven't any time to lose. I've got to leave for that train in ten minutes. And I want you to set the day.

LORETTA: But we're not engaged, Billy. So there can't be any setting of the day.

BILLY: (*with confidence*). But we're going to be. (*Suddenly breaking out.*) Oh, Loretta, if you only knew how I've suffered. That first night I didn't sleep a wink. I haven't slept much ever since. (*Nudges chair forward.*) I walk the floor all night. (*Solemnly.*) Loretta, I don't eat enough to keep a canary bird alive. Loretta . . .

Nudges chair forward.

LORETTA: (*nudging her chair back maternally*). Billy, what you need is a tonic. Have you seen Doctor Haskins?

BILLY: (*looking at watch and evincing signs of haste*). Loretta, when a girl kisses a man, it means she is going to marry him.

LORETTA: I know it, Billy. But . . . (*She glances toward letters on table.*) Captain Kitt doesn't want me to marry you. He says . . .

She takes letter and begins to open it.

BILLY: Never mind what Captain Kitt says. He wants you to stay and be company for your sister. He doesn't want you to marry me because he knows she wants to keep you.

LORETTA: Daisy doesn't want to keep me. She wants nothing but my own happiness. She says—

She takes second letter from table and begins to open it.

BILLY: Never mind what Daisy says—

LORETTA: (*taking third letter from table and beginning to open it*). And Martha says—

BILLY: (*angrily*). Darn Martha and the whole boiling of them!

LORETTA: (*reprovingly*). Oh, Billy!

BILLY: (*defensively*). Darn isn't swearing, and you know it isn't. *There is an awkward pause. Billy has lost the thread of the conversation and has vacant expression.*

BILLY: (*suddenly recollecting*). Never mind Captain Kitt, and Daisy, and Martha, and what they want. The question is, what do you want?

LORETTA: (*appealingly*). Oh, Billy, I'm so unhappy.

BILLY: (*ignoring the appeal and pressing home the point*). The thing is, do you want to marry me? (*He looks at his watch.*) Just answer that.

LORETTA: Aren't you afraid you'll miss that train?

BILLY: Darn the train!

LORETTA: (*reprovingly*). Oh, Billy!

BILLY: (*most irascibly*). Darn isn't swearing. (*Plaintively.*) That's

the way you always put me off. I didn't come all the way
here for a train. I came for you. Now just answer me one
thing. Do you want to marry me?

LORETTA: (*firmly*). No, I don't want to marry you.

BILLY: (*with assurance*). But you've got to, just the same.

LORETTA: (*with defiance*). Got to?

BILLY: (*with unshaken assurance*). That's what I said—got to.
And I'll see that you do.

LORETTA: (*blazing with anger*). I am no longer a child. You
can't bully me, Billy Marsh!

BILLY: (*coolly*). I'm not trying to bully you. I'm trying to save
your reputation.

LORETTA: (*faintly*). Reputation?

BILLY: (*nodding*). Yes, reputation. (*He pauses for a moment,
then speaks very solemnly.*) Loretta, when a woman kisses
a man, she's got to marry him.

LORETTA: (*appalled, faintly*). Got to?

BILLY: (*dogmatically*). It is the custom.

LORETTA: (*brokenly*). And when . . . a . . . a woman kisses a
man and doesn't . . . marry him . . . ?

BILLY: Then there is a scandal. That's where all the scandals
you see in the papers come from.
Billy looks at watch.
Loretta in silent despair.

LORETTA: (*in abasement*). You are a good man, Billy. (*Billy
shows that he believes it.*) And I am a very wicked woman.

BILLY: No, you're not, Loretta. You just didn't know.

LORETTA: (*with a gleam of hope*). But you kissed me first.

BILLY: It doesn't matter. You let me kiss you.

LORETTA: (*hope dying down*). But not at first.

BILLY: But you did afterward, and that's what counts. You let
me kiss you in the grape arbor. You let me—

LORETTA: (*with anguish*). Don't! Don't!

BILLY: (*relentlessly*). —kiss you when you were playing the piano. You let me kiss you that day of the picnic. And I can't remember all the times you let me kiss you good night.

LORETTA: (*beginning to weep*). Not more than five.

BILLY: (*with conviction*). Eight at least.

LORETTA: (*reproachfully, still weeping*). You told me it was all right.

BILLY: (*emphatically*). So it was all right—until you said you wouldn't marry me after all. Then it was a scandal—only no one knows it yet. If you marry me, no one ever will know it. (*Looks at watch.*) I've got to go. (*Stands up.*) Where's my hat?

LORETTA: (*sobbing*). This is awful.

BILLY: (*approvingly*). You bet it's awful. And there's only one way out. (*Looks anxiously about for hat.*) What do you say?

LORETTA: (*brokenly*). I must think. I'll write to you. (*Faintly.*) The train? Your hat's in the hall.

BILLY: (*looks at watch, hastily tries to kiss her, succeeds only in shaking hand, starts across stage toward left*). All right. You write to me. Write tomorrow. (*Stops for a moment in doorway and speaks very solemnly.*) Remember, Loretta, there must be no scandal.

Billy goes out.

Loretta sits in chair quietly weeping. Slowly dries eyes, rises from chair, and stands, undecided as to what she will do next. Ned enters from right, peeping. Discovers that Loretta is alone, and comes quietly across stage to her. When Ned comes up to her, she begins weeping again and tries to turn her head away. Ned catches both her hands in his and compels her to look at him. She weeps harder.

NED: (*putting one arm protectingly around her shoulder and drawing her toward him*). There, there, little one, don't cry.

LORETTA: (*turning her face to his shoulder like a tired child, sobbing*). Oh, Ned, if you only knew how wicked I am.

NED: (*smiling indulgently*). What is the matter, little one? Has your dearly beloved sister failed to write to you? (*Loretta shakes head.*) Has Hemingway been bullying you? (*Loretta shakes head.*) Then it must have been that caller of yours? (*Long pause, during which Loretta's weeping grows more violent.*) Tell me what's the matter, and we'll see what I can do.

He lightly kisses her hair—so lightly that she does not know.

LORETTA: (*sobbing*). I can't. You will despise me. Oh, Ned, I am so ashamed.

NED: (*laughing incredulously*). Let us forget all about it. I want to tell you something that may make me very happy. My fondest hope is that it will make you happy, too. Loretta, I love you—

LORETTA: (*uttering a sharp cry of delight, then moaning*). Too late!

NED: (*surprised*). Too late?

LORETTA: (*still moaning*). Oh, why did I? (*Ned somewhat stiffens.*) I was so young. I did not know the world then.

NED: What is it all about anyway?

LORETTA: Oh, I . . . he . . . Billy . . . I am a wicked woman, Ned. I know you will never speak to me again.

NED: This . . . er . . . this Billy—what has he been doing?

LORETTA: I . . . he . . . I didn't know. I was so young. I could not help it. Oh, I shall go mad, I shall go mad!

Ned's encircling arm goes limp. He gently disengages her and deposits her in big chair.

Loretta buries her face and sobs afresh.

NED: (*twisting mustache fiercely, regarding her dubiously, hesitating a moment, then drawing up chair and sitting down*). I . . . I do not understand.

LORETTA: (*wailing*). I am so unhappy!

NED: (*inquisitorially*). Why unhappy?

LORETTA: Because . . . he . . . he wants to marry me.

NED: (*his face brightening instantly, leaning forward and laying a hand soothingly on hers*). That should not make any girl unhappy. Because you don't love him is no reason— (*Abruptly breaking off.*) Of course you don't love him? (*Loretta shakes her head and shoulders vigorously.*) What?

LORETTA: (*explosively*). No, I don't love Billy! I don't want to love Billy!

NED: (*with confidence*). Because you don't love him is no reason that you should be unhappy just because he has proposed to you.

LORETTA: (*sobbing*). That's the trouble. I wish I did love him. Oh, I wish I were dead.

NED: (*growing complacent*). Now, my dear child, you are worrying yourself over trifles. (*His second hand joins the first in holding her hands.*) Women do it every day. Because you have changed your mind, or did not know your mind, because you have—to use an unnecessarily harsh word—jilted a man—

LORETTA: (*interrupting, raising her head and looking at him*). Jilted? Oh, Ned, if that were all!

NED: (*hollow voice*). All!

Ned's hands slowly retreat from hers. He opens his mouth as though to speak further, then changes his mind and remains silent.

LORETTA: (*protestingly*). But I don't want to marry him!

NED: Then I shouldn't.

LORETTA: But I ought to marry him.

NED: *Ought* to marry him? (*Loretta nods.*) That is a strong word.

LORETTA: (*nodding*). I know it is. (*Her lips are trembling, but she strives for control and manages to speak more calmly.*) I am a wicked woman. A terrible, wicked woman. No one knows how wicked I am . . . except Billy.

NED: (*starting, looking at her queerly*). He . . . Billy knows?
(*Loretta nods. He debates with himself a moment.*) Tell me
about it. You must tell me all of it.

LORETTA: (*faintly, as though about to weep again*). All of it?

NED: (*firmly*). Yes, all of it.

LORETTA: (*haltingly*). And . . . will . . . you . . . ever . . .
forgive . . . me?

NED: (*drawing a long breath, desperately*). Yes, I'll forgive you.
Go ahead.

LORETTA: There was no one to tell me. We were with each other
so much. I did not know anything of the world . . . then.
Pauses.

NED: (*impatiently*). Go on.

LORETTA: If I had only known.
Pauses.

NED: (*biting his lip and clenching his hands*). Yes, yes. Go on.

LORETTA: We were together almost every evening.

NED: (*savagely*). Billy?

LORETTA: Yes, of course, Billy. We were with each other so
much. . . . If I had only known . . . There was no one to
tell me. . . . I was so young. . . .
Breaks down crying.

NED: (*leaping to his feet, explosively*). The scoundrel!

LORETTA: (*lifting her head*). Billy is not a scoundrel. . . . He
. . . he . . . is a good man.

NED: (*sarcastically*). I suppose you'll be telling me next that it
was all your fault. (*Loretta nods.*) What!

LORETTA: (*steadily*). It was all my fault. I should never have
let him. I was to blame.

NED: (*paces up and down for a minute, stops in front of her,
and speaks with resignation*). All right. I don't blame you
in the least, Loretta. And you have been very honest. It
is . . . er . . . commendable. But Billy is right, and you are
wrong. You must get married.

LORETTA: (*in dim, faraway voice*). To Billy?

NED: Yes, to Billy. I'll see to it. Where does he live? I'll make him. If he won't, I'll . . . I'll shoot him!

LORETTA: (*crying out with alarm*). Oh, Ned, you won't do that?

NED: (*sternly*). I shall.

LORETTA: But I don't want to marry Billy.

NED: (*sternly*). You must. And Billy must. Do you understand? It is the only thing.

LORETTA: That's what Billy said.

NED: (*triumphantly*). You see, I am right.

LORETTA: And if . . . if I don't marry him . . . there will be . . . scandal?

NED: (*calmly*). Yes, there will be scandal.

LORETTA: That's what Billy said. Oh, I am so unhappy!

Loretta breaks down into violent weeping.

Ned paces grimly up and down, now and again fiercely twisting his mustache.

LORETTA: (*face buried, sobbing and crying all the time*). I don't want to leave Daisy! I don't want to leave Daisy! What shall I do? What shall I do? How was I to know? He didn't tell me. Nobody else ever kissed me. (*Ned stops curiously to listen. As he listens, his face brightens.*) I never dreamed a kiss could be so terrible . . . until . . . until he told me. He only told me this morning.

NED: (*abruptly*). Is that what you are crying about?

LORETTA: (*reluctantly*). N-no.

NED: (*in hopeless voice, the brightness gone out of his face, about to begin pacing again*). Then what are you crying about?

LORETTA: Because you said I had to marry Billy. I don't want to marry Billy. I don't want to leave Daisy. I don't know what I want. I wish I were dead.

NED: (*nerving himself for another effort*). Now, look here,

Loretta, be sensible. What is this about kisses? You haven't told me everything after all.

LORETTA: I . . . I don't want to tell you everything.

NED: (*imperatively*). You must.

LORETTA: (*surrendering*). Well, then . . . must I?

NED: You must.

LORETTA: (*floundering*). He . . . I . . . we . . . I let him, and he kissed me.

NED: (*desperately, controlling himself*). Go on.

LORETTA: He says eight, but I can't think of more than five times.

NED: Yes, go on.

LORETTA: That's all.

NED: (*with vast incredulity*). All?

LORETTA: (*puzzled*). All?

NED: (*awkwardly*). I mean . . . er . . . nothing worse?

LORETTA: (*puzzled*). Worse? As though there could be. Billy said—

NED: (*interrupting*). When?

LORETTA: This afternoon. Just now. Billy said that my . . . our . . . our . . . our kisses were terrible if we didn't get married.

NED: What else did he say?

LORETTA: He said that when a woman permitted a man to kiss her, she always married him. That it was awful if she didn't. It was the custom, he said; and I say it is a bad, wicked custom, and it has broken my heart. I shall never be happy again. I know I am terrible, but I can't help it. I must have been born wicked.

NED: (*absentmindedly bringing out a cigarette and striking a match*). Do you mind if I smoke? (*Coming to himself again and flinging away match and cigarette.*) I beg your pardon. I don't want to smoke. I didn't mean that at all. What I mean is . . .

He bends over Loretta, catches her hands in his, then sits on arm of chair, softly puts one arm around her, and is about to kiss her.

LORETTA: (*with horror, repulsing him*). No! No!

NED: (*surprised*). What's the matter?

LORETTA: (*agitatedly*). Would you make me a wickeder woman than I am?

NED: A kiss?

LORETTA: There will be another scandal. That would make two scandals.

NED: To kiss the woman I love . . . a scandal?

LORETTA: Billy loves me, and he said so.

NED: Billy is a joker . . . or else he is as innocent as you.

LORETTA: But you said so yourself.

NED: (*taken aback*). I?

LORETTA: Yes, you said it yourself, with your own lips, not ten minutes ago. I shall never believe you again.

NED: (*masterfully putting arm around her and drawing her toward him*). And I am a joker, too, and a very wicked man. Nevertheless, you must trust me. There will be nothing wrong.

LORETTA: (*preparing to yield*). And no . . . scandal?

NED: Scandal fiddlesticks. Loretta, I want you to be my wife.
He waits anxiously.
Jack Hemingway, in fishing costume, appears in doorway to right and looks on.

NED: You might say something.

LORETTA: I will . . . if . . .
Alice Hemingway appears in doorway to left and looks on.

NED: (*in suspense*). Yes, go on.

LORETTA: If I don't have to marry Billy.

NED: (*almost shouting*). You can't marry both of us!

LORETTA: (*sadly, repulsing him with her hands*). Then, Ned, I cannot marry you.

NED: (*dumbfounded*). W-what?

LORETTA: (*sadly*). Because I can't marry both of you.

NED: Bosh and nonsense!

LORETTA: I'd like to marry you, but . . .

NED: There is nothing to prevent you.

LORETTA: (*with sad conviction*). Oh, yes, there is. You said yourself that I had to marry Billy. You said you would s-s-shoot him if he didn't.

NED: (*drawing her toward him*). Nevertheless . . .

LORETTA: (*slightly holding him off*). And it isn't the custom . . . what . . . Billy said.

NED: No, it isn't the custom. Now, Loretta, will you marry me?

LORETTA: (*pouting demurely*). Don't be angry with me, Ned. (*He gathers her into his arms and kisses her. She partially frees herself, gasping.*) I wish it were the custom, because now I'd have to marry you, Ned, wouldn't I?

Ned and Loretta kiss a second time and profoundly.

Jack Hemingway chuckles.

Ned and Loretta, startled, but still in each other's arms, look around. Ned looks sillily at Alice Hemingway. Loretta looks at Jack Hemingway.

LORETTA: I don't care.

CURTAIN

THE BIRTHMARK

for Robert and Julia Fitzsimmons

One of the club rooms of the West Bay Athletic Club. Near center front is a large table covered with newspapers and magazines. At left a punching-bag apparatus. At right, against wall, a desk, on which rests a desk telephone. Door at rear toward left. On walls are framed pictures of pugilists, conspicuously among which is one of Robert Fitzsimmons.* Appropriate furnishings, etc., such as foils, clubs, dumbbells and trophies.

Enter Maud Sylvester.

She is dressed as a man, in evening clothes, preferably a tuxedo. In her hand is a card, and under her arm a paper-wrapped parcel. She peeps about curiously and advances to table. She is timorous and excited, elated and at the same time frightened. Her eyes are dancing with excitement.

MAUD: (*pausing by table*). Not a soul saw me. I wonder where everybody is. And that big brother of mine said I could

---

* The prizefighter Robert Fitzsimmons (1863–1917) won world titles in three weight divisions: middleweight, light heavyweight, and heavyweight. Born at Helston, Cornwall, England, he began fighting professionally in New Zealand and Australia and then moved to the United States to further his career. In his later years he also worked as a vaudevillian and in 1903 married Julia May Gifford, his third wife, who was a singer in a touring company to which he also belonged.

not get in. (*She reads back of card.*) "Here is my card, Maudie. If you can use it, go ahead. But you will never get inside the door. I consider my bet as good as won." (*Looking up, triumphantly.*) You do, do you? Oh, if you could see your little sister now. Here she is, inside. (*Pauses and looks about.*) So this is the West Bay Athletic Club. No women allowed. Well, here I am, if I don't look like one. (*Stretches out one leg and then the other and looks at them. Leaving card and parcel on table, she struts around like a man, looks at pictures of pugilists on walls, reading aloud their names and making appropriate remarks. But she stops before the portrait of Fitzsimmons and reads aloud.*) "Robert Fitzsimmons, the greatest warrior of them all." (*Clasps hands and, looking up at portrait, murmurs.*) Oh, you dear! (*Continues strutting around, imitating what she considers are a man's stride and swagger; returns to table and proceeds to unwrap parcel.*) Well, I'll go out like a girl, if I did come in like a man. (*Drops wrapping paper on table and holds up a woman's long automobile cloak and a motor bonnet. Is suddenly startled by sound of approaching footsteps and glances in a frightened way toward door.*) Mercy! Here comes somebody now!

Glances about her in alarm, drops cloak and bonnet on floor close to table, seizes a handful of newspapers, and runs to large leather chair to right of table, where she seats herself hurriedly. One paper she holds up before her, hiding her face as she pretends to read. Unfortunately the paper is upside down. The other papers lie on her lap.

Enter Robert Fitzsimmons.

He looks about, advances to table, takes out cigarette case, and is about to select one when he notices motor cloak and bonnet on floor. He lays cigarette case on table and picks them up. They strike him as profoundly curious things to be in a club room. He looks at Maud, then sees card on table. He picks it up and reads it to himself, then looks at her with comprehension. Hidden by her newspaper, she sees nothing. He looks at card again and reads and speaks in an aside.

FITZSIMMONS: "Maudie. John H. Sylvester." That must be Jack Sylvester's sister Maud. (*Fitzsimmons shows by his expression that he is going to play a joke. Tossing cloak and bonnet under the table, he places card in his vest pocket, selects a chair, sits down, and looks at Maud. He notes paper is upside down, is hugely tickled, and laughs silently.*) Hello! (*Newspaper is agitated by slight tremor. He speaks more loudly.*) Hello! (*Newspaper shakes badly. He speaks very loudly.*) Hello!

MAUD: (*peeping at him over top of paper and speaking hesitatingly*). H-h-hello!

FITZSIMMONS: (*gruffly*). You are a queer one, reading a paper upside down.

MAUD: (*lowering newspaper and trying to appear at ease*). It's quite a trick, isn't it? I often practice it. I'm real clever at it, you know.

FITZSIMMONS: (*grunts, then adds*). Seems to me I have seen you before.

MAUD: (*glancing quickly from his face to portrait and back again*). Yes, and I know you you are Robert Fitzsimmons.

FITZSIMMONS: I thought I knew you.

MAUD: Yes, it was out in San Francisco. My people still live there. I'm just, ahem, doing New York.

FITZSIMMONS: But I don't quite remember the name.

MAUD: Jones—Harry Jones.

FITZSIMMONS: (*hugely delighted, leaping from chair and striding over to her*). Sure.

Slaps her resoundingly on shoulder.

She is nearly crushed by the weight of the blow and at the same time shocked. She scrambles to her feet.

FITZSIMMONS: Glad to see you, Harry. (*He wrings her hand so that it hurts.*) Glad to see you again, Harry.

He continues wringing her hand and pumping her arm.

MAUD: (*struggling to withdraw her hand and finally succeeding. Her voice is rather faint.*) Ye-es, er . . . Bob . . . er . . . glad to see you again.

She looks ruefully at her bruised fingers and sinks into chair. Then, recollecting her part, she crosses her legs in a mannish way.

FITZSIMMONS: (*crossing to desk at right, against which he leans, facing her*). You were a wild young rascal in those San Francisco days. (*Chuckling.*) Lord, Lord, how it all comes back to me.

MAUD: (*boastfully*). I was wild—some.

FITZSIMMONS: (*grinning*). I should say! Remember that night I put you to bed?

MAUD: (*forgetting herself, indignantly*). Sir!

FITZSIMMONS: You were . . . er . . . drunk.

MAUD: I never was!

FITZSIMMONS: Surely you haven't forgotten that night! You began with dropping champagne bottles out of the club windows on the heads of the people on the sidewalk, and you wound up by assaulting a cabman. And let me tell you, I saved you from a good licking right there and squared it with the police. Don't you remember?

MAUD: (*nodding hesitatingly*). Yes, it is beginning to come back to me. I was a bit tight that night.

FITZSIMMONS: (*exultantly*). A bit tight! Why, before I could get you to bed, you insisted on telling me the story of your life.

MAUD: Did I? I don't remember that.

FITZSIMMONS: I should say not. You were past remembering anything by that time. You had your arms around my neck—

MAUD: (*interrupting*). Oh!

FITZSIMMONS: And you kept repeating over and over, "Bob, dear Bob."

MAUD: (*springing to her feet*). Oh! I never did! (*Recollecting herself.*) Perhaps I must have. I was a trifle wild in those days, I admit. But I'm wise now. I've sowed my wild oats and steadied down.

FITZSIMMONS: I'm glad to hear that, Harry. You were tearing off a pretty fast pace in those days. (*Pause, in which Maud nods.*) Still punch the bag?

MAUD: (*in quick alarm, glancing at punching bag*). No, I've got out of the hang of it.

FITZSIMMONS: (*reproachfully*). You haven't forgotten that right-and-left, arm-elbow, and shoulder movement I taught you?

MAUD: (*with hesitation*). N-o-o.

FITZSIMMONS: (*moving toward bag to left*). Then, come on.

MAUD: (*rising reluctantly and following*). I'd rather see you punch the bag. I'd just love to.

FITZSIMMONS: I will, afterward. You go to it first.

MAUD: (*eyeing the bag in alarm*). No, you. I'm out of practice.

FITZSIMMONS: (*looking at her sharply*). How many drinks have you had tonight?

MAUD: Not a one. I don't drink—that is, er, only occasionally.

FITZSIMMONS: (*indicating bag*). Then go to it.

MAUD: No, I tell you I am out of practice. I've forgotten it all. You see, I made a discovery.
Pause.

FITZSIMMONS: Yes?

MAUD: I—I—you remember what a light voice I always had—almost soprano? (*Fitzsimmons nods.*) Well, I discovered it was a perfect falsetto. I've been practicing it ever since. Experts, in another room, would swear it was a woman's voice. So would you, if you turned your back and I sang.

FITZSIMMONS: (*who has been laughing incredulously, now*

becomes suspicious). Look here, kid, I think you are an imposter. You are not Harry Jones at all.

MAUD: I am, too.

FITZSIMMONS: I don't believe it. He was heavier than you.

MAUD: I had the fever last summer and lost a lot of weight.

FITZSIMMONS: You are the Harry Jones that got soused and had to be put to bed?

MAUD: Y-e-s.

FITZSIMMONS: There is one thing I remember very distinctly. Harry Jones had a birthmark on his knee.

He looks at her legs searchingly.

MAUD: *(embarrassed, then resolving to carry it out).* Yes, right here.

She advances right leg and touches it.

FITZSIMMONS: *(triumphantly).* Wrong. It was the other knee.

MAUD: I ought to know.

FITZSIMMONS: You haven't any birthmark at all.

MAUD: I have, too.

FITZSIMMONS: *(suddenly springing to her and attempting to seize her leg).* Then we'll prove it. Let me see.

MAUD: *(in a panic backs away from him and resists his attempts until, grinning in an aside to the audience, he gives over. She, in an aside to audience.)* Fancy his wanting to see my birthmark.

FITZSIMMONS: *(bullying).* Then take a go at the bag. *(She shakes her head.)* You're not Harry Jones.

MAUD: *(approaching punching bag).* I am, too.

FITZSIMMONS: Then hit it.

MAUD: *(resolving to attempt it, hits bag with several nice blows and then is struck on the nose by it).* Oh! *(Recovering herself and rubbing her nose.)* I told you I was out of practice. You punch the bag, Bob.

FITZSIMMONS: I will, if you will show me what you can do with that wonderful soprano voice of yours.

MAUD: I don't dare. Everybody would think there was a woman in the club.

FITZSIMMONS: (*shaking his head*). No, they won't. They've all gone to the fight. There's not a soul in the building.

MAUD: (*alarmed, in a weak voice*). Not—a—soul—in—the building?

FITZSIMMONS: Not a soul. Only you and I.

MAUD: (*starting hurriedly toward door*). Then I must go.

FITZSIMMONS: What's your hurry? Sing.

MAUD: (*turning back with new resolve*). Let me see you punch the bag—er—Bob.

FITZSIMMONS: You sing first.

MAUD: No, you punch first.

FITZSIMMONS: I don't believe you are Harry—

MAUD: (*hastily*). All right, I'll sing. You sit down over there and turn your back.

Fitzsimmons obeys.

Maud walks over to the table toward right. She is about to sing, when she notices Fitzsimmons's cigarette case, picks it up, and in an aside reads his name on it and speaks.

MAUD: "Robert Fitzsimmons." That will prove to my brother that I have been here.

FITZSIMMONS: Hurry up.

Maud hastily puts cigarette case in her pocket and begins to sing.

During the song Fitzsimmons turns his head slowly and looks at her with growing admiration.

MAUD: How did you like it?

FITZSIMMONS: (*gruffly*). Rotten. Anybody could tell it was a boy's voice—

MAUD: Oh!

FITZSIMMONS: It is rough and coarse, and it cracked on every high note.

MAUD: Oh! Oh! (*Recollecting herself and shrugging her*

shoulders.) Oh, very well. Now let's see if you can do any better with the bag.

Fitzsimmons takes off coat and gives exhibition.

Maud looks on in an ecstasy of admiration.

MAUD: (*as he finishes*). Beautiful! Beautiful!

FITZSIMMONS: (*as he puts on coat and goes over and sits down near table*). Nothing like the bag to limber one up. I feel like a fighting cock. Harry, let's go out on a toot, you and I.

MAUD: Wh-a-a-t?

FITZSIMMONS: A toot. You know—one of those rip-snorting nights you used to make.

MAUD: (*emphatically, as she picks up newspapers from leather chair, sits down, and places them on her lap*). I'll do nothing of the sort. I've—I've reformed.

FITZSIMMONS: You used to joyride like the very devil.

MAUD: I know it.

FITZSIMMONS: And you always had a pretty girl or two along.

MAUD: (*boastfully, in mannish fashion*). Oh, I still have my fling. Do you know any—well—er—nice girls?

FITZSIMMONS: Sure.

MAUD: Put me wise.

FITZSIMMONS: Sure. You know Jack Sylvester?

MAUD: (*forgetting herself*). He's my brother—

FITZSIMMONS: (*exploding*). What!

MAUD: —in-law's first cousin.

FITZSIMMONS: Oh!

MAUD: So, you see, I don't know him very well. I only met him once—at the club. We had a drink together.

FITZSIMMONS: Then you don't know his sister?

MAUD: (*starting*). His sister? I—I didn't know he had a sister.

FITZSIMMONS: (*enthusiastically*). She's a peach. A queen. A little bit of all right. A—a lulu.

MAUD: (*flattered*). She is, is she?

FITZSIMMONS: She's a scream. You ought to get acquainted with her.

MAUD: (*slyly*). You know her, then?

FITZSIMMONS: You bet.

MAUD: (*aside*). Oh, ho! (*To Fitzsimmons.*) Know her very well?

FITZSIMMONS: I've taken her out more times than I can remember. You'll like her, I'm sure.

MAUD: Thanks. Tell me some more about her.

FITZSIMMONS: She dresses a bit loud. But you won't mind that. And whatever you do, don't take her to eat.

MAUD: (*hiding her chagrin*). Why not?

FITZSIMMONS: I never saw such an appetite—

MAUD: Oh!

FITZSIMMONS: It's fair sickening. She must have a tapeworm. And she thinks she can sing.

MAUD: Yes?

FITZSIMMONS: Rotten. You can do better yourself, and that's not saying much. She's a nice girl, really she is, but she is the black sheep of the family. Funny, isn't it?

MAUD: (*weak voice*). Yes, funny.

FITZSIMMONS: Her brother Jack is all right. But he can't do anything with her. She's a—a—

MAUD: (*grimly*). Yes. Go on.

FITZSIMMONS: A holy terror. She ought to be in a reform school.

MAUD: (*springing to her feet and slamming newspapers in his face*). Oh! Oh! Oh! You liar! She isn't anything of the sort!

FITZSIMMONS: (*recovering from the onslaught and making believe he is angry, advancing threateningly on her*). Now I'm going to put a head on you, you young hoodlum.

MAUD: (*all alarm and contrition, backing away from him*). Don't! Please don't! I'm sorry! I apologize. I—I beg your pardon, Bob. Only I don't like to hear girls talked about that way, even—even if it is true. And you ought to know.

FITZSIMMONS: (*subsiding and resuming seat*). You've changed a lot, I must say.

MAUD: (*sitting down in leather chair*). I told you I'd reformed. Let us talk about something else. Why is it girls like prizefighters? I should think—ahem—I mean it seems to me that girls would think prizefighters horrid.

FITZSIMMONS: They are men.

MAUD: But there is so much crookedness in the game. One hears about it all the time.

FITZSIMMONS: There are crooked men in every business and profession. The best fighters are not crooked.

MAUD: I—er—I thought they all faked fights when there was enough in it.

FITZSIMMONS: Not the best ones.

MAUD: Did you—er—ever fake a fight?

FITZSIMMONS: (*looking at her sharply, then speaking solemnly*). Yes. Once.

MAUD: (*shocked, speaking sadly*). And I always heard of you, and thought of you, as the one clean champion who never faked.

FITZSIMMONS: (*gently and seriously*). Let me tell you about it. It was down in Australia. I had just begun to fight my way up. It was with old Bill Hobart out at Rushcutters Bay. I threw the fight to him.

MAUD: (*repelled, disgusted*). Oh! I could not have believed it of you.

FITZSIMMONS: Let me tell you about it. Bill was an old fighter. Not an old man, you know, but he'd been in the fighting game a long time. He was about thirty-eight, and a gamer man never entered the ring. But he was in hard luck. Younger fighters were coming up, and he was being crowded out. At that time it wasn't often he got a fight, and the purses were small. Besides, it was a drought year in Australia. You don't know what that means. It means that the rangers are starved. It means that the sheep are starved and die by the millions. It means that there is no money and no work and that the men and women and kiddies starve. Bill Hobart had a missus and three kids, and at the time of his fight with me they were all starving. They did not have enough to eat. Do you understand? They did not have enough to eat. And Bill did not have enough to eat. He trained on an empty stomach, which is no way to train, you'll admit. During that drought year there was little enough money in the ring, but he had failed to get any fights. He had worked at longshoring, ditch-digging, coal-shoveling—anything to keep the life in the missus and the kiddies. The trouble was the jobs didn't hold out. And there he was, matched to fight with me, behind in his rent, a tough old chopping block, but weak from lack of food. If he did not win the fight, the landlord was going to put them into the street.

MAUD: But why would you want to fight with him in such weak condition?

FITZSIMMONS: I did not know. I did not learn till at the ringside just before the fight. It was in the dressing rooms, waiting our turn to go on. Bill came out of his room, ready for the ring. "Bill," I said—in fun, you know. "Bill, I've got to do you tonight." He said nothing, but he looked at me with the saddest and most pitiful face I have ever seen. He went back into his dressing room and sat down. "Poor Bill!" one of my seconds said. "He's been fair starving these last weeks. And I've got it straight, the landlord chucks him out if he loses tonight." Then the call came and we went into the ring. Bill was desperate. He fought like a tiger, a madman. He was fair crazy. He was fighting for more than I was fighting for. I was a rising fighter, and I was fighting for the money and the recognition. But Bill was fighting for life—for the life of his loved ones. Well, condition told. The strength went out of him, and I was fresh as a daisy. "What's the matter, Bill?"

I said to him in a clinch. "You're weak." "I ain't had a bit to eat this day," he answered. That was all. By the seventh round he was about all in, hanging on and panting and sobbing for breath in the clinches, and I knew I could put him out anytime. I drew my right for the short arm jab that would do the business. He knew it was coming, and he was powerless to prevent it. "For the love of God, Bob," he said, and—

Pause.

MAUD: Yes? Yes?

FITZSIMMONS: I held back the blow. We were in a clinch. "For the love of God, Bob," he said again, "the missus and the kiddies!" And right there I saw and knew it all. I saw the hungry children asleep, and the missus sitting up and waiting for Bill to come home, waiting to know whether they were to have food to eat or be thrown out in the street. "Bill," I said, in the next clinch, so low only he could hear. "Bill, remember the La Blanche swing. Give it to me, hard." We broke away, and he was tottering and groggy. He staggered away and started to whirl the swing. I saw it coming. I made believe I didn't, and started after him in a rush. Biff! It caught me on the jaw, and I went down. I was young and strong. I could eat punishment. I could have got up the first second. But I lay there and let them count me out. And making believe I was still dazed, I let them carry me to my corner and work to bring me to. (*Pause.*) Well, I faked that fight.

MAUD: (*springing to him and shaking his hand*). Thank God! Oh! You are a man! A—a—a hero!

FITZSIMMONS: (*dryly, feeling in his pocket*). Let's have a smoke.

He fails to find cigarette case.

MAUD: I can't tell you how glad I am you told me that.

FITZSIMMONS: (*gruffly*). Forget it.

He looks on table and fails to find cigarette case. Looks at

*her suspiciously, then crosses to desk at right and reaches for
telephone.*

MAUD: (*curiously*). What are you going to do?

FITZSIMMONS: Call the police.

MAUD: What for?

FITZSIMMONS: For you.

MAUD: For me?

FITZSIMMONS: You are not Harry Jones. And not only are you
an imposter, but you are a thief.

MAUD: (*indignantly*). How dare you?

FITZSIMMONS: You have stolen my cigarette case.

MAUD: (*remembering and taken aback, pulls out cigarette case*).
Here it is.

FITZSIMMONS: Too late. It won't save you. This club must be
kept respectable. Thieves cannot be tolerated.

MAUD: (*growing alarm*). But you won't have me arrested?

FITZSIMMONS: I certainly will.

MAUD: (*pleadingly*). Please! Please!

FITZSIMMONS: (*obdurately*). I see no reason why I should not.

MAUD: (*hurriedly, in a panic*). I'll give you a reason—a—a
good one. I—I—am not Harry Jones.

FITZSIMMONS: (*grimly*). A good reason in itself to call in the
police.

MAUD: That isn't the reason. I'm—a— Oh! I'm so ashamed.

FITZSIMMONS: (*sternly*). I should say you ought to be.
Reaches for telephone receiver.

MAUD: (*in rush of desperation*). Stop! I'm a—I'm a—a girl.
There!
Sinks down in chair, burying her face in her hands.
Fitzsimmons, hanging up receiver, grunts.
*Maud removes hands and looks at him indignantly. As she
speaks, her indignation grows.*

MAUD: I only wanted your cigarette case to prove to my
brother that I had been here. I—I'm Maud Sylvester, and

you never took me out once. And I'm not a black sheep.
And I don't dress loudly, and I haven't a—a tapeworm.

FITZSIMMONS: (*grinning and pulling out card from vest pocket*).
I knew you were Miss Sylvester all the time.

MAUD: Oh! You brute! I'll never speak to you again.

FITZSIMMONS: (*gently*). You'll let me see you safely out of here.

MAUD: (*relenting*). Ye-e-s. (*She rises, crosses to table, and is about to stoop for motor cloak and bonnet, but he forestalls her, holds cloak, and helps her into it.*) Thank you.
She takes off wig, fluffs her own hair becomingly, and puts on bonnet, looking every inch a pretty young girl ready for an automobile ride.

FITZSIMMONS: (*who, all the time, watching her transformation, has been growing bashful, now handing her the cigarette case*). Here's the cigarette case. You may k-k-keep it.

MAUD: (*looking at him, hesitates, then takes it*). I thank you—er—Bob. I shall treasure it all my life. (*He is very embarrassed.*) Why, I do believe you're bashful. What is the matter?

FITZSIMMONS: (*stammering*). Why—I—you— You are a girl—and—a—a—deuced pretty one.

MAUD: (*taking his arm, ready to start for door*). But you knew it all along.

FITZSIMMONS: But it's somehow different now, when you've got your girl's clothes on.

MAUD: But you weren't a bit bashful—or nice—when—you—you—(*blurting it out*)—were so anxious about birthmarks.
They start to make exit.

CURTAIN

SELECTED BIBLIOGRAPHY

The Son of the Wolf (1900) – stories
The God of His Fathers and Other Stories (1901) – stories
Children of the Frost (1902) – stories
The Cruise of the Dazzler (1902) – novel
A Daughter of the Snows (1902) – novel
The Call of the Wild (1903) – novel
The Kempton–Wace Letters (1903)[1] – fiction
The People of the Abyss (1903) – nonfiction
The Faith of Men and Other Stories (1904) – stories
The Sea Wolf (1904) – novel
The Game (1905) – novel
Tales of the Fish Patrol (1905) – stories
War of the Classes (1905) – essays
Moon Face and Other Stories (1906) – stories
Scorn of Women (1906) – play
White Fang (1906) – novel
Before Adam (1907) – novel
Love of Life and Other Stories (1907) – stories
The Road (1907) – nonfiction
The Iron Heel (1908) – novel

1. Written with Anna Strunsky.

Martin Eden (1909) – novel
Burning Daylight (1910) – novel
Lost Face (1910) – stories
Revolution and Other Essays (1910) – essays
Theft (1910) – play
Adventure (1911) – novel
The Cruise of the Snark (1911) – nonfiction
South Sea Tales (1911) – stories
When God Laughs and Other Stories (1911) – stories
The House of Pride and Other Tales of Hawaii (1912) – stories
Smoke Bellew (1912) – stories
A Son of the Sun (1912) – stories
The Abysmal Brute (1913) – novel
John Barleycorn (1913) – nonfiction
The Night-Born (1913) – stories
The Valley of the Moon (1913) – novel
The Mutiny of the Elsinore (1914) – novel
The Strength of the Strong (1914) – stories
The Scarlet Plague (1915) – novel
The Star Rover (1915) – novel
The Acorn Planter (1916) – play
The Little Lady of the Big House (1916) – novel
The Turtles of Tasman (1916) – stories
The Human Drift (1917) – stories
Jerry of the Islands (1917) – novel
Michael, Brother of Jerry (1917) – novel
The Red One (1918) – stories
On the Makaloa Mat (1919) – stories
Hearts of Three (1920) – novel
Dutch Courage and Other Stories (1922) – stories
The Assassination Bureau, Ltd. (1963)[2] – novel
Jack London Reports (1970) – articles
The Letters of Jack London (1988) – letters

2. Left unfinished by London; completed by Robert L. Fish.

ORIGINAL PUBLICATION SOURCES

Scorn of Women (New York: Macmillan, 1906).

"The Scorn of Women": In *The God of His Fathers and Other Stories* (New York: McClure, Phillips, 1901). Originally appeared in *Overland Monthly,* May 1901.

Theft (New York: Macmillan, 1910).

The Acorn Planter (New York: Macmillan, 1916).

"The First Poet": In *The Turtles of Tasman* (New York: Macmillan, 1916). Originally appeared in *Century Magazine,* June 1911.

"A Wicked Woman": In *The Human Drift* (New York: Macmillan, 1917).

"The Birthmark": In *The Human Drift.*

A NOTE ON THE TEXT

The plays and "The Scorn of Women" are drawn from their original publication sources. Obvious errors in the original texts have been emended. Where appropriate, modern standards in spelling and punctuation have been imposed to enhance readability.